TRADING OPTIONS IN TURBULENT MARKETS

Since 1996, Bloomberg Press has published books for financial professionals on investing, economics, and policy affecting investors. Titles are written by leading practitioners and authorities, and have been translated into more than 20 languages.

The Bloomberg Financial Series provides both core reference knowledge and actionable information for financial professionals. The books are written by experts familiar with the work flows, challenges, and demands of investment professionals who trade the markets, manage money, and analyze investments in their capacity of growing and protecting wealth, hedging risk, and generating revenue.

For a list of available titles, please visit our web site at www.wiley.com/go/bloombergpress.

TRADING OPTIONS IN TURBULENT MARKETS

Master Uncertainty through Active Volatility Management

Second Edition

Larry Shover

BLOOMBERG PRESS
An Imprint of
WILEY

Cover Design: C. Wallace
Cover Image: Ocean waves © Irina Belousa/iStockphoto

Published by John Wiley & Sons, Inc., Hoboken, New Jersey.
The First Edition of *Trading Options in Turbulent Markets* was published by Bloomberg Press in 2010.
Published simultaneously in Canada.

For general information on our other products and services or for technical support, please contact
our Customer Care Department within the United States at (800) 762-2974, outside the United States
at (317) 572-3993 or fax (317) 572-4002.

Wiley publishes in a variety of print and electronic formats and by print-on-demand. Some material
included with standard print versions of this book may not be included in e-books or in print-on-demand.
If this book refers to media such as a CD or DVD that is not included in the version you purchased,
you may download this material at http://booksupport.wiley.com. For more information about Wiley
products, visit www.wiley.com.

Library of Congress Cataloging-in-Publication Data:

Shover, Larry.
    Trading options in turbulent markets : master uncertainty through active volatility management /
Larry Shover. — 2nd ed.
        p. cm.
    Includes index.
    ISBN 978-1-118-34354-8 (cloth); ISBN 978-1-118-41663-1 (ebk);
    ISBN 978-1-118-43403-1 (ebk); ISBN 978-1-118-42021-8 (ebk)
        1. Options (Finance)   2. Risk management.   I. Title.
HG6024.A3S537   2012
332.64'53—dc23
                                                                    2012038304
Printed in the United States of America.

10 9 8 7 6 5 4 3 2 1

To Maribeth, Megan, Tim, & Andy

Contents

Preface

Trading Options in Turbulent Markets, Second Edition further reveals how volatility in options trading relates to today's stormy marketplace and shows you how to manage risk and take advantage of market volatility when investing in derivatives. This book addresses how to use historical volatility to help predict the future value of a security, or the implied volatility, and offers suggestions for dealing with that odd feature of options trading known as skew—in which the options market has, in recent decades, essentially developed its own consciousness and can respond to market conditions that defy all logic. Skew is uncertainty squared, and here, I describe how to work with or around it.

This book also includes proven tools for evaluating options trading decisions: the Greeks—delta, vega, theta, and gamma. We will define the values carefully and describe how each relates to volatility. In addition, you will discover effective strategies for trading options contracts in uncertain times, explore the decision-making process in broad terms, and learn how to become a steel-nerved trader. Along the way, this book answers complex issues such as: How does a trader know when to tolerate risk? How does a successful trader think or respond to adversity? How does a trader lose well?

Trading Options in Turbulent Markets also looks at specific options trading strategies that help you offset risk and reach for profit. These include the covered call, the naked and married puts, collars, straddles, vertical spreads, calendar spreads, butterflies, along with a new chapter on wing-spreads. This second edition features a deeper dive into the vastly popular VIX—the fear gauge—along with the uncovering of various volatility terms once reserved for the institutional world that are now becoming more mainstream.

Filled with in-depth insights and practical advice, this important resource explores how to turn turbulent markets into profitable opportunities and reveals why options are the best tool to use in such a difficult endeavor.

Acknowledgments

I would like to begin by saying thank you to the hundreds of brokers, traders, clerks, and exchange personnel with whom I've shared both the opportunity and privilege to grow and learn as a trader over the years. Spending countless hours jammed shoulder-to-shoulder with other traders and trading staff produces a bond—a familial link—that transcends both emotions and time. I started in this industry as an 18-year-old boy. Now, looking back, I reflect on the lessons learned, the emotions, the broken dreams, the vast fortunes made and lost, as well as the raging hostility of my fellow traders at times, and the fear. All of this I have collected and filed away. The ink spilt during the writing of this book is the result of this experience, and for that I am most grateful.

A very special thanks to my original editor, Stephen Isaacs, of Bloomberg Press. To date, Stephen's phone is never far away—he continues to be available to me for anything and everything!

Thanks also to my John Wiley & Sons family! To Kevin Commins and Marty Schecter, both of whom worked vigorously crafting the vision necessary for this second edition; always moving the mountain in the right direction! To Meg Freeborn—a senior development editor that most authors could only hope for. To my senior publicist, Stacy Smith, who took my book quite personally—doing whatever it took to help it become a true evergreen!

A big round of applause to Josh Suckenic of OptionsXpress, who early on appreciated the uniqueness of my book and helped create the vision for this second edition.

Jim Bittman of the Chicago Board Options Exchange and Option Institute is, in my estimation, the industry's most stimulating and capable instructor on options trading. Jim has written two very successful books and was always very encouraging and supportive of my writing efforts. I'm grateful to have a friend like Jim to emulate.

Curt Zuckert of the CME Group's Trading Knowledge Center (TKC) regularly greeted me with a smile even though he knew full well that my sole intention was to camp out in his "library," using it as my personal office (for my personal gain) while researching this second edition. Although I had plenty of places where I could have gone to write, the atmosphere at TKC gave me both hope and inspiration.

Matthew Curtis once again did nothing short of save me from my technical deficits by designing and editing most of the initial charts and graphs. I count myself very fortunate to be able to defer to Matthew, coming to him mostly empty-handed and leaving with a stunning piece of art. Matthew truly saved me from countless failed and frustrated efforts.

A very big thanks to my chief technical writer, Mark Dawson. Mark is not only one of the greatest technical writers in the options field, he also carries with him a sixth sense. Mark had a continuous feeling for where this second edition was heading and kept me swimming in the right direction. When I ran out of ink, Mark was there—he possessed an uncanny ability to keep me focused on the book, its intention, and the audience I was hopefully trying to reach.

Introduction

The United States used to be a good place to make assumptions.

Young men and women were admitted to college without creating marketing videos of themselves and without pledging their teenaged years to an extracurricular cloister. College arrived, and college led to graduation (four years), a cubicle, modest debt, spouse, offspring, real estate, health insurance, trips to Disneyland. Nurses and math teachers did not need resumes. Single-family homes increased in value every year. That's written in the *Bible* somewhere. People in their 50s and 60s owned homes that were paid off. If you had been working somewhere for 20 years or more you could safely hide in your office until you turned 65, and at that point, with your golden years ahead, Social Security would be waiting patiently. Forever would Americans buy Kodak film, books at Borders, tools and trousers at Sears. When recession did arrive (the non-Great kind) a company like Circuit City might dally with Chapter 11, but only long enough to get reorganized and draw enough investment capital to return to health. If a developer was stuck with an office tower or apartment project that was still unfinished when economists announced that the downturn had started, the investors pushed to finish the property anyway, and then made an effort to find tenants. Walking away from a property with rebar sticking out of the top was unthinkable. And regardless of the economy, talk of Chapter 11 for icons like General Motors or Bank of America was the province of conspiracy theorists with greasy hair and smudged glasses.

The end of the last century offered engineers writing software in Mumbai and Moscow and Chinese factories that assembled, well, everything. The Internet shook the planet even more than Gutenberg's invention did more than five centuries earlier. And then the strangely old-fashioned financial panic of 2008 arrived.

The panic has subsided, but the rubble remains:

- The venerable United States Postal Service lost a third of its first-class mail volume and started talking of eliminating Saturday delivery for the first time ever as one of the possible cutbacks needed to remain solvent.
- Public libraries across the country closed their doors. Firefighters and police officers were laid off. The town of Vallejo, California, filed for bankruptcy.
- For 15 years, from 1991 through 2005, Bill Miller, the chairman and chief investment officer of Legg Mason Capital Development, was a superhero for investors. Every year he outperformed the Standard & Poor's 500, a record unmatched by any competitor, and his fund assets peaked in 2006 at $20 billion. But after the financial crisis started, the old wisdom of the markets no longer worked for him. Miller snapped up bank stocks in the midst of the crisis, expecting them to recover. They didn't. In 2008, his fund lost more than half of its value, investors headed for the exit, and by the time Miller retired at the end of 2011, his fund's balance had slid to less than $3 billion.
- Greeks responded to talk of austerity with riots, and Italy (a G6 member) trembled close to defaulting on its bonds, as its debt-to-GDP ratios reached levels not seen since the end of World War II. Europeans talked of abandoning the euro—and their southern neighbors—to their fates.
- By the end of 2011, the U.S. middle class had watched $8 trillion in home equity vanish. Some 11 million families lost their homes to foreclosure, and throughout 2011 as many as one out of every three homeowners found that their properties were worth as much as 25 percent less than the amount remaining on the mortgage. The term "underwater" had to be invented in 2008 to describe homes that were impossible to refinance and hopeless to sell. By January 2012, U.S. homes had lost, on average, a staggering 40 percent of their value.
- The total amount of student loan debt passed the total amount of credit card debt for the first time ever. New graduates struggled with crushing debt burdens even as they faced crippling levels of unemployment. Books and articles for the first time repeatedly questioned whether a college degree was really worth the money.
- The Federal Reserve and European Central Bank offered stimulus. Again. Did anyone notice? U.S. Treasury bills remained at least a safe investment, but yields on these bonds fell below 2 percent, and on 30-year bonds, below 4 percent, their lowest rates ever.
- Egypt, the largest country in the Middle East, saw mass demonstrations that overturned a dictator. Nothing like that had happened in the nation's

5,000-year history. Civil war toppled a dictator in Libya and threatened Syria to the north. Mass protests swept the United States, too.

- The longest war in U.S. history stumbled on in Afghanistan, though still without clear goals. Relations soured further with a critical ally, Pakistan. Troops were at last withdrawn from Iraq. The U.S. government could not convince the Iraqis to allow it to maintain a military presence, leaving the country—and its oil reserves—to a very uncertain future. Meanwhile, talk of an attack on Iran persisted, prompting the Iranian government to threaten to close the Strait of Hormuz to shipping. This act, easily within the reach of the Iranian military, would lead inevitably to a disastrous spike in oil prices.

- The U.S. House of Representatives pushed the U.S. Federal government to within a few weeks of defaulting on its loans and a new global depression in a debate over raising the debt ceiling. For the first time in U.S. history there was discussion of invoking the Fourteenth Amendment to guarantee the government's solvency; for the first time ever, the government's credit rating was lowered.

- Who wins the Oval Office in 2012? What will Congress—facing approval levels in the single digits—look like? Will the government start to actually work again? And what vision would guide the government if, in fact, it does manage to start producing something in 2013 other than parliamentary maneuvers, stalled appointments, and filibusters?

Welcome to 2012, the Age of Uncertainty. Nobody knows.

The same amount of uncertainty applies to the modern investment community. Computer models still press on, but traders no longer dare to make predictions, because they frequently no longer have any idea what to expect. A trader's judgment can be reduced to coincidence, or a gamble. Maybe a market swings simply because a single hedge fund completes a large off-floor trade or a major bank starts buying up puts to cover its exposure after issuing warrants. Or one might decide to make a trading decision only when the moon is full, or find that based on past experience, on the third Friday of March or December, if the S&P 500 index has dropped three days in a row, it's a good time to start buying Swedish municipal bonds. A careful review of these trends six months later might show that they were in fact accurate. But that doesn't make them any less silly. You can find a lot of truth in using hindsight to explain past performance but still find that hindsight useless in predicting what happens next, especially now.

Trading is all about human frailty. We live in a world with people who become greedy and shortsighted, who panic, who make blunders and then try to hide them, who try to protect their jobs, who lack experience, or who grow complacent. And all of this frailty and folly is in high relief in a modern world where nothing makes sense any longer. Seasoned traders talk of a time when they could sense where the market was going, when they could manage positions without desperation, when certain rules applied to how the markets would behave next month or next year. For many years, people with PhDs working at trading firms on Wall Street produced models that efficiently predicted market value for securities. However, these scholars failed to plan—or were unable to plan—for rare events, much less the current era of violent volatility and fiscal and social chaos. Further, the very value of experience itself has been called into question of late. A trader with 25 years of experience and a career noted for its rigorous success can now be found to be losing money six months in a row, while a new graduate—with a freshly minted MBA—can have a run on the market that can make him the toast, and the envy, of his older peers. Why? Skill or luck? Something else? We can no longer estimate how well a given trader will do based on that trader's background.

As of this writing, it appears that the 25-year period of the "great moderation" is over, and, in fact, may have been somewhat of an historical anomaly. Since 2008, we've found ourselves struggling to deal with markets and an economy besieged by uncertainty.

Trading Options in Turbulent Markets is a book about how to think about options trading in terms of our modern world of randomness and volatility. This book was written with the hope of filling the void in traditional financial literature by combining theory and real-world practice with the awareness that the world we live in is completely random and that volatility is nothing but an expression of that randomness. The book draws from the premise that volatility isn't just standard deviation or a number generated from the Black-Scholes calculator. It is the sum of all the information we simply don't possess.

In an era full of so much uncertainty in all of the financial markets, and with the global investment community arguing about how well supercomputers can predict rare events—predict the unpredictable—I decided to write an expanded second edition about options trading. One can find an abundance of high-quality books about options trading, and plenty that address volatility analysis. I sought to write this second edition uniquely combining options trading and volatility in a universe that is beyond control and sometimes terrifying.

Face it; the past three decades have been the exception, not the norm, for investors in equity markets. To this day, Wall Street seems to be dedicated to the principle that when it comes to trading the markets, there is such a thing as expertise; that skill and insight count in trading, just as skill and insight count in surgery or baseball. But the common thread of this book is to show that options do not behave in the way that physical phenomena such as mortality statistics do. Physical events, whether death rates or card games, are the predictable function of a limited and stable set of factors and tend to follow what statisticians call a "normal distribution," or a bell curve. Markets do not follow any normal distribution. Markets are not normal. This book is intended to help you understand that even though you may hear that 90 percent of all options expire as worthless, the 10 percent that don't can create devastating results. The best computer modeling tools often fail to predict option contract prices and which options contracts are likely to be exercised. This uncertainty is largely caused by investors and traders who don't act with any statistical orderliness. We change our minds on a whim. We do stupid things. We copy each other. We panic.

The options market has grown at a record pace over the past 25 years. Today, you can bet on whether a stock goes up or down. You can buy or sell options on bonds, on foreign currency, on mortgages, or on the relationship among any number of financial instruments of your choice; you can bet on whether the market booms or crashes or stays the same. Options allow investors to gamble heavily and turn 1 dollar into 50. They also allow investors to manage their risk. What drives the options market is the notion that the risks represented by all of these bets can be quantified, that by looking at the past behavior of a stock, you can calculate out the precise likelihood that the stock will reach a share price of $25.45 by next November 30, and whether the option is a good or bad investment at that price. Actually, the process is a lot like the way insurance companies analyze actuarial statistics in order to determine how much to charge for life insurance premiums.

But despite all the growth and the vast sums invested in derivatives trading today, we still face a stunning amount of uncertainty in the markets as in life. Addressing this uncertainty as options traders is what this book is about.

Part One focuses on how volatility in options trading relates to today's stormy marketplace. The book reflects on the 2008–2012 era—a period full of randomness, uncertainty, and risk—and how this uncertainty leads to volatility in the financial markets. Of course the world has always been random, uncertain, and risky. But the financial markets were not so complicated even 25 years ago, the trade volumes and dollars invested were not nearly so vast, the markets were not dependent on enormously complex computer modeling tools, and the financial marketplace did not experience unprecedented volatility as it has over the last few years.

Part One also addresses how to manage risk and how to take advantage of market volatility when investing in derivatives. The book demonstrates how to take advantage of market volatility when investing in derivatives. It shows how to use historical volatility to predict the future volatility for a security, or the implied volatility. Part One deals with that odd feature of options trading known as skew, in which the options market has, in recent decades, essentially developed its own consciousness and can respond to market conditions that defy all logic. Skew is uncertainty squared. I describe how to work with skew or work around it.

Lastly, Part One confronts the overwhelming fixation with VIX—the self-proclaimed fear gauge of the market! This section helps to unpack VIX, providing the investor with practical application on what VIX is—what it isn't—and how it can lead or even mislead in making options trading decisions.

Part Two digs into the tools for evaluating options trading decisions, the Greeks: delta, vega, theta, and gamma. It defines the values carefully and describes how each relates to volatility. Part Two takes this discussion one step further with an in-depth look into some of the more intricate details of volatility in an informative, easy-to-understand format. Institutional terms such as "realized volatility," "term-structure," "vol of vol," and "correlations" are dissected with the investor in mind—boiling them down to where they can be both helpful and relevant to readers of all stripes.

Part Three provides strategies for trading options contracts in uncertain times. First, we address the decision-making process in broad terms and discuss how to become a steel-nerved trader. When does a trader know how to tolerate risk? How does a successful trader think or respond to adversity? How does a trader lose well?

Moving on, the book looks at specific options trading strategies to offset risk and reach for profit. These include the covered call, the naked and married puts, collars, straddles, vertical spreads, calendar spreads, butterflies, and condors, along with other various and sundry wingspreads. Part Three focuses on ways to use these strategies in a volatile market, how volatility affects each method of investing, and how to blend these strategies to control for risk. It explores how to open doors to making a profit even when nobody has any idea what is likely to happen next, when it seems there are long odds on any event other than the sun perhaps rising the next morning.

You can prosper in options trading, even in the midst of chaos. And despite the risks, options trading can be fun, invigorating, and, for a wise trader, an excellent means to profit, even in uncertain times.

PART I

Understanding the Relationship between Market Turbulence and Option Volatility

CHAPTER 1

Managing Risk and Uncertainty with Options

Trading in the financial markets can be summarized by the phrase, "You just don't know what you don't know." On one hand, an investor can spend hours with research, due diligence, charts, and mathematical models only to end up with a worthless stock certificate, the result of a rare event that could not have been predicted. On the other hand, an investor can reap a bountiful reward on any stock, option, or future with less due diligence than that performed when purchasing a microwave oven. No charts or formulas involved—just plain profit resulting from old-fashioned intuition.

Today, the flow of information and the speed of its dissemination are simply astounding. In this age of electronic financial instruments, one can review information from a myriad of up-to-the-minute sources and subsequently amass a large trading position via a few clicks on the computer. Equally astounding is the sheer depth and liquidity of the exchange markets, where options are often quoted pennies wide and in multiple thousands on both the bid and offer. The markets have evolved from a disjointed fragmentation of phone calls and hand signals to a symphony of speed and synchronization.

Yet despite all the growth and development of the financial markets, there remains a great equalizer. Within the trading space there lies an element that is applicable equally to the eighteenth-century bourse trader, who anxiously awaited the latest information flow via flag signals along the stagecoach line between New York and Philadelphia, and to the twenty-first-century day trader, enveloping himself with television screens, statistical forecasts, and computer monitors.

The great equalizer—the factor that surpasses both time and knowledge—is volatility. Volatility is the ultimate unknown. No matter what is said, modeled, or written about it, volatility simply cannot be forecasted. Volatility amounts to risk to the investor. Learning to harness that risk is the subject of this book. Volatility and risk can be construed synonymously, and both terms are derived from uncertainty. In terms of the financial markets, *uncertainty generates volatility, and volatility results in risk.*

What Is Risk?

Risk is the direct result of a random event which has a quantifiable probability. The probability of an event—whether it is tomorrow's weather, the outcome of a baseball game, or the closing price of a stock—can be determined by using either the practical observance of the frequency of past events or theoretical forecasting models. For instance, an observer with high school math skills can work out the probabilities of the possible outcomes of a card game. Similarly, economists use complex theoretical models to construe probability distributions for stock market returns.

It is also possible to calculate probabilities from past patterns of behavior when theoretical models are not available or reliable. For example, an insurance actuarial can estimate the probability that a motorcyclist will suffer a head injury by observing how frequently such injuries have occurred in the past. Similarly, casinos review probability distributions for blackjack winners on the basis of past winners.

What Is Uncertainty?

Uncertainty is . . . The concept of uncertainty is more intricate than that of risk. Whereas risk can be observed and quantified, uncertainty cannot. Uncertainty applies to situations in which the world is not well charted. The way in which the world operates is always changing—at least to the extent that observations of past events offer little guidance for the future.

Years ago, National Football League (NFL) owners were reluctant to televise games, believing that doing so would decrease ticket sales. Yet in actuality, the opposite occurred. Ticket sales in the NFL have increased significantly over the years, due in part to increased exposure through televised games. Ironically, concerns about the relationship between television and ticket sales changed when NFL owners began managing the observed ticket sales risk on the basis of previously observed relations between cause and effect.

All decisions typically involve some degree of both risk and uncertainty. Many choices are made in circumstances encountered for the first time, and uncertainty thrives in the relationship between cause and effect. Given that risk is quantifiable and more accessible to theoretical treatment than uncertainty is, it should be no surprise that literature on market randomness deals specifically with risk. Dismissing uncertainty—the conduit to volatility—can prove perilous to the investor.

Seven Lessons Learned from Market Volatility

An unprecedented number of financial crises have occurred in the past few decades. Without the benefit of hindsight, who could have predicted any of the turbulent market conditions over the preceding thirty-plus years? The list is formidable, including the breakdown of the Bretton Woods Agreement, the first oil crisis of 1973, Black Monday, the Japanese stock market crash, the collapse of Long-Term Capital Management (LTCM), the Russian ruble crisis, the Asian currency crisis, 9/11, Hurricane Katrina, the 2008 credit crisis, and the recent volatility of commodity prices. These rare events have had both short-term and long-term effects on market volatility.

Researchers who are conveniently removed in both time and emotion from such events have carefully documented and learned from them, whereas the average investor is still reeling from the too-recent, hard-hitting, real-life lessons of volatility and risk.

Macroeconomic data and fine points aside, several simple lessons about volatility seem relevant.

Lesson One

Financial crisis and market volatility often appear in waves. Like a tsunami, volatility is felt first on the shores of one country, followed by fierce waves appearing on other shores, often in very close succession. These financial tsunamis are often unleashed by episodes of economic weakness, political instability, and financial turmoil.

Lesson Two

The next wave of crises is sure to be different from the last. Money is made and money is lost in crises. Those who lose money typically set up safety measures to avoid incurring loss in the same fashion twice. As institutions evolve, those who profit during crises and other periods of volatility look elsewhere for weak points. From this simple dynamic, it follows that the next series of financial crises will be distinctive and different from previous debacles.

Lesson Three

Market volatility tends to be persistent. That is, periods of both high and low volatility typically persist for extended periods of time. In particular, periods of high volatility tend to occur when stock prices are falling and continue throughout rare events. The persistence of volatility is derived from the overall health of the economy, including volatility in economic variables such as inflation, industrial production, and debt levels in the corporate sector.

Lesson Four

Volatility is the product of an inefficient financial marketplace. It is rational to expect that financial markets will be efficient, setting prices at their real values, since buyers and sellers both behave according to rational self-interest based on broadly shared information about the economy and its individual parts. Yet people are often caught off guard when unexpected shocks—for example, severe drought, a sudden bankruptcy, or an aggressive change in government policy—disrupt the norm. Markets can and will move for any reason or for no reason at all.

Lesson Five

Volatility directly affects the average investor's willingness to hold what is perceived to be a risky asset. In uncertain markets—volatile markets—humans tend to engage in a type of behavior that economists refer to as the "herding effect" and which floor traders effectively name a "bull rush." This tendency creates a self-fulfilling prophecy: As more investors sell, it becomes increasingly likely that others will be convinced that there must be a good reason for them to sell also. The subsequent panic can actually serve to magnify trends instead of countering them. As a result, the implied volatility of stocks or options can move drastically without any real news to justify such a move.

Lesson Six

Sharp changes in the level of market volatility can discourage market participants from providing deep, two-way price quotations. The absence of a deep, two-way quotation, or liquidity, could potentially trigger adverse price reactions, which in turn can force irrational decision making, resulting in the wholesale liquidation of a position. It is absolutely essential that investment goals and theoretical knowledge about options are combined with an assessment of the possible hazards of ill liquidity.

Lesson Seven

Both the intensity and the frequency of investors' changing beliefs about market fundamentals will directly affect market volatility. When investors' sense of what the future holds is in flux, stock prices and option volatility will change rapidly, frequently, and significantly. This lesson is not necessarily intuitive, since one might expect uncertainty to generate only tentative volatility oscillations rather than huge waves of selling. However, such irrational behavior is what causes a trader to be convinced on Monday that the world is ending, and by Friday to be equally convinced that the world has weathered the storm.

Lessons Summary

Volatility is an alternate for investment risk. The persistence of volatility suggests that the risk and return tradeoff adjusts in a predictable fashion. That being said, options perform well as both potential portfolio enhancers and volatility reducers. However, options are not good or suitable if they cause an investor to make irrational judgments, chase returns, double up on losers, or engage in risks that are better absorbed by those who are more capable and more appropriately positioned to take them.

Understanding Derivatives

Derivatives are financial instruments whose value and guaranteed payoffs are derived from the value of something else, generally called the underlying. This underlying is often a singular company or a government's interest rate, but it definitely does not have to be. For instance, derivatives exist based on the price of the Standard & Poor's 500, the temperature at O'Hare Airport, the number of bankruptcies filed among a group of selected companies, or even the implied volatility of the market.

There are two variations of derivative products: plain vanilla and exotic. Plain vanilla derivatives are defined as either an option or future contract.

Exotics conjure up names like "knock-outs," "double-touch," or even "barrier options," and they are far beyond both the intention and scope of this book.

Options Defined

An option is a contract to buy or sell a specified quantity of an asset at a fixed price at or before a predetermined date in the future. An option can be bought or sold at the asset's current price (at the money), well below the current price (in the money), or far above the prevailing traded price (out of the money). In addition, options contracts can be traded with expiration dates ranging from one day to several years in the future. Exchange-traded options can be bought or sold at any time, although there is a specific difference in expiration style. An American style option can be exercised at any time on or before its expiration date. A European style option can be exercised only on its expiration date.

Futures Defined

A futures contract refers to a standardized contract to buy or sell a particular commodity of consistent quality at a predefined date in the future at a market-determined price.

For example, a corn future is a contract to buy or sell a specified amount of physical corn at the market-determined price. Similarly, a futures contract on XYZ stock gives the buyer of the futures contract the right to buy a predefined quantity of XYZ at the present market price. The vast majority of futures contracts end up being closed out as a result of buying or selling in the marketplace. Physical delivery does occur, but only on the future's settlement date, which transpires at a predefined time once per quarter.

Understanding Options

Although options can be traded on just about anything imaginable, let's use options on common stock as an example. A call option gives its buyer or holder the right—not the obligation—to buy a fixed number of shares at a given price at some future date. A put option gives its buyer the right to sell a fixed number of shares at a given price at some future date. The specified price is called the exercise price. The seller of an option at its beginning is called the writer. When the buyer (holder) of an option takes advantage of his right, he is said to have exercised his option. A holder (purchaser) who cannot gain from exercising his option before expiration either sells his option to close or allows the option to expire. The purchase price of an option is called the option premium. Options enable buyers to leverage their resources while limiting their risk.

The Six Benefits of Options

Although exchange-traded options have existed since 1973, many investors have chosen to avoid them, deeming them to be either too risky or difficult to understand. Others have had bad experiences with options because neither they nor their brokers were properly trained in how to handle them strategically. Although options can be difficult, risky, and downright frustrating if not strategically employed, they don't necessarily need to be. A game plan that includes a reasonable risk/reward profile and an ironclad exit strategy can help the investor reduce the ill effects of volatility and improve the possibility of enhanced returns.

Benefit One: The Ability to Leverage

Options provide both individuals and firms with the ability to leverage. In other words, options are a way to achieve payoffs that would usually be possible only at a much greater cost. Options can cause markets to become more competitive, creating an environment in which investors have the ability to hedge an assortment of risks that otherwise would be too large to sustain.

Benefit Two: Creating Market Efficiency

Options can bring about more efficiency in the underlying market itself. Option markets, in and of themselves, tend to produce information flow. Options enable investors to access and trade on information that otherwise might be unobtainable or very expensive. In the equity market, for instance, short sales of stock are often difficult to apply. This difficulty slows down the speed with which adverse information is incorporated into stock prices and makes markets less efficient. With put options, investors can more easily take advantage of adverse information about stock prices.

Benefit Three: Cost Efficiency

Derivatives are cost efficient. Options can provide immense leveraging ability. An investor can create an option position that will imitate a stock position identically, or almost identically, although at a large cost savings. For example, in order to buy 500 shares of a $20 stock, an investor must outlay $10,000 (500 shares × $20 = $10,000). However, if the investor were to purchase five $20 call options (with each contract representing 100 shares), the total outlay could be far less. For example, if the investor bought five 30-day $20 calls for, say, $2 each, he would spend $1,000 ($2 × 100 shares × = contracts = $1,000) to somewhat replicate the stock for a 30-day period. In practice, stock replication is not always as straightforward as this example implies. The investor must choose the right call to purchase, determine the optimum time frame, have a solid understanding of the implications of volatility, and be familiar with the greeks.

Benefit Four: 24/7 Protection

Options provide relative immunity to potential catastrophic effects of gap openings in the underlying. There are numerous circumstances in which buying options is riskier than owning the underlying, but there are also times when options can be used to reduce risk. It really depends on how you utilize them. Employed efficiently, options can serve as the most dependable form of hedging.

For instance, when an investor purchases stock, a stop-loss order is often placed to protect the position and to prevent losses below a predetermined price set by the investor. The stop order is executed when the stock trades at or below the limit indicated on the order. The risk with stop orders is inherent in the nature of the order itself.

For example, suppose you purchase XYZ stock at $30. You do not wish to lose any more than 15 percent of your investment, so you place a $25.50 stop order. This order will become a market order to sell if the stock trades at or below $25.50. This type of order is effective during the day, but it could prove disastrous after the market closes. Suppose that the next morning there is terrible news about XYZ, and the stock is expected to open at around $5. When the market opens, your stop-loss will be triggered at $5, since it is the first price below your initial stop-loss implementation—which means you end up taking a considerable loss on the trade. The stop-loss strategy simply did not work when you needed it most.

Had you purchased a put option for downside protection, you would not be subject to such a catastrophic loss. Unlike stop-loss orders, options do not shut down when the market closes. They offer insurance twenty-four hours a day, seven days a week—something that stop orders can't do.

Benefit Five: Flexibility

Options are flexible tools that offer a variety of investment alternatives. Options can present the investor with a means to capture downside opportunity or to hedge downside risk. Many brokers charge a cost-prohibitive margin when the investor wants to short a stock. Other brokers simply do not allow for the shorting of stocks. This inability to trade or to effectively hedge the downside virtually handcuffs the investing public, forcing them onto an uneven playing field with the professional trading community. Options offer the individual investor a way to hedge a myriad of risks under specific circumstances.

Benefit Six: Trading Additional Dimensions

Implementation of options opens up opportunities of additional asset classes to the investor that are embedded in the options themselves. Options allow the investor not only to trade underlying movements, but to allow for the passage of time and the harnessing of volatility. The investor can take advantage of a stagnant market or a range-bound market. Unlike the traditional "buy and hope" investment theory, options, if applied correctly, can serve to limit downside exposure, stop a loss, and lock in a range for possible profit. Options can provide flexibility and a genuine risk/reward profile like no other investment. In many ways, options are profoundly confusing. But at the same time, they can be easy to understand.

CHAPTER 2

Making Sense of Volatility in Options Trading

Volatility is a measure of instability. A volatile substance will tend to change its form easily—for example, a liquid with a low boiling point readily turns into a gas. Gasoline is volatile; this doesn't mean that gasoline can catch fire easily (although it can), but rather that gasoline gives off fumes even at low temperatures. The volatility of gasoline increases its flammability because in its vapor form, it is much more likely to be ignited by, say, static electricity than it is as a liquid.

In the financial markets, volatility refers to the likelihood that securities or indexes will change in value over time, which can be determined on the basis of either past events or implications for the future. Usually the term is applied to stocks and to options contracts based on those stocks. The share price for a volatile stock will tend to fluctuate considerably over time. But this simplistic approach to volatility lacks nuance. An uninformed investor may think volatility is all about risk and liability—in other words, volatility in the market results in losing money. But if volatility is managed properly, it can be used to derive benefit. Either way, most traders tend to think of volatility as both an opportunity and a plague. It can be difficult to live with, but option contracts cannot be traded without it.

Volatility is a fundamental market force, and it must include risk. But traders can also take advantage of market volatility and prosper from it. Those who see profit in volatility understand that the volatility measurement for any security is based on market forces and anticipates the likely future value of the underlying security. They also understand that volatility describes how the value of a security moves *up* as well as down over time. Volatility is not merely an indicator that shows how share prices are likely to drop.

Volatility as an Asset Class

An asset class is a group of related securities, such as stocks or futures contracts. All assets are defined by how fair market value is calculated. *Real assets*, including stocks, bonds, real estate, commodities, and even collectibles such as rare baseball cards, have an intrinsic and identifiable value. Currencies are considered *nominal assets*, because dollars or euro or yen have no value apart from the good faith of the issuing government and the economic strength of the host country. A *wasting asset* has a limited shelf life and loses value over time. If tomatoes (perhaps homegrown ones) were considered assets, they would be wasting assets. So are options contracts. Options contracts are valuable only as long as they can be exercised. When an options contract expires, it becomes worthless. Most options contracts tend to lose value as they approach the expiration date, because a change in share price that would make an out-of-the-money contract worth exercising becomes less likely as time runs out.

Some traders consider volatility itself as an asset class, and they trade in volatility for underlying stocks or for the options contracts based on those stocks. Any asset can be traded if it has a risk dynamic that can be marketed. A risk dynamic is a market exposure that can be protected through hedging but which is hard to flatten out or diversify. Risk factor can be traded by calculating its value and assigning a price to it. This applies to volatility as well. Volatility is an expected result of any asset that features risk, and this volatility can be estimated for an asset in the future. Volatility values are quoted in real time and trade on options markets throughout the world.

Any asset's future volatility is unknown, so traders developed models in the 1970s, not long after the Chicago Board of Options Exchange (CBOE) opened, to project volatility over the lifetime of options contracts. Consequently, the concept of implied volatility was born. Market makers are specially designated traders under contract to provide price quotes for buying and selling specific securities on exchanges in order to set a price range to facilitate trading. Options market makers sometimes believe that options contracts are mispriced and thus trade based on the implied volatility in order to profit from this mispricing.

Volatility *buyers* believe that the implied volatility for an options contract will cost less than the underlying volatility likely to occur over the lifetime of the contract. Volatility *sellers* believe the opposite—implied volatility is expensive relative to the underlying volatility expected to occur between today and the options expiry. It is tempting to think that implied volatility should more or less follow the historical volatility observed for the underlying asset. That is, it would make sense to think that the likely change in share price for a given stock over the next six months would tend to follow the share prices for that same stock over the last six months. Actually, however, option traders and investors have varying time lines, perspectives, and objectives, so how they project implied volatility for a given asset tends to vary significantly.

How Does Volatility Work?

There are two ways to measure volatility: historical volatility and implied volatility.

Historical volatility gauges the change in the value of an underlying security based on historical prices over a distinct period of time. Generally, traders determine historical volatility by calculating the daily average percentage change in price for an underlying security over a given time period. This average is then presented as an annualized percentage. Historical volatility is often referred to as *actual volatility* or *realized volatility* and is discussed in detail in Chapter 3.

Implied volatility is the current volatility of an underlying asset, as shown by the changes in the price of the option based on that asset. To calculate the price for an options contract, traders use the following values:

- Strike price
- Expiration date
- Current share price of the underlying stock
- Projected dividend payments for the stock
- Current interest rates

If a trader can come up with all of these values for an options contract, except volatility, he can use them, plus the price of the contract itself, to change his pricing model and calculate the implied volatility for the options contract. This mathematical approach to implied volatility is discussed in Chapter 3.

Any given stock is likely to serve as an underlying asset for many different options contracts, each with its own strike price and expiration date. As a result, each options contract will have its own implied volatility value. Generally, the implied volatilities of call and put contracts show separate patterns, called the *skew*. Implied volatility tends to be higher for options contracts that are out of the money than for contracts that are in the money. This tendency exists partly because out-of-the-money options contracts face more risk on large market changes. To counteract this risk, such contracts tend to be priced higher. Because out-of-the-money calls and puts do not automatically have the same implied volatility as in-the-money contracts, the difference in implied volatility between the two represents a biased, or skewed, market. If a large demand exists for an options contract, it will push the implied volatility for the contract even higher.

Analyzing Volatility with Implied Volatility

To use implied volatility, traders must calculate the implied volatility for the option on the basis of the underlying asset. This calculation is simply an average of the implied volatilities of the different options on that underlying asset. However, no customary value is in place for the specific implied volatility to use. Many traders simply draw on the median implied volatility of the at-the-money options contracts over the next several expiration cycles. Others use a more elegant approach by incorporating several at-the-money and out-of-the-money options.

Implied volatility acts as an approximation of the value of an options contract over time. It is the one factor in option pricing that is not readily apparent from the market and cannot be easily hedged or compensated by using some other trading instrument. Because all other option variables can be defined—the strike price, interest rates, expiration date, and so on—the price of the contract relies entirely on the implied volatility. To compare the relative value of two option contracts, traders need only to look at the relative implied volatilities.

What Does Implied Volatility Reveal?

Implied volatility corresponds to the market's belief in what the share price of an underlying asset should be in the future. High implied volatility indicates that the market anticipates the stock will continue to be volatile, or keep moving significantly, either in the same direction or up and down. Low implied volatility shows that the market expects share price changes to be moderate. But implied volatility can also reveal much more than general market expectations.

Since implied volatility stands in, to some extent, for option value, a variation in implied volatility suggests there is a change in the option value itself. Sometimes large changes appear in the implied volatility of call versus put contracts in an underlying asset. Such fluctuations may hint at a change in the bias of the market, or even that something is going on behind the scenes that is not readily apparent to the marketplace.

For example, consider the market for E. F. Hutton options contracts in the mid-1980s. Rumors were flying that either Transamerica or Travelers Insurance were making plans to take over E. F. Hutton, so implied volatility in E. F. Hutton contracts soared with every passing rumor and ensuing denial. Something was up in the market, yet no one seemed to have a good handle on it, which made the stock price highly volatile. E. F. Hutton wasn't taken over until later in the decade, and by that time the implied volatility acted far differently. When Shearson Lehman Brothers announced its intention to acquire E. F. Hutton in late 1987, the implied volatility of E. F. Hutton collapsed, pending the closing of the deal. This collapse in implied volatility was natural—since the price of the sale was fixed, the price of E. F. Hutton shares was expected to remain stable.

Implied volatility sometimes offers insight into the current collective opinion of the marketplace. For example, when an underlying stock is dropping, it is common to notice implied volatility rising as well, indicating that traders are edgy about the underlying common stock. Even so, in early 2000, the market witnessed a phenomenon in which financial stocks across the board took some serious hits. During the course of this mini-crash in the financial sector, implied volatilities remained flat or even, in some cases, dropped as low as the historical volatility of the individual stocks. In hindsight, this implied volatility event showed that although the market felt the financial sector may have been overvalued, it was not concerned with long-term prospects for the industry.

Making Trading Decisions Based on the Disparity between Historical and Implied Volatility

Professional market makers typically trade volatility by maintaining "delta-hedged" positions. In other words, they buy or sell options and consequently hedge against (protect) the option position by buying shares of the underlying stock or with other complementary options contracts.

Delta is an estimate of how much the price of an options contract is likely to change if the share price for the underlying stock changes by $1 up or down. The delta comes from dividing the dollar amount of change in the value of an options contract by the change in value of the underlying stock at any given time. The delta is based on historical prices and is expressed as a whole number from 0 to 100. A delta of 50 shows that the price of an options contract has changed historically by 50 percent of the value of the underlying share price. If the delta is negative, the value of the options contract will tend to go up if the share price falls.

A hedge is an investment strategy to reduce the risk of another investment. The idea is to buy one security to offset or cancel the risk of another. A trader could buy 1,000 shares of stock and then hedge that investment by also buying 10 put contracts (100 shares each), giving the trader the right to sell those shares at a specific price. This strategy would limit the trader's loss if the share prices fall. On the other hand, a stock hedge can be also used to secure an option requirement. A trader may sell (write) call contracts that require him to sell shares at a specific price if the other party holding those contracts decides to exercise them. To hedge against that risk, the trader might decide to buy shares to have on hand in case he is forced to sell them.

As a trader, if you sell 100 option call contracts, representing 10,000 shares of stock, you might not want to buy all 10,000 shares to hedge your options position. Such a strategy would be expensive. Other investment opportunities might be more interesting to you, or you might not have enough cash available. You can't know how likely it is that the other trader will exercise the contracts, forcing you to sell those 10,000 shares to him. One way to respond to the risk would be to buy only a portion of the shares—say, 5,000—so that if the contracts are assigned to you, you don't need to buy as many shares on the market when it happens. The greater the risk that the contracts will be in the money, and thus exercised, the more shares you would be inclined to buy. The delta value of the options contract provides a clue. As a rule, the higher the delta, the more likely the contracts are going to be in the money before they expire. So you might want to use the delta value as a guide in deciding how many shares to buy. If the delta is 50 (50 percent), you might want to buy 50 percent of the shares you might need, or 5,000. This is called *delta hedging*. As mentioned above, you could also hedge a set of options contracts with another set of options contracts. For example, you could sell 100 call contracts and also buy 100 put contracts for the same security.

This type of hedging protects you if the share price of the underlying stock changes suddenly. Generally, you will want to keep an eye on the market and adjust your positions as the market moves, such as buying or selling additional shares of stock to account for daily changes in the delta value.

Because the hedge commonly involves shares of the underlying stock, traders for practical purposes are exposed to *historical volatility* on the hedges while being exposed to *implied volatility* on the option price. That is, if they buy options contracts at a lower implied volatility than the historical volatility of the hedge, they will theoretically make money. The same would be true if they sell options at a higher implied volatility than the historical volatility of their hedges.

In practical terms, however, it is important to first recognize the historical volatility of the stock. It might seem logical that the higher the implied volatility of an options contract, the better the underlying stock would be as a candidate for selling options contracts. Conversely, it might also seem reasonable that the lower the implied volatility of an options contract, the better the underlying stock would be as a candidate for buying options.

Yet such reasoning is not always applicable. If historical volatility is extremely high, it indicates that the share price of the underlying stock moves a lot, and thus the share price is more likely to move away from the strike price on a given options contract. In other words, if a stock has high historical volatility, it should also have high implied volatility. Past performance tells us what the future performance should look like. With that principle in mind, the best trading situations often involve those instances in which historical volatility differs sharply from implied volatility.

Another hedging technique is to compare the current implied volatility for a security to the past range of implied volatility originally estimated for the same asset. How does the implied volatility for a stock projected over the next six months compare to what traders *thought* the implied volatility would be for the same stock over the previous six months? If the implied volatilities for a security are near the *historical* highs or lows for implied volatility, while the historical volatility *itself* is not, it may be a good time to trade volatility for that stock. Most traders view each new trading day as full of sunshine and hope and opportunity for random, unpredictable madness in any market. Thus, they don't pay too much attention to historical charts and statistical probabilities. However, you can still use charts showing how implied volatility (not historical volatility) has worked for a security over time to provide yourself with an extra trading edge.

Appreciating Volatility for All It Is Worth

The risk embedded in the underlying asset establishes the fair value for implied volatility for that asset. The apparent fair value of volatility may often, and for long periods, diverge from its market price, or cited implied volatility. A trader who disagrees with the implied volatility in the market for an asset will buy or sell accordingly. That is, if a trader believes the share price for a stock is likely to gain value slowly over the next three months, he might decide to buy the stock even if the implied volatility for the options based on that stock is high, showing that the market believes that the share price is likely to move sharply up or down in the same time period.

This difference between apparent value and projected value can appear without regard to any specific factor that would suggest the future direction for the underlying stock, such as an unusual earnings report or merger plans. Determining a fair value for implied volatility is comparable to assessing the fair value of a piece of antique furniture bought at an auction house. Like any other object of sale or trade, the value of an options contract is what someone is willing to pay for it.

However, unlike nearly all other assets, volatility has a distinctive element of time decay. Since implied volatility approximates the future of the options market, the value of any options contract is tied to a predetermined expiration date. When a contract expires, the implied volatility also expires, and its fair value quickly becomes zero. Of course, options that expire in the money have intrinsic value because they can be exercised. But this value is separate from implied volatility, which must go to zero at expiration.

Volatility can be fully valued based on a simple supply–demand model. For example, demand for out-of-the-money put contracts by portfolio traders more often than not surpasses supply. This causes a *skew* wherein the implied volatilities are greater for options with lower strike prices in equity and index options. On the other hand, a surplus of options with higher strike prices, stemming from investors who are buying contracts with lower strike prices, may well serve to lower the subsequent price of implied volatility. The advent of individual structured products may affect option pricing. These forces of supply and demand could create additional opportunities for investors who disagree with the observed skew prevalent in many option markets.

How Volatility Really Works on the Trading Floor

Implied volatility should move along with historical volatility. Future volatility tends to follow the volatility observed more recently, especially when the time periods involved are short. But implied volatility can sometimes spike in response to unusual market events.

Historical volatility is often lopsided. Equity markets tend to fall much faster than they rise. Sell orders tend to intensify in falling markets. While rising markets tend to attract investors who see a trend, investors don't flock to rising markets with the same passion they bring to falling markets. Therefore, falling volatility does not necessarily look like rising volatility.

A period of volatility for a security or market, either high or low, can continue for a very long time before slowly returning to the historical norm. For instance, it seems that periods of low volatility are generally followed by comparable periods of high volatility before returning to more standard levels. With that in mind, making an educated guess as to near-term volatility in the future may be as simple as considering the most recent historical volatility.

But we have already considered how sometimes the implied volatility for a given stock has no relationship to the history of its actual share price. For example, smaller companies could potentially present bigger business risk and earnings volatility as compared with that for larger, more-established firms. In other words, regardless of past performance, the greater the risk, the greater the likely volatility. For example, when a company's market value rises, its debt ratios get better, and the risk of bankruptcy or failure retreats. Naturally, the apparent risks of smaller companies shrink as they graduate to large-company status. So sometimes a company's volatility could increase with falling stock prices.

Volatility and Uncertainty: Lessons for the Irrational Option Trader

Brokers usually warn customers before investing in any product:

Past performance is not a guarantee of future results.

No one can predict the future, but when considering volatility and uncertainty, many people tend to regard that statement in terms of risk, nothing but risk—as something to avoid, or as a prediction of future loss. Yet history tells us that the market can provide large surprises on both the upside and the downside. Relevant examples include technological innovations nobody could have imagined earlier, or great ideas that improve efficiency or lower cost.

The last twenty-five years have been a period of low volatility for various economic variables. During that period, the United States has endured only two recessions, and they were rather mild. If you were to look at quarterly changes in real gross domestic product (GDP) or any other real economic factors, unpredictability certainly went down. These facts, among others, lulled many investors and traders into thinking that the country had achieved, once and for all, a stable economic environment. That long-term stability and a general complacency, among other things, probably encouraged firms to take on massive amounts of leverage and thus contributed to the most recent economic tsunami.

People with PhDs working at trading firms on Wall Street created models that were designed to efficiently predict market value for securities. However, they failed to plan for rare events or comprehend the nature of volatility itself. As of this writing, it appears that the twenty-five-year period of "great moderation" is over, and in fact may have been an historical anomaly. We return to markets and an economy besieged by uncertainty.

In options and in life, probabilities don't really matter. In fact, you could argue that the idea of probability doesn't make sense. In the end, it matters little whether an event has a 1 percent chance or a 99 percent chance of occurring. Whether or not the incident actually happens, and the ultimate payoff or loss, is what counts. That potential payoff or loss is what should motivate options traders, clearinghouses, and investors alike.

Think about it. In 1839, Charles Goodyear declared personal bankruptcy in his demoralizing search for a process to cure rubber. If Goodyear had been influenced by the statistical probability of eventually making this discovery, one could assume that the rubber-curing process would not have been implemented until far in the future. Likewise, Thomas Edison's relentless efforts to develop a workable light bulb might have been significantly dampened by a realistic assessment of probability. It's possible that during all his years of labor, Edison never knew for sure whether his experiments would ever pay off.

In options trading, the opportunity for a payoff (or an unbalanced payoff) matters. If a future payoff (or loss) is inconsistent with the current state of financial matters, the traders should take full advantage. That is, if an event occurs in the future, the payoff should be superior to the effort it takes to get to that event in the future. That notion is what gives options trading its component of volatility.

Option volatility isn't necessarily efficient and can't be explained with rational analysis. Sometimes the price of equities under- or overreact and are either too low or too high as compared with essential numbers related to the corporate or industrial sector. This happens because traders are not rational, but emotional. Volatility represents the collective emotions of all participants motivated by the availability of inadequate information. This volatility—

based on emotion—eventually decides the price of equities and their corresponding option prices.

Varieties of Option Volatility Trading

Option volatility trading comes in three typical varieties.

First, there are positions, or spreads, in which volatility is uniformly long or short and the vega, gamma, and theta are all on the same side of the market—all three are positive or all three are negative. Vega shows how the price of an options contract changes when the volatility in the price of the underlying stock changes by 1 percent. The theta refers to how the price of an options contract will change as time passes. Also called time decay, the theta allows you to estimate how much the value of an options contract might decrease from one day to the next if the stock price or volatility does not change. Options contracts tend to lose value over time simply because they eventually expire, and they are worthless at that date if they are not exercised first. Delta describes how the price of an options contract changes due to a change in the share price of the underlying stock. The gamma refers to the change in the delta itself when the share price changes. The gamma describes the stability of the delta. A large gamma suggests that the delta might start changing even with a small change in the stock price.

A straddle or strangle would fit this first category of volatility trading. A straddle trade includes buying two sets of options contracts, one call and one put, with the same strike price and expiration date. In a strangle trade, you would buy a set of call contracts and a set of put contracts, all expiring on the same date, but they would have different strike prices. The different parts of a trade are referred to as *legs*. Simple trades have two legs—one set of call contracts and one set of put contracts, as described above. More complex trades may have multiple sets of trades or legs.

For volatility trading, when working with a straddle or strangle trade, both legs of the trade are always either both long or both short volatility. A trader who is short an index strangle for a given stock (i.e., the trader sold an out-of-the-money call and an out-of-the-money put) expects that stock's index volatility to drop and would thereby profit.

A second type of volatility trade involves both buying and writing (issuing and selling) options contracts at the same time and combining various strikes and/or expiration dates for these contracts. The contracts you buy or sell are all based on the same underlying asset. An example would be a vertical spread (either call or put) where you are long one strike against being short another strike in equal amounts. To be more specific, you could buy 100 call contracts with a strike price of $32 per share and write another 100 call contracts with a strike price of $34, both for the same underlying stock. Buying 100 one-month call contracts on a stock while selling 100 contracts of a three-month call on the same stock, but with the same strike price, would fit the description as well. The defining characteristic of these trades is that the greek values and volatility can reverse from positive to negative somewhere along the break-even path.

The third type of volatility trade involves what is called trading the volatility of volatility, using back spreads or ratio spreads. A ratio or back spread essentially includes a unequal net position of options in two different strikes. For example, if a trader buys out-of-the-money options and in effect pays for these options by selling a smaller quantity of at-the-money options, so that the net position generates a positive theta with a long volatility position, the trader has taken a volatility of volatility bet. Depending on factors such as time till expiration, the strike prices, and the implied options skew, the volatility of volatility position will have net long vega (volatility), long theta (positive cash flow), and short gamma.

CHAPTER 3

Working with Volatility to Make Investment Decisions

The subject of volatility, as any experienced trader will attest, is itself a volatile subject. Volatility has undergone remarkable changes during the past couple of decades in terms of how it's calculated, predicted, and utilized by investors and traders alike.

In the financial markets, volatility refers to the likelihood that securities or indexes change in value over time, either measured as a series of past events or implied for the future. Usually, the term is applied to stocks and to the options contracts based on those stocks. The share price for a volatile stock will tend to go up and down a lot over time. Traders seek to predict the future volatility of a stock or options contract based on a wide variety of factors. The volatility that a stock price has shown over time is called the historical volatility. The projected, or estimated, volatility for share prices or options contract prices for a future time period—say, the next two weeks or thirty days—is called the implied volatility.

On Predicting the Future

For options traders, successfully predicting implied volatility for contracts is crucial. But that expectation leads to a central problem related to performance for options traders, and traders in general, over the years—traders are obliged to be prophets. The most obvious issue, of course, is the dress code.

Goat-hair robes, oak staves, and waist-length beards tend to interfere with trading, especially floor trading. However, much more important than the prophet's garb is the prophet's results. Predicting the future is arguably the only area in which humans are always spectacularly incompetent.

Stanley Kubrick's classic science fiction film *2001: A Space Odyssey*, based on the novel by Arthur C. Clarke, features a Howard Johnson's restaurant in a rotating space station. Futurists in 1968 never imagined that the Howard Johnson's chain would disappear from the nation's roads and highways, so in the movie a HoJo franchise appears in orbit. A recent exhibit at Chicago's Museum of Science and Industry, "Yesterday's Visions of the Future," featured a happy suburban housewife at the dawn of the twenty-first century tidying her living room by blasting the vinyl furniture and carpeting with a fire hose. In July 1988, *Chicago Tribune* columnist Mike Royko responded to Donald Casselberry's 1987 letter predicting the imminent death of Ronald Reagan by suggesting that the psychic shouldn't quit his day job just yet. The 1939 New York World's Fair, "The World of Tomorrow," expected that the future of long-distance air travel belonged to dirigibles. About ten years ago, a dedicated web guru described fifteen sundry attempts to predict the end of the world before 1900 and forty more doomsdays slated for the twentieth century, including six in 1999 or 2000. In his 1973 apocalyptic title *The Vision*, David Wilkerson (already famous for *The Cross and the Switchblade*) prophesied that in the near future, marijuana would be legalized and that the 1980s would be noteworthy for violent hailstorms with massive chunks of ice. On the other hand, he sort of missed the Internet, the collapse of the Soviet Union, the HIV virus, cell phones, and the rise of Islamic fundamentalism.

Despite this track record, traders and financial analysts attempt to estimate the future value of options contracts. However, they swap dreams and visions and crystal balls for complex mathematical calculations, and often, it turns out, they are right. Traders and investors seek to project future or implied volatility, or the likelihood that the share price of an underlying stock will change during a certain time period in the future. These projected volatilities are based on the actual historic volatility of the security, and they utilize the best available current market data plus advanced computer systems and models to manage the heavy lifting. Traders reflect on past events such as the performance of certain sectors of the economy and the markets during recessions in previous decades, they study the likely impact of future events such as new product announcements or earnings reports, and they watch the market performance itself to look for near-term trends.

If you are a wise trader, you use all this data and evaluation to weigh what you stand to gain if your projections are right against what you may lose if you are wrong. And you always need to keep in mind that the only certainty in the modern market is ever-present uncertainty. Calculating the implied volatility for an options contract is a useful tool in determining which contracts to buy and sell. But it is only a tool. The markets are full of random events, so you should consider any calculation of implied volatility to be a well-reasoned guess.

Starting with Historical Volatility

Implied volatility is central to options trading because it projects how the share price of the underlying stock will perform. The price of the options contract is based on the share price; the closer the share price moves toward being in the money, the more the value of the options contract increases. So if you can accurately project how the underlying stock price is likely to perform in coming weeks, you can estimate the likely value of the options contract as well.

Calculating implied volatility starts with knowing historical volatility. First, consider how the underlying stock performed over the last six months or the last ten years. Then choose the time period for estimating the future implied volatility, such as the next thirty days, and the time between changes in share price. Commonly, implied volatility is based on the daily closing share price, but you could use a weekly average or an even longer range. Note that this interval doesn't have much impact on the implied volatility. If a contract is volatile for four days in one week, it will likely continue to be volatile if the values are averaged out from one month to the next.

Market data vendors who provide historical volatility records for stocks generally base their calculations on daily settlement-to-settlement price changes. Those who don't usually explain how their volatility values are calculated. If, for example, a service calculates the volatility of a contract for the month of August as 21.5 percent, you can assume that the calculations were made using the daily settlement-to-settlement price changes for all the business days during that month.

Calculating Historical Volatility

Historical volatility, sometimes referred to as realized volatility, measures what has already happened with a stock's value. It also projects how much the share price might move in the future, although such projections are limited by plenty of borders and boundaries. Suppose a driver plans to travel from

Seattle to Miami, a distance of nearly 3,400 miles. If we assume that the car averages a speed of 75 miles per hour, we can project that the trip will take about 45 hours. But that 45-hour calculation does not allow for the driver to stop for gas, to eat, or to spend the night. The projection doesn't take into account two days spent exploring St. Louis, or a week backpacking in Montana, or a side trip to visit Grandma in Denver. And how can we know that the speed will average 75 miles per hour? What if the water pump gives out and the car needs to be towed back to Seattle, or if the driver turns around because he learns about an emergency at work? Although historical volatility can serve as a good tool, it is important to recognize it's just that—a tool. In practice, underlying asset distributions often depart significantly from the lognormal.

Some markets are more volatile than others. Oil sold for about $60 a barrel in July 2007. A year later, on July 11, 2008, a barrel of West Texas crude reached a record price of $147.27, climbing steadily from an average of nearly $85 a barrel in January. But prices fell just as quickly, reaching an average below $100 a barrel by September. And a nation of weary drivers got a Christmas present that year, with oil plummeting to $33.87 a barrel by December 21, 2008. Few of us would have predicted that the Dow Jones Industrial Average would more than double in value in the space of a year and then fall from that height by 75 percent over the following six months. A commodity trader knows that oil and precious metals are generally more volatile than interest rate instruments. Stock traders know that high-tech issues tend to be more volatile than utility stocks.

Stocks and futures contracts are likewise unpredictable. Prices move back and forth over time, at varying rates. But the future of a share price is calculated on the basis of how fast it was moving in the recent past, and in what direction. Therefore, we rely on the daily percentage of price change.

How Traders Have Calculated Volatility Has Itself Been Volatile over Time

The science of calculating volatility has changed significantly over the years. When implied volatility was first used to project prices for options contracts in the 1970s and 1980s, analysts preferred quantity over quality. They collected a lot of historical data on share prices, providing an excellent baseline for estimates. In response, analysts routinely projected volatilities for one, three, and even five years in advance. Soon, however, financial specialists discovered that recent volatilities are more relevant in terms of predicting market performance in the near future. Traders rapidly followed their example, using ever-smaller samples of data to estimate volatility. As the use of delta and gamma hedging (in options) also increased, traders increasingly used implied volatilities with computer models to spot new profit-making opportunities.

The historical volatility value is nothing more than a percentage that describes past changes in the price of an underlying asset. You can use past share prices to calculate this percentage, either simply or painstakingly. Below are two methods for calculating historical volatility. The first is a simple approach that doesn't require an Excel spreadsheet or an advanced degree in statistics. The second offers more detail in terms of using standard deviation techniques to come up with historical volatility values.

Method 1: A Piece of Paper and a Pencil

We start with a set of closing prices for five days of trading for a new stock issue:

Date	Closing Price
Day 1	$1
Day 2	$3
Day 3	$4
Day 4	$6
Day 5	$9

1. Find the mean, or average. Add the share prices listed above ($23) and divide by 5. The mean is $4.60.
2. Subtract this mean from each price to create a list of deviations, as shown below. Some values may be negative.

Closing Price	Minus the Mean	Deviation
$1	$4.60	$3.60
$3	$4.60	$1.60
$4	$4.60	$ .60
$6	$4.60	$1.40
$9	$4.60	$4.40

3. Square the resulting list of values in the Deviation column (multiply the deviation by itself), as shown here.

Deviation	Multiplied by Itself	Result
3.6	3.6	12.96
1.6	1.6	2.56
0.6	0.6	0.36
1.4	1.4	1.96
4.4	4.4	19.36

4. Add up the numbers in the Result column. The sum is 37.20.
5. Take the sum of deviations (37.20) and divide it by one less than the total number of values. In this example, divide 37.20 by 4, yielding 9.3.
6. Calculate the square root of 9.3. The result is 3.05.

Therefore, the standard deviation is 3.05 for this stock. You can multiply that by the square root of the number of trading days in a year, 254 (15.937), to calculate a historical volatility of 48.61 percent for this stock. Keep in mind, this historical volatility is unusually high because the stock in this example is a new initial public offering (IPO). Very few stocks will triple in value in one day and double again two days later. However, the calculated historical volatility tells us how much the share price is likely to change in the future based on how much the share price changed in the recent past. The historical volatility for this particular issue suggests that the price may jump or fall by half (!) from one day to the next for the remainder of the trading days (254) in the year.

Of course, this example clearly demonstrates the limitations inherent in using historical volatility numbers. For this particular stock, it would make more sense to wait a month or two for the new IPO to settle down, and then take a historical volatility reading for ten days at that point. Likewise, be wary of using a ten-day value when, for example, a company struggles with losses and traders short its stock, or when big gains occur following a promising earnings report. Or, more generally, simply be cautious and avoid applying historical volatility values for stocks more than a few days or a week into the future.

Traders use a variety of methods to calculate historical volatility for a stock. The most common way, based on percentage changes in daily closing price, is demonstrated above. But you could also work with average daily high or low share prices to capture a sense of intraday activity.

Another issue involves the calculation of historical volatility and trending versus trading range markets. It is possible for a strong trend to develop up or down without any change in the size of daily percentage price changes (e.g., the magnitudes remain the same but more positive days develop). The average of daily price changes can become larger while historical volatility calculated via the popular method described above becomes smaller. Likewise, it could also be shown that if average daily price change declines in size, historical volatility can rise even when the market is trending stronger.

Method 2: A Piece of Paper, a Pencil, and Excel

Begin by taking the share prices from market close to close for each day in the recent past, such as the last ten days. Then calculate the average of those price changes as a percentage. When you have the average percentage price change over ten days, subtract the percentage change in share price for each of the ten days. This gives you the daily average change in the share price over the ten-day period. An example of this method can be seen below.

Date	Daily Closing Price	Daily Percentage Change
9/1/2009	$102.00	
9/2/2009	$102.21	0.002
9/3/2009	$100.13	−0.0203
9/4/2009	$100.00	−0.0012
9/8/2009	$101.12	0.0112
9/9/2009	$101.08	−0.0004
9/10/2009	$102.43	0.0133
9/11/2009	$102.19	0.0018
9/15/2009	$102.21	0.00019
9/16/2009	$102.23	0.00019

The middle column lists the daily closing prices for the stock between September 1 and September 16, 2009. The right column contains the daily percentage change in share price. To calculate this value, subtract today's closing price from yesterday's closing price and divide the result by yesterday's closing price. This is the raw material for computing historical volatility.

The data from the table below can then be used to compute the standard deviation of daily price changes, which can be done easily in an Excel spreadsheet using the STDEV function. Using the share price data for the calculation, the table below presents current ten-day historical volatility for the stock.

Standard Deviation	Square Root, 254 Days	Historical Volatility
0.009	15.937	0.14%

In this case, the historical volatility of .014 percent is an annualized figure. Normally we present both historical and implied volatility as annual values. Multiply the standard deviation, .009, by 15.937, the square root of 254 trading days in an average year. Keep in mind that although we are talking about the speed of price changes in the underlying shares, we interpret this as an expected .014 percent up or down potential move at current price changes over the next 254 trading days.

We should pause here to describe standard deviation. Standard deviation is a statistics and probability tool that describes how a group or population varies from the average. You can think of the standard deviation as the average of the average; it can make statistics tell a story. As such, this tool has a wide range of applications when estimating future population changes, environmental factors, economic trends, political values, popularity of media and entertainment concepts, and other fields that require the prediction of trends or the evaluation of current market or demographic forces. Scientists and statisticians use standard deviation to determine how many Irish teenagers or butterflies or stock prices or textile manufacturers fall close enough to an average range of values to precisely estimate their future behavior.

A great many values, such as the heights of American men, or closing prices, or the productivity of California farms and orchards, can be charted on a graph that takes the shape of a bell curve, as seen in **Exhibit 3.1**. The bulge in the middle of the curve represents the primary group, with the average or mean for all values being a line down the middle. The first standard deviation is the 34 percent of individuals who are closest to this mean value, either above or below. So the first standard deviation is 68 percent of all individuals. The second deviation includes the next 27 percent, so within two deviations you cover 95 percent of all possible outcomes. If the population is very close to the mean value, the bell curve will be very high in the middle. Very few American men are shorter than 5 foot 6 inches or taller than 6 foot 6 inches. If you have a broad spread of values, the bell curve will be flatter and taper toward the edges. In this case, fewer individuals fall in the first standard deviation of 68 percent.

Implied Volatility

Volatility, the square root of the variance of returns of an asset, is used to show the variability of an asset's value around an average price. It has been the standard measure of risk for the trading population for the last four decades. Volatility measures how much the value of an asset can move over a specific

EXHIBIT 3.1 Standard Deviation Graph

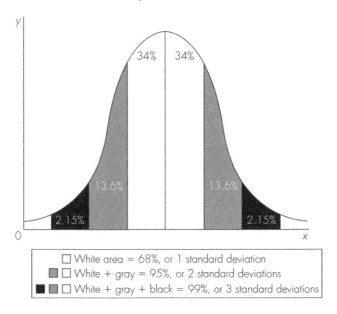

amount of time, and for options contracts it is defined as the standard deviation of daily percentage changes of the underlying share price. For options, implied volatility is simply the difference between the market price of a contract and its projected theoretical value at any given moment in the future. Volatility is usually expressed in annual terms, and it represents a one-standard-deviation move in the value of the underlying asset.

When dealing with actual numbers, what does it mean if an options contract has an implied volatility of 10 percent or 90 percent? You may recall from the discussion about standard deviation that one standard deviation represents two-thirds of all occurrences in a pool of values, or two-thirds of all members of a defined community. So if the implied volatility is 25 percent for a contract, it means that over the next year (254 business days) the contract is likely to move up or down in value by 25 percent. But most contracts expire within a few weeks or, at the most, within sixty days. So the annual value must be scaled down to a more recent time frame.

Consider a stock that is understood to have an annualized volatility of 25 percent. What does that translate to in terms of how much it may move in one day, one week, or even one month? Understand that standard deviation increases proportionately to the square root of time. If there are 254 trading days in one year, multiply 25 percent by the square root of 1/254 to arrive at the one standard deviation for one day, approximately 1.6. Therefore, two-thirds of the time, the underlying will move up or down 1.6 percent on an average trading day.

To get the standard deviation for a range of trading days, such as a week (five days) from the current date, multiply 25 percent by the square root of the number of days divided by 254. For a range of the next ten days, multiply 25 percent by the square root of 10/254. For twenty days, multiply 25 percent by the square root of 20/254. Theoretically, two-thirds of the time over the next five days, the stock price will rise or fall by 3.50 percent.

Believe it or not, this tool can be applied to help estimate the potential risk of an options position. Consider a hypothetical thirty-day at-the-money straddle. XYZ stock is currently trading at $40, and the thirty-day at-the-money options have an implied volatility of 30 percent. This value suggests that over the next thirty days, XYZ will theoretically trade up or down by 10.31 percent, or between $35.88 and $44.12 per share, two-thirds of the time. This information may or may not cause a trader to think twice about selling this particular straddle, or it could instigate a different volatility strategy altogether. In any event, it can serve as a tool to help evaluate both a trade and its implied volatility.

Implied volatilities in options markets tend to vary according to the strike price; this is especially true in equity markets. For example, if the comparative volatilities of options contracts that are out of the money, at the money, and in the money are all plotted with the same underlying stock data and expiration dates, usually the volatilities for the out-of-the-money and the in-the-money contracts will differ from the volatility of the at-the-money contracts. This is known as the volatility skew. The skew replicates the market's perception regarding the amount by which options contract prices are likely to rise and fall. The volatility skew is not essentially proportioned. It may be distorted to one side or the other based on how the market responds to in-the-money versus out-of-the-money options.

Calculating Implied Volatility

The theoretical fair value of an options contract is calculated on the basis of five factors:

1. Current share price
2. Strike price of the contract
3. Historical volatility of the share price
4. Number of days until the contract expires
5. Interest rates

After plugging these variables into a pricing model, the output would be the theoretical price of an option. However, if you have any experience with comparing theoretical values to market values, you know that the fair price is not always the price the market sets for the same option.

The theoretical value of a contract, however, often varies from the actual market price. Other traders and financial analysts might come up with differing values for the implied volatility for a contract, based on different inputs or different models. Everybody will use the same interest rate, number of days remaining until expiration, and strike price. But experts might disagree on the current appropriate bid and ask price for the underlying stock or on the estimated future share price over the next thirty days.

The difference in pricing, or the culprit, is normally volatility. What volatility is the market using to arrive at the current fair value of an option? To discover what volatility the market is using, you must hold all inputs (i.e., time to expiry, exercise price, underlying price, risk-free interest rate) constant and feed a volatility into the pricing model which will yield a price equal to the current market price. It's really that simple.

Why Do Volatilities Increase as Equities Fall?

Generally, the implied volatility of a stock or stock index rises when the share price starts to fall. This might seem confusing at first glance. A stock price can't fall any farther than $0, but it could continue to climb indefinitely, at least in theory. So shouldn't volatilities rise only when stock prices go up?

As equity prices begin to fall, the put options contracts on the market approach being in the money. This makes these contracts more desirable and thus more expensive. At the same time, nervous investors start to buy more put contracts to protect their positions against further losses, driving up the price even more.

The price of any put option contract is based on the implied volatility. With all other factors remaining the same, if the price of an options contract goes up, the implied volatility for that contract will rise in concert. In fact, the implied volatility is a proxy for the option price. Therefore, if the stock price falls, the value of the put contracts based on that equity go up in value. In turn, the implied volatility of the stock itself increases.

When equity prices decline, implied volatility increases due to the leverage effect. When the share price for a corporation falls, the debt-to-equity ratio of the firm goes up. That is, the total market value of the company drops because the market value is the share price times the number of shares outstanding. But the amount of money the firm owes remains the same. So as the share price falls, the firm's debt burden in effect increases, weakening the company's ability to service that same debt. The firm has less in the way of assets to offset its indebtedness. If the firm is heavily in debt already, the credit rating for the firm may also fall, making further borrowing more expensive or impossible, prompting more investors to start selling the stock, or even to sell short, provoking the share price to fall further. That leads to yet more implied volatility. There is a close relationship between the implied volatility of a stock and the likelihood that the company issuing the stock will default on its debt.

Implied versus Historical Volatility

The implied volatility of an options contract can be considered to be a market agreement of sorts. The traders, analysts, and other participants with an interest in projecting the change in the value of a stock and the options contracts based on that stock collectively arrive at an estimated amount of volatility over the remaining life of the contract. Just as an individual trader is likely to alter his volatility forecast in reaction to changing historical volatility, the marketplace as a whole will also modify its consensus volatility forecast. As the market becomes increasingly volatile, implied volatility can be expected to rise; as the market becomes less volatile, implied volatility can be expected to fall.

Market participants plausibly presume that what has happened in the past is a good indicator of what will happen in the future. The options and equity marketplace tends to behave as a living thing, a collective consciousness capable of making its own decisions. It is as if the marketplace continuously polls all traders and investors and obliges them to agree on a volatility value for each contract. As bids and offers are made, the trade price of an option will represent the equilibrium between supply and demand. This equilibrium can be translated into future, or implied, volatility. **Exhibit 3.2** demonstrates implied versus historical volatility for a particular market index, Standard & Poor's 500.

Note that in an efficient market, the implied volatility will normally be greater than the historical volatility. In other words, the market always predicts that the underlying share price will change more than it actually does. For example, compare the historical volatility values for a stock over a given three-month period to the implied volatility that had been projected for the same stock at the beginning of that period.

EXHIBIT 3.2 Implied versus Historical Volatility Comparison for Standard & Poor's 500, 2003–2009

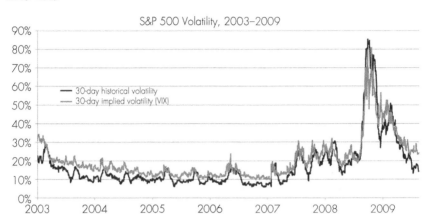

Source: Reprinted by courtesy of Condor Options, © Condor Options

Justification for the Disparity between Historical and Implied Volatility

Over long stretches of time, the historical volatility of an underlying asset seems to be the driving force affecting implied volatility. However, over shorter time spans, various and sundry factors can and do play a considerable role. For instance, suppose the market anticipates an event that could cause instability (e.g., a surprise earnings report, geopolitical event, or weather-related tragedy). The short-term market reaction to this event may trigger implied volatility to change in ways that are not necessarily in harmony with the asset's historical volatility. Indeed, any imminent event that could have unforeseen consequences can have an effect on implied volatility despite the asset's historical volatility.

On the other hand, if the market has the conviction that no large events are likely to occur in the very near future, ambiguity is removed from the market, and the implied volatility may fall even if the historical volatility has been comparatively high. This explains why implied volatility sometimes drops right after large moves in an underlying asset. In the case of an equity, for example, if a company issues an earnings report that falls far short of the experts' forecasts, causing the stock to drop 10 percent in one day, it is not uncommon for the implied volatility to drop. The reasoning is this: The news is out; what else can possibly go wrong?

Regardless of short-term changes in implied volatility, remember that, in the end, the actual volatility of the underlying stock price eventually overwhelms any considerations of implied volatility. Implied volatility—the future price predicted for a contract—is still important in making trading decisions. But in order to perform intelligently, a trader must know value as well as price. The value of an options contract is determined by how the share price of the underlying stock moves over the life of that contract. Many trading firms employ people with PhDs in mathematics and physics to build complex computer models that provide theoretical prices and quotes for options contracts. These modern prophets, it turns out, have created sophisticated tools that work very well in predicting how the market will move in the future. That is, these models work very well—until they don't. In the chaos of fourth quarter 2008, traders and investors had to rely on their knowledge and experience to stay afloat. And that a good lesson for the future. Don't let twenty-first-century computer systems get in the way of old-fashioned instincts. Implied volatility calculations can be enormously helpful when making investment decisions with options contracts, but they are a poor substitute for your own judgment as a trader.

CHAPTER 4

Volatility Skew: Smile or Smirk?

In 1986, traders used the Black-Scholes pricing model to compute the theoretical fair value of an options contract. At the time, most traders assumed that the same implied volatility would apply for all options contracts based on a single underlying stock and with the same expiration date. It was also assumed that all options contracts based on a single stock or stock index should trade with the same measure of volatility, and at-the-money calls and puts with the same strike price and expiration date should have the same volatility.

But that was before the crash of October 19, 1987. On a single day, the Dow Jones Industrial Index fell by 508 points, or 22.6 percent. During that month the index lost nearly a third of its value. Since then, prices for stocks and options contracts have shown a strong negative skew. Mathematically speaking, a negative skew means that projected future prices for contracts tend to move down over time regardless of market conditions. Higher implied volatility is also more common for out-of-the-money puts as compared with put contracts at the money or in the money. The result has come, over time, to be referred to as the risk premium.

Academics who write books and earn PhDs offer explanations for the phenomenon of the negative skew. The implied volatility for put contracts is higher than it "should be" because market liquidity is driven by demand shocks or short supply, because banks and clearinghouses are unwilling to take excessive risk, or because traders and investors are afraid of the next rare event. No one knows exactly why options trading features now work in this way; however, since October 1987, any investor who is paying attention needs to account for this negative skew with every trading decision.

39

Considering Some Examples

Volatility skew is the tendency of options contracts at different exercise prices to trade at different implied volatilities.

The table below shows a sampling of the settlement prices and implied volatilities for October cash-settled options expiring in thirty days on the Standard & Poor's index (SPX) traded on the CBOE. These prices reflect the characteristics of option markets with which traders have become accustomed.

The implied volatilities at various exercise prices do not line up.

This is a problem if one believes that the Black-Scholes or any other model is supposed to be flawless in predicting option prices. In fact, the projected prices don't make sense. If the SPX is trading at $1,064 and expires in thirty days, how can it be that the $1,070 call should have a volatility of 21.5 percent, whereas the $1,110 call should have a volatility of 20 percent? Why should the call contract with the higher strike price have nearly identical volatility, given that it is so far out of the money? And why should the volatility for *both* put and call contracts fall within a range of 18.5–29 percent across a range of $200 in strike prices?

Strike Price	Call Price	Put Price	Strike Volatility
$970	$98.00	$ 4.00	29.0%
$990	$80.00	$ 6.00	27.5%
$1,010	$63.00	$ 8.85	26.0%
$1,030	$47.00	$ 13.05	24.5%
$1,050	$33.35	$ 19.35	23.0%
$1,070	$21.80	$ 27.80	21.5%
$1,090	$12.95	$ 39.00	20.5%
$1,010	$ 7.25	$ 53.00	20.0%
$1,130	$ 3.60	$ 69.40	19.5%
$1,150	$ 1.75	$ 88.10	19.0%
$1,170	$ 0.80	$106.50	18.5%

SPX = $1,064.00, cash settled. Thirty days to expiration, interest rate = 2 percent.

There are clearly real problems associated with the use of a traditional theoretical pricing model as the only means to value options. Volatility may vary over the life of an option; the real world does not end up looking like a lognormal distribution. Before going further, it probably makes sense to explore the mathematical assumptions made when looking at theoretical pricing.

A Primer on Random Walk and Normal Distribution

Consider a coin toss, a roll of the dice, a spin of a roulette wheel, or a hand of cards. When the beautiful concept of randomness encounters each probability, there is a predetermined percentage chance of heads or tails, of a specific combination of the dice, a ball falling on a certain number on the roulette wheel, or a three of hearts being turned over by the dealer.

The arbitrary path the coin or roulette wheel or dice follows is known as the random walk. After the coin is flipped or wheel spun or dice cast, nothing can be done to change the course or predict the outcome. Gamblers commonly think of themselves as being hot or cold, of having a lucky run, of probability pointing to a sudden and likely success at the tables or slot machines because they've been losing lately, or because they have been winning lately, or because today is 09/09/09, or because today is September 23 and twenty-three is the gambler's lucky number. Casino operators gain from the gamblers' foolishness; they know that wheels and dice and decks of cards have no memory. Every wager has the same statistical probability of success as the previous attempt. The only predictable outcome is that 98.5 percent of gamblers will leave the casino with less money than when they walked in.

Even given all of this, if enough coins are flipped, a pattern or distribution of coin flips similar to that in **Exhibit 4.1** might begin to emerge.

EXHIBIT 4.1 Normal Distribution Graph

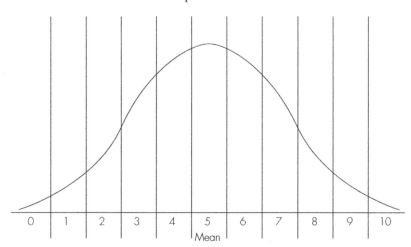

A similar graph was shown in Chapter 3. The graph in Exhibit 4.1 is a normal distribution, or a bell curve. When a seemingly random set of values is plotted from just about any statistical source—income, obesity, tooth decay, winnings at blackjack tables, options contract prices, you name it—the random, jumbled set of values tend toward a predictable shape.

Suppose New York City has a total of 13,000 registered cabs—6,500 yellow cabs and 6,500 white cabs. A person is stationed on the corner of 42nd Street and 7th Avenue to count the number of cabs of each color for every ten cabs that drive by. Typically, one might come up with a variety of combinations—three yellow and seven white, four yellow and six white, and so on. But the longer one stands on that corner counting groups of ten cabs, the more the outcomes will smoothly fall into a bell curve distribution.

The shape in Exhibit 4.1 might represent the outcome of counting cabs for a very long time. Each channel in the exhibit represents the possible number of yellow cabs for every ten cabs that go by. An outcome in Channel 0 represents ten yellow cabs in a row (ten yellow cabs and no white cabs). An outcome in Channel 5 represents five yellow cabs and five white cabs, whereas Channel 10 represents no yellow cabs at all (zero yellow cabs and ten white cabs).

Given the time and patience to stand on the corner long enough, the result might be a distribution very similar to that seen in **Exhibit 4.2**. Most of the observations will tend to assemble near the center, with a decreasing

EXHIBIT 4.2   Normal Distribution of Taxi Cab Sightings in New York City

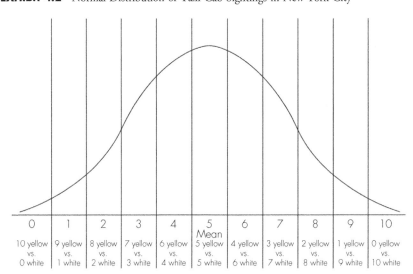

number of groupings finishing up in the channels farther away from the center. The distribution resulting from this study of the randomness of cabs barreling down 7th Avenue is referred to as a normal distribution.

Now consider the ten consecutive cab observations as the up and down price change of an underlying asset, and each set of ten observations as the passage of time. Furthermore, suppose that each day the underlying asset moves up or down by, say, $2. In that case, the price distribution after thirty days might correspond to the curve shown in Line 1 of **Exhibit 4.3**. If the price moves up or down by $2 every five days, the price distribution after thirty days might be represented by Line 2 of Exhibit 4.3. If the price moves up or down $5 each day, the price distribution might be represented by Line 3 of Exhibit 4.3.

Line 1 is a normal distribution. Line 2 shows lower volatility. That is, the same range of price changes ($2) occurs once a week rather than every day, so the bell curve is steeper. The prices have less variation. Line 3 is flat. It represents high volatility, or extreme outcomes, as prices can change much more ($5) within a single day. The higher the volatility, the more the values are spread out, and thus the distribution curve becomes flatter.

So how is this information converted into the volatility for the underlying option price? With thirty days to go to expiration, how is a thirty-day,

EXHIBIT 4.3 Volatility Distribution

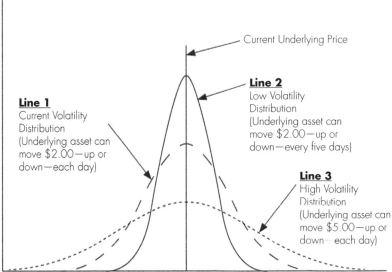

$55 call appraised when the stock currently trades at $50? One could assume that share prices will follow a random walk distribution over the next thirty days, and so one of the lines (1, 2, or 3) in Exhibit 4.3 will characterize the possible distribution before the contract expires. The ways in which the thirty-day, $55 call contract might vary in price under each of these scenarios—average volatility, medium volatility, and high volatility—is illustrated in **Exhibit 4.4**.

Given a normal distribution, comparable to Line 1 in Exhibit 4.3, the underlying share price has a small but realistic chance of getting to $55. The value of the $55 contract will, in turn, have a low implied volatility. In the case of low volatility, a distribution comparable to Line 2, the stock is less likely to reach $55 a share, so intuitively, the call contract premium would be less. Finally, with high volatility, a distribution similar to Line 3, the $55 call contract is very likely to finish in the money. As a result, the value of the options contract increases noticeably as measured against the other examples.

At first glance, the comparative price distributions in Exhibit 4.4 look proportional; it may seem that increased volatility should have no bona fide effect on the value of an options contract. After all, higher volatility may increase the possibility of sizeable upward movement, but this should be counterbalanced by the equally greater likelihood of large downward movement.

EXHIBIT 4.4   Volatility Distribution with $55 Call Strike Price

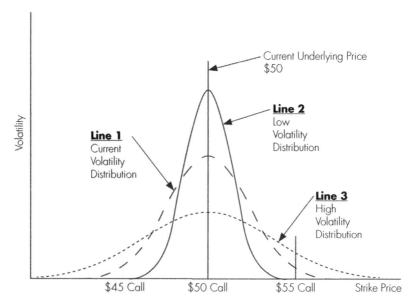

However, herein lies a chief dissimilarity concerning an options position versus a position in the underlying stock. If you buy options contracts, your potential loss is controlled. That control does not apply to the stock on which the contract is based. No matter how much the market plummets, a call option can only go to zero. In the previous example, whether the stock drops to $10 a share or stays at $55 when the contract expires, the $55 call contract will be worthless. The loss—that is, the premium you spent to buy the contract in the first place—is the same. You might even consider that loss to be an *insurance* premium and part of the cost of doing business. But if you own the stock at $50 a share and its price falls to $10, you take a huge hit. When you are trading in stocks, all outcomes are important. With an options contract, the only outcome that counts is whether the contract finishes in the money or out of the money. In Exhibit 4.4, only price outcomes to the right of the exercise price are relevant. Everything else is futile.

This difference leads to the primary divergence between the appraisal of a stock and that of an options contract. If we presume that prices are disseminated along a normal curve, the worth of an underlying stock share price depends on the pinnacle of the curve—the highest possible share price. The value of an option depends on how quickly the curvature spreads itself out.

In the end, the Black-Scholes options pricing model tells us that the price of the call option today is the sum total of all probability-weighted payoffs at expiration. In other words, if we suppose that the share prices track a normal distribution over time, the average call option should match the sum of all the potential and/or likely option payoffs at expiration. You don't know whether the option will conclude in the money or out of the money. All you can know for certain is that the asset returns at expiration will reflect a normal probability distribution. For all asset values—from $0 to infinity—that are possible when the contract expires, every call/put option payoff related to that specific asset value will have a significant chance of in fact taking place. This probability is depicted directly in a normal probability distribution.

Dealing with the Higher Moments of the Normal Distribution

In the early 1980s there was an elitist group of option traders who actually understood and could articulate the higher moments of a distribution. These days, however, it appears that every quantitative derivatives book talks about the higher moments. In today's world of trading you would be hard-pressed to go too far in a derivatives roundtable without the third and fourth moments being thrashed out.

The concept of "moment" in mathematics developed from the concept of "moment" in physics. The moments articulate the nature of the distribution. Any distribution can be characterized by a number of features, such as the mean, the variance, the skewness, the kurtosis, and so forth.

Whether you are a trader or a passive buy-writer, you are forced to live with these higher moments each and every day. So what are these moments, why are we living with them, and how do they affect our trading decisions?

The first moment of a normal distribution: Determine the expected value of a variable from an average of previous values (finding the mean). Analysts, traders, and investors alike are all concerned with the problem of figuring out the likelihood or expectation of a certain outcome. An analyst, after hours of research, places a value on a stock for a future period. A street-smart day trader may take the average of the last three months of XYZ and quickly conclude that XYZ will trade at such and such a price. In this case, both the analyst and the day trader are toying with the expected value of XYZ—the first moment of a normal distribution.

You may, for example, take the average of the share price for the last three months and use that to develop a value. You aren't predicting a price for a specific future date or series of dates; you are simply finding the average for past performance and using that to get an idea of where the share price might go next.

The second moment of a normal distribution: Estimate the variance or volatility of that asset over time. Next, options traders try to estimate the odds that the stock price will trade between, for example, $30 and $40 over the next thirty days. They seek to refine an estimated future share price into the variability of that price over time. The standard deviation—or implied volatility, in financial terms—is the second moment. The second moment tries to capture the dispersion of values around the single expected value that you estimated in the first moment described above. Thus, the second moment captures the risk or volatility of a financial asset.

The second moment—the volatility—of the distribution is one of the most valuable notions in financial philosophy. Financial derivatives are based on this second moment. The second moment of the normal distribution is the "stress" in the orderliness which prompts asset prices to diverge from what everyone assumes them to be, thus stirring up risk in the system.

The third moment of a normal distribution: The skew or shape in the distribution. Options traders seek to make money by accurately predicting when the market will rally or drop. But often the market goes against the traders, causing them to lose money. Sometimes they confront sizeable negative returns, a situation they may not have anticipated at all. This is the skew. If a distribution has a skew—and all normal distributions in actuality do—it insinuates the ever-present possibility of large negative returns. This is actually negative skew.

Skew is the contour, or the unevenness, in a distribution, the dent in the bell curve. A negative skew suggests that the left half of the normal distribution (the left side of the mean) is twisted in such a way that the prospect of achieving negative returns is superior to that of achieving large positive returns. Recall that in a theoretically precise, ideal normal distribution, positive returns and negative returns of equivalent magnitudes have more or less equivalent probabilities. Hence the distribution is symmetrical, or balanced. Of course, a distribution can possess positive skew as well, which signifies the prospect of a large positive return.

When dealing with skew, traders strive to resolve how frequently in the trading time horizon they will obtain negative returns rather than positive returns. A skew demonstrates the relationship between the movement of an underlying asset and its volatility.

The fourth moment of a normal distribution: Kurtosis or varying variance, the volatility of volatility. Mathematicians have a fearsome term for the fourth moment of a normal distribution—kurtosis. The fourth moment is a gauge of whether the distribution curve is tall and skinny or short and squat, measured up to the normal distribution of the same exact variance. It means varying volatility or, more precisely, varying variance.

The fourth moment is something that all options traders can relate to, although they may not know its name or be able to provide details. It signifies volatility of the volatility of an underlying asset. What happens to the distribution of the curve when volatility changes? What occurs to the extreme downside skew if volatility changes? A changing volatility can cause the tails of the normal distribution to become "fatter" or "skinnier" than otherwise predicted, thereby increasing the potential risk. This is the work of the fourth moment.

Skew Is High, Skew Is Low. So What?

Traders should be wary of statistical studies done on the skew, since the epitome of skew is indeed a rare event. For example, New Yorkers in 2001 could have looked at two hundred years of data and never seen any reason to expect a massive terrorist attack.

Whenever there is a skew, traditional statistical methods do not unite properly. Nor is there a means to determine whether the sample size is ample to draw adequate conclusions. A once-heroic statistical analyst might end up looking like a muttering madman scribbling on endless legal pads in a lifetime mission to disprove Einstein. Traders can no longer accept hypotheses; they can only refuse them. One cannot count on the hypothesis of a tip for a good trade, but one can refuse it if the trade proves to be a poor choice.

So what use does skew have to a trader or investor? Skew points to a probability, and a large probability in some cases, of losing a lot of money in a transaction or investment strategy. But if an underlying asset has a probability of large negative returns, especially a very small probability, how should it affect how the trader of investor looks at skew when trading?

One approach is to think about what one might do in a different situation. If you think a baseball card or a 1966 Ford Mustang or a rare print found at a garage sale is underpriced, you buy it. If you believe it's overpriced, you sell it. In terms of skew, if you have an idea of what direction the market is heading and an opinion about skew, you could trade accordingly. For instance, if you were bullish on a particular equity index and also believed skew to be high, you could buy the index while shorting the skew by selling a slightly out-of-the-money put spread. This trade would accomplish both of your convictions.

Does a "Flat" or "Steep" Skew Predict the Future?

When the market skew is steep—out-of-the-money puts are priced higher than equally distanced out-of-the-money calls—does that indicate the market is going down? When market skew is deemed steep or expensive, the market is more than likely to trade higher. Major market downturns or other rare events seem to occur as shocks. When you have an exceptionally steep skew, it means that an event or crash has been built into the market; people are willing to shell out this risk premium (or crash premium) with the fear of the impending crash. And that's precisely why it doesn't happen, since the aspect of surprise is gone.

A strong up or down move in the market can also be coincident with a low level of volatility, regardless of the skew's shape. When volatilities are higher, the premium that people are willing to pay is too expensive, and the market typically doesn't end up moving as much as the implied volatility suggests it will. Simply put, the implied volatilities are pricing in a premium that is just too high.

In low periods of volatility, skew gives all the appearances of growing steeper. The longer the volatility lulls, the steeper the skew becomes. This appearance of a steep skew is just that—an appearance; there is nothing in the history of the options market to suggest it means anything other than simple supply and demand. As implied volatilities go lower, it tends to affect the at-the-money part of the curve as compared to the left or right side. The skew seems to be the last thing to fall.

A Fair Warning about Thinking about Skew too Much

When the moon is waning, the skew is high in the SPX, the Dow Jones Industrial Average has gone down three days in a row, and it's Friday (though maybe not Friday the 13th), you can make a profit by buying cattle futures or Hungarian municipal bonds. You could be especially confident in this analysis if it turns out to be correct a month later. You can find a lot of truth in hindsight by exploring past performances. But computer models and statistical analysis can't generate future hindsight. Traders have to rely on predictions instead.

When skew is higher than average or lower than average, you may well learn something from that. But analyzing skew involves a variety of components that more often than not can only be described with the benefit of hindsight. And again, hindsight is now something that can be included in an options trading model. Changes in skew can be produced by ordinary supply and demand, the opinions of options market makers, or from a hedge resulting from a large off-floor trade. There have been periods where skew was so cheap that a trader's chief concern became how many puts the market makers could actually afford to finance. With that quantity of long (skew) supply being held by market makers, the skew became as flat as anyone had seen in modern memory. In that scenario, would a flat skew necessarily imply anything? Maybe.

For example, consider a large bank that recently issued a sizable number of warrants and accordingly begins purchasing puts to cover its downside exposure. Suddenly market makers are short a lot of puts; their prospective clearinghouses and/or risk managers command them to buy those puts back. As a result, the skew goes up. This is one of a seemingly infinite number of possible scenarios that could cause a short squeeze and drive the put volatility (skew) up.

Keep in mind human frailty. Skew is all about possible loss that you can't predict and can't control. It's the result of living in an imperfect world with imperfect people who become greedy and short-sighted, who panic, who make blunders and then try to hide them, who try to protect their jobs, who lack experience, or who have too much experience and grow complacent. Skew rises from an unpredictable world with too many human factors to count. And nothing is more unpredictable in markets and trading than the humans who are behind it all.

CHAPTER 5

Fixated on Volatility and the VIX

What Is Volatility, Anyhow?

What is volatility, anyway? It is both a deeply profound yet extraordinarily easy question to answer. We all know what volatility is and yet most of us have difficulty articulating it with any degree of clarity. The arduous quest for a clear, crisp explanation exists largely because volatility can—and does— represent different things to different people and in different contexts. Is it a fear gauge? Is it a statistical quantity? Is it a parameter in an options pricing model? Is it an asset? In fact, volatility is all of these things and probably a great deal more if the truth were known.

Volatility is the most theoretical and yet the most elusive hypothesis— both in the financial markets and in the theory of quantitative finance. Whether you are a particle physicist who cut his teeth on quarks and leptons or a casual options trader, you at one point have been perplexed by the entire notion of volatility—especially when the conversation goes via. VIX as the fathoming of the topic is quite impossible to imagine. You learn quickly to allow volatility to provide you with a meaningful way to think about the market—though not necessarily giving you an answer regarding which way the market is headed. You've most likely discovered that in most cases the world doesn't really behave in exactly the way you planned—that models, financial advice, volatility, and the VIX are more often than not a mediocre approximation of reality. You constantly remind yourself that you are immersed in an industry that involves the behavior of humans and that data alone doesn't speak—you need to think and draw conclusions. You must remember that no one truly knows what volatility is and everything you learn, devise, or contrive concerning the topic, while certainly helpful, is merely a beginning (see **Exhibit 5.1**).

What We (Think) We Know

Historical volatility is measured by the standard deviation of asset price returns around a mean (see Chapter 2). Implied volatility is a common metric used by options traders and other market participants to value options and other financial derivatives in addition to attempting to sum up their risk (see Chapter 3). In spite of this, volatility, whether historical or implied, cannot be directly observed in the market. Truthfully, it is the only parameter in an option-pricing model that cannot be observed in the market precisely but has to be either mathematically projected or, as traders do, backed out from a Black-Scholes-type option pricing formula. When the volatility is extracted from a Black-Scholes-type model, it is known as implied volatility. As the name suggests, it is that volatility that is implied by the put and call option prices that are traded on the exchange markets.

The notion that volatility has a significant part in determining asset valuation has long been a pillar of finance. Volatility measures, generally defined, are considered to be helpful tools for consolidating how opinions of uncertainty about economic fundamentals are apparent in prices. Derivative prices, where volatility plays a major part, are therefore especially germane for unraveling the connections between uncertainty, the dynamics of economy, preference, and prices.

For decades, options traders have been obsessed with implied volatility along with additional measures of volatility, including historical volatility, realized volatility, or even the volatility surface, that are resultant of the options price quoted on the trading floors around the world. Now, it appears there is a brand new fixation, the VIX, or the volatility index on the Standard & Poor's 500 stock index. Not only the derivative traders, but everyone else—from the financial bloggers, to the financial television talking heads, to the regulators, it seems, is now talking about the VIX index. This wholesale talk of VIX has caused me some concern as I'm afraid most people who talk about it perhaps don't truly understand what it is or even what it is supposed to measure. When discussions go down the path of anything mathematically hazy—especially when the topic turns to volatility—I often remind myself of something Albert Einstein said, actually I'm told Einstein engraved this onto his desk at Princeton: "Not everything that can be counted counts, and not everything that counts can be counted."

EXHIBIT 5.1 Historical SPX Implied and Realized Volatility

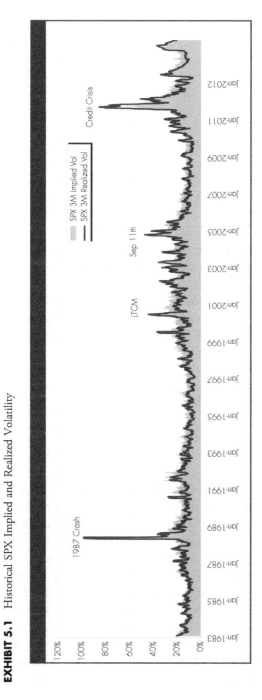

Source: CS Derivatives Strategy

Definitions of VIX

The VIX is an implied-volatility index that calculates the market's expectation of 30-day S&P 500 volatility embedded in the prices of near-term S&P 500 index options. However, the majority of investors, including some exceedingly seasoned ones, view VIX as merely the "fear gauge." Some people suppose that an elevated VIX simply implies increasingly justified worries by the option traders regarding a looming market disaster. On the other hand, a reasonably low or falling VIX level sometimes dupes the mainstream into thinking that options prices are indicating that a significant bull market is under way. To complicate things further, there is a contrarian mind-set that believes a relatively high VIX reading is a buy signal for equities, and conversely, a relatively low reading is a signal pointing to a pending correction. The reason for this, I think, is the somewhat flawed interpretation on the part of these traders and the far-reaching public in the financial markets that VIX by hook or by crook solely measures the expected volatility in the Standard & Poor's 500 stock index. They mistakenly believe that VIX somehow sums up the expected movement of the market in the next day, week, or month. Although it is true that the VIX theoretically measures the expected volatility of the S&P 500 stock index, there is more—much more—to the story.

Grasping the VIX Index

VIX is an index, like the Dow Jones Industrial Average (DJIA) or the Goldman Sachs Commodity Index (GSCI), calculated in real time throughout the trading day. The key difference is that VIX measures the movement in the options implied volatility—not the price path. VIX was launched in 1993 to provide investors with a tangible benchmark of expected short-term implied volatility changes. In an effort to smooth the progress of comparisons—comparing apples to apples—of the current VIX levels with historical levels, minute-by-minute values were compared and calculated using index options pricing back to the very beginning of 1986. This back-testing was especially essential as increased data mining tends to inspire confidence amongst mathematicians, modelers, and traders alike. More important, this comparison included the worst stock market crash since the Great Depression—Black Monday 1987. No doubt, the 1987 stock market crash provided vital benchmark information in estimating the level of volatility experienced throughout that gut-wrenching period of time.

Also, VIX was proposed as a means to provide options and futures trading for those who wanted to express their convictions about S&P 500 stock index implied volatility.

In an attempt to truly understand VIX, it is critical to stress that VIX is an attempt—a mere snapshot of looking ahead—assessing volatility that we look forward to see. It is not in any way backward-facing, looking at volatility that has been recently observed as some of us are taught. It may prove helpful to think in the abstract and conceptualize VIX the same way as you would a bond's yield to maturity. A yield to maturity is the discount rate that equates a bond's price to the present value of its promissory payments. A bond's yield is therefore "implied" by its current trading price. And that price characterizes the expected future return of the bond over its residual life. Similarly, the VIX index price is inferred or implied by the current prices of S&P 500 stock index options and thus provides a portrayal of sorts of expected future volatility over the next 30 days.

VIX—A (Very) Brief History

The VIX was introduced in 1993 by Robert Whaley—a world-renowned expert in the field of derivatives including volatility, derivative valuation, and risk management. I would encourage everyone to take a tour of Whaley's body of work. He's a rare breed in that he's able to write with a style that bridges that broad chasm between academicians and the rest of us. Further, I'd like to point out that Whaley was the innovator who developed additional volatility products along with the groundbreaking and highly successful BuyWrite Monthly Index (BXM) for the Chicago Board Options Exchange.

Whaley's original index was based on the prices of the S&P 100 (OEX), not the S&P 500 (SPX) as, believe it or not, OEX options accounted for approximately 75 percent of total exchange-traded index volume up until that point. Another unique feature of the original VIX is that it was based on the prices of just eight at-the-money OEX puts and calls. However, looking back to the early 1990s this made complete sense, as option trading (open interest) was much different from what it is today given that the majority of trading was done at or near the money strikes. With that, an accurate index needed to be based on actively traded pricing—calculating anything beyond the at-the-money strikes would risk an inaccurate index that used stale quotes and/or wide and illiquid markets.

Since those early days of the VIX, the markets have changed in dramatic ways, forcing the VIX to reflect those changes. In 2003, the CBOE began to use SPX rather than OEX prices as SPX became the overwhelmingly dominant volume leader in index options. The CBOE also began to include out-of-the money options in the VIX computation. The evolution of stock index option trading had reached a point where volumes of all strikes were big enough and fresh enough to warrant inclusion in the calculation. Furthermore, including out-of-the-money strikes helped to create a somewhat better representation of true volatility expectations as out-of-the-money strikes do provide market clues that may be different from at-the-money strike prices.

VIX: Calculation and Interpretation with a Simple Calculator

It would be easy to fill the pages with all types of highbrow math to justify the VIX, however, I feel what is so often is missing is a clear explanation of what this number actually means. To be clear, I'm of the conviction that VIX is an indicator of sorts—it means what you want it to mean. In other words, this talk of VIX is trying to interpret something that most likely can't be interpreted. It's severely limiting as it's an expectation of an expectation. It works until it doesn't work.

The VIX is quoted in percentage points and roughly deciphers the expected movement in the S&P 500 stock index over the next 30-day period, which is then annualized.

For example, if the VIX is 20, this represents an expected change of 20 percent over the next 30 days. One can infer that the market expects the S&P 500 to move up or down 20 percent/standard deviation of 12 (3.4641016) = 5.77 percent over the next 30-day period. More precisely, due to the math of the probability distribution, S&P 500 index options are priced (if the VIX is 20) with the assumption of a 68 percent certainty (one standard deviation) that the magnitude of the S&P 500's 30-day return will be less than 5.77 percent.

VIX Reading	Divided by Standard Deviation of 12	Magnitude of the S&P 500's 30-Day Return Will Be Less than
10	3.464	2.89%
15	3.464	4.33%
20	3.464	5.77%
25	3.464	7.22%
30	3.464	8.66%
35	3.464	10.10%
40	3.464	11.54%

Important Insights on the VIX Index

This brings us back to where we started, with VIX providing insights to the market as the fear gauge. When it was introduced 20 years ago, VIX became popular quickly as a simple number that could be used to express expected volatility in the market. But as the years crowded into each other and chaos danced with calamity over and over again, the VIX benchmark took on an apocalyptic role. VIX spoke to flummoxed traders and the general public as an indicator of market meltdown in an era of unprecedented—and frequently, terrifying—levels of volatility. But for both the VIX and for the markets in general, that was too simple.

VIX is not simply a stand-alone fear index. For that matter, trading options is not a pastime for the fearful, but that's the subject of another chapter. VIX is designed to measure what the market expects to see in terms of implied volatility for options contracts based on stocks in the S&P 500 stock index. That's it. VIX can help to estimate prices of options contracts and the best times to buy and sell, and it can help measure risk. But it can also point to future volatility over the next several months, and sometimes VIX points to a turbulent market settling down. After all, record-breaking states anywhere—in the market, in baseball, in new car sales, in condo starts, or oil production—are, by nature, unsustainable. Volatility is, too. If the markets show extreme volatility, investors tend to respond by backing away and waiting. Traders and investors either retreat from the risk itself, and look for low-yield havens like U.S. Treasury bonds, or they grow reluctant to pay premium prices for options contracts that by definition are intended to shield against that same risk. Unless, of course, they are forced to! So when the VIX soared close to 100 during the financial collapse in October of 2008, suggesting daily price changes of 6 percent, the VIX future volatility index passed 80, suggesting future daily price changes of 5 percent. That pointed to levels of volatility that could not last. And, in fact, governments around the world in late 2008 scrambled to calm jittery markets. As a result, the VIX had fallen by half or more by early 2009.

Also, VIX is used to measure volatility of prices for options contracts. Options contracts get more expensive when people get nervous, and that same wave of anxiety also tends to hammer stock prices. But not always. VIX and the S&P 500 tend to move in opposite directions, but that doesn't make it a good idea to try to use VIX to predict stock prices. This is because the idea of using the VIX to predict the S&P 500 index doesn't always work. It isn't foolproof! A wide variety of factors affect how options are priced. For example, if hard times last long enough that traders and investors get used to

EXHIBIT 5.2 VIX® and S&P 500® Indexes

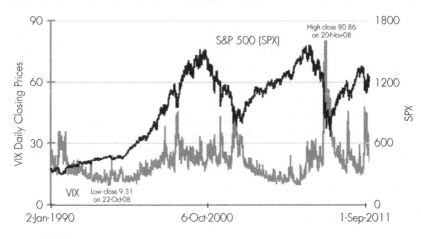

Source: CBOE

them and start seeing sagging stock prices as the norm, volatility levels out as
a result. If the risk is known, volatility tends to drop, right? In general, we can
sometimes use VIX to predict future stock prices. High VIX levels might
point to a market bottoming out, and low VIX levels have been seen as a sign
of a market waiting for a correction. But when considered over the long term,
high levels of the S&P 500 index frequently do not line up with low VIX
levels, and vice versa (see **Exhibit 5.2**).

What Does the VIX Tell Us?

So what does VIX tell us? VIX numbers have been predictive of market
changes over the last five years, but that doesn't mean that we can count on
the same effectiveness in the years ahead. The last five years featured extreme
volatility, and that means that the last five years became known for relentless
uncertainty and unpredictability. So were successful efforts to apply VIX all
just luck in the end? Maybe. But financial analysts across the markets have
confidence in VIX. And traders and investors tend to like warnings. If the
VIX falls significantly below its own moving average for the quarter, traders
and investors are wise to watch the market carefully.

Still, historical volatility does not predict rare events well. When considered over five or six years it might look like statistics related to VIX values
line up nicely with unusual downturns or surges. But it is hard to line up

future events with VIX values for the simple reason that if an event almost never happens, you don't have much information available to describe that event. So using these historical data to try to estimate when the next rare event will show up, or what it will look like, is at best ill-advised. Also, no matter how good the charts and graphs for the last six months may look, the longer the base line of data you have to evaluate, the more complex the environment you have to consider, and the more likely it is that important factors will be left out. Maybe over the past year you see that the VIX value correlates well with a few days of exotic volatility and also with a sudden market downtown. So what? Many other market factors and social and economic conditions might have contributed to both the market performance and the VIX values. These factors might have made it look like VIX was predicting rare events from a safe distance after the event was over. Assuming that VIX will be successful in predicting another rare event six months hence based on a complex historical model could lead to disappointment—or worse.

VIX and Perhaps the Biggest Misnomer of All!

I'm shocked by the number of traders and risk managers who still believe that because VIX results from liquid option prices on the S&P 500 stock index it in some way reflects the implied volatility of at-the-money S&P 500 options. This is dangerous thinking as nothing could be further from the truth. Although the VIX is computed from liquid options prices on the S&P 500 index, it is neither in relation to implied volatility resulting from these option prices nor is it in relation to expected volatility of the S&P 500 stock index. The best way to decipher the VIX, which is connected to S&P 500 option prices across a substantial series of strikes, considers the level of volatility "smile" at any one given point in time. In a chart of volatility values, if the VIX goes up, the S&P 500 index appears to have a broader smile. This is because options contracts that are in-the-money and out-of-the-money will have a higher implied volatility than at-the-money contracts. Hence the smiley face curve. A lower VIX value makes the S&P 500 volatility values more somber, at least in the diagram. In real life, many traders and investors welcome a VIX value that draws a less cheerful face on the markets. VIX values can be used to predict likely risk, and while this method is not as accurate as frequently thought, it does serve well when guiding the trader and investor to make prudent decisions when trading derivatives. Refer to **Exhibit 5.3**.

EXHIBIT 5.3   Skew as a Volatility Differential and Skew Measured as a Volatility Ratio

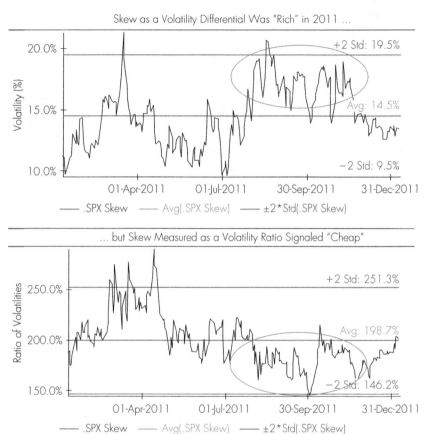

Source: Credit-Suisse Locus and Credit Suisse Derivatives Strategy

Understanding Option Volatility and its Relationship to Option Greeks, Personal Decision Making, and Odds Creation

CHAPTER 6

Extreme Volatility and Option Delta

The risks associated with options include, among other things, asset prices moving up or down, implied volatility moving up or down, and options losing value as time passes. These risks can be quantified with numbers generated by mathematical formulas known as *greeks*, because most use Greek letters as names. Each greek estimates the risk for one variable.

- *Delta* measures the change in the option price due to a change in the asset price.
- *Gamma* measures the change in the option delta due to a change in the asset price.
- *Theta* measures the change in the option price due to the passage of time.
- *Vega* measures the change in the option price due to a change in volatility.
- *Rho* measures the change in the option price due to a change in interest rates.

The Misnomer of Delta and Probability of Exercise

Over the years, a tricky issue regarding the delta of an option has emerged. It makes intuitive sense to illustrate delta initially using a simple equiprobable tree (i.e., 50 percent probability of either an up or down change in an asset) to price a call option and explain the concept of option sensitivity. However, this approach is flawed because of the conceptual problem of equating the delta of an option with the probability that the asset will finish in the money.

Delta ≠ The Probability of Exercise

Old-school traders, who learned the options business on the floor and not through a mathematical degree, experience a sharp learning curve to fully understand delta. During the first days of trading, countless traders have the propensity to equate the delta of an option to the probability of exercise. That belief sticks until experience—such as a volatility explosion—proves it to be flawed.

Probability is a magnificent yet dangerous concept when applied to financial markets, greeks, financial risk management, and especially delta. What exactly is probability? In its simplest form, probability can be defined as the chance that a particular event will occur. But this chance, or probability measure, doesn't exist in practice for the following reasons.

1. Probability exists only to the extent of the information one possesses.
2. Probability is pure randomness and can be observed only after the fact.

Probability Does Not Actually Exist in Practice

Probability exists to the extent of the information one possesses. Imagine a friend has a dollar bill in one of his back pockets and asks you, "What is the probability that the currency is in my right pocket?" You will likely answer, "Fifty percent." Since you don't know which pocket holds the dollar bill, you must make an investigation. There are only two possibilities, and the total probability is one, so you reason that the probability that the dollar bill is in your friend's right pocket is 50 percent. *Your analysis is wholly predicated on your lack of information.*

However, since your friend knows which of his pockets contains the dollar bill, from his perspective, the probability that the dollar is in his right pocket is 100 percent. Inversely, the probability that the dollar bill is in his left pocket is 0 percent. You see, the game is fixed! The person holding the dollar bill always knows with confidence where the dollar bill is while everyone else is guessing in the dark.

As tongue-in-cheek or oversimplified as this example may be, the world of financial markets seems to boil down figuratively to someone holding a dollar bill in one of his pockets, leaving everyone else to guess which pocket it is.

Probability is pure randomness and can only be observed after the fact. Stock prices, and indeed the prices of all financial assets, whether currencies, commodities, or interest rates, follow a completely unsystematic course. This randomness is the sheer essence of probability. To suggest the movement of an asset price, choose a random number from a probability distribution, multiply it by the volatility of the underlying asset, and you get a product that is merely an estimate of where the underlying asset will be trading in the very next instant. This random number represents a probability measure with infinite possibilities regarding the price of the underlying asset tomorrow given where it is at the present.

These unlimited possibilities overwhelm our limited minds. No one knows precisely what is going to happen to the price of an underlying asset. There is no statistical formula or equation that can determine an asset's exact value *tomorrow* given today's asset price and some observable input parameters. It's really all unsettled and vague.

Astronomers can predict the next lunar eclipse. Veterinarians can specify a reasonably accurate due date for a pregnant horse. Their scientific models produce dates and times, sometimes precisely, for these occasions. But an analyst who forecasts stock prices does not have this confidence. He is at the mercy of a model that is wholly dependent on probability distributions and the idea of randomness.

Therefore, as a trader desperately tries to model the evolution of stock prices and to value financial derivatives, she observes a distinct randomness which, in reality, is nothing more than an illusion. The next day, when reality arrives, the stock affirms its value and randomness evaporates. The probability measure that was used yesterday to predict today's stock value no longer applies. The trader now is in need of a new probability for predicting tomorrow's price.

For the sake of verification, and contrary to what is frequently written and said about it, delta is not the probability that the option will expire in the money.

Delta Defined

Delta is a number that measures how much the theoretical value of an option will change if the underlying asset moves up or down one point. It is the sensitivity of an option with respect to the underlying asset price. Delta is often described as the measure of the relationship between the price of an option and the price of its underlying. Delta is also referred to as a hedge ratio: the amount by which a trader needs to "hedge" to be dollar/ delta neutral.

Positive delta means that the option will rise in value if the asset price rises and drop in value if the asset price falls. Negative delta means that the option position will theoretically rise in value if the asset price falls and theoretically drop in value if the asset price rises.

Delta is sensitive to changes in volatility and time to expiration. The delta of at-the-money options is relatively immune to changes in time and volatility. This means that at-the-money options with 120 days to expiration and at-the-money options with 20 days to expiration both have deltas very similar to 50. But the more in the money or out of the money an option is, the more sensitive its delta will be to changes in volatility or time to expiration. Fewer days to expiration or a decrease in volatility push the deltas of in-the-money calls closer to 1.00 (−1.00 for puts) and the deltas of out-of-the-money options closer to 0.00. Hence, as an example, an in-the-money option with 120 days to expiration and a delta of .80 could see its delta grow to .90 (or more) with only a couple days to expiration without any movement in the underlying.

Running the Delta Numbers

The delta of a call can range from 0.00 to 1.00; the delta of a put can range from 0.00 to −1.00. Long calls have positive delta; short calls have negative delta. Long puts have negative delta; short puts have positive delta. Long underlying has positive delta; short underlying has negative delta. The closer an option's delta is to 1.00 or −1.00, the more the price of the option responds like the actual long or short underlying when the underlying price moves (see **Exhibit 6.1**).

EXHIBIT 6.1   Positive and Negative Delta

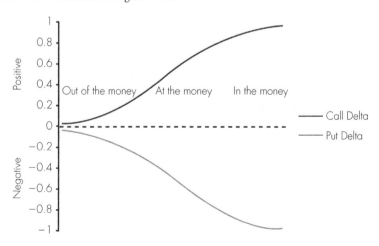

Assume the XYZ December 50 call has a value of 1.00 and a delta of +.40, and the price of XYZ is at $47. If XYZ rises to $48, the value of the XYZ December 50 call will theoretically rise to $1.40. If XYZ falls to $46, the value of the XYZ December 50 call will theoretically drop to $0.60 (see below).

Stock Price	Delta	December 50 Call Theoretical Value
$48	0.4	1.4
$47	0.4	1.0
$46	0.4	0.6

XYZ December 50 call; XYZ underlying price = $47.00, delta = +.40.

If the December 50 put has a value of $3.25 and a delta of −.60 with the price of XYZ at $47, if XYZ rises to $48, the value of the XYZ December 50 put will theoretically drop to $2.65. If XYZ falls to $46, the value of the XYZ December 50 put will theoretically rise to $3.85 (see below).

Stock Price	Delta	December 50 Put Theoretical Value
$48	−0.6	$2.65
$47	−0.6	$3.25
$46	−0.6	$3.85

XYZ December 50 put; XYZ underlying price = $47.00, delta = −.60.

These numbers assume that nothing else changes, such as a rise or fall in volatility or interest rates or the passage of time. Alterations in any one of these parameters can change delta, even if the price of the underlying asset doesn't move.

Notice in the above example that the delta of the XYZ December 50 call is .40 and the delta of the December 50 put is −.60. The sum of the absolute values is 1.00 (.40 + −.60 = 1.00). This is true for every call and put of the same month and strike price, since long underlying has a delta of +1.00. *Synthetic long underlying is long a call and short a put at the same strike price in the same month.* Therefore, the delta of a long call plus the delta of a short put (at the same strike in the same month) must equal the delta of long underlying. In the case of the XYZ December call and put, .40 + −.60 = 1.00. Conversely, *synthetic short underlying is short a call and long a put at the same strike in the same month*.

It must be understood that delta can be calculated with various input formulas, which won't be discussed here. Using the Black-Scholes model for European style options, the sum of the absolute values of the call and put is equal to 1.00. Using other input models for American style options and under specific circumstances, the sum of the absolute values of the call and put (at the same strike in the same month) can be slightly more or slightly less than 1.00.

Portfolio Delta

You can add, subtract, and multiply deltas to determine the delta of a position and underlying. The position delta is a means to see the risk/reward character of your position in terms of underlying. The calculation is very straightforward, as can be seen here:

Position Delta = option's theoretical delta × quantity of options contracts

If you are long five of the XYZ December 50 calls, each with a delta of +.40, and short one hundred shares of the XYZ stock, you will have a position delta of +100 (short 100 shares of stock = −100 deltas, long 5 calls with delta +.40, with 100 shares of stock per contract = +200 − 100 + 200 = +100).

A way to explain this delta is that if the price of XYZ rises $1.00, you will theoretically make $100. If XYZ falls $1.00, you will theoretically lose $100. It is vital to be aware that these numbers are theoretical. In actuality, delta is precise for only very small changes and for short time periods in the stock price. Nevertheless, it is still a practical tool for a $1.00 change, and it is a decent way to evaluate your risk.

Cardinal Rules of Delta

1. The delta of an option is not equal to and may never be even close to the probability of exercise of the option.
2. Calls have delta ranging from 0 to 100.
3. Puts have delta ranging from 0 to −100.
4. The underlying asset has a delta of 100. If you are short it would be −100.

5. At-the-money options, no matter where they are in the term structure, will have a delta very close to 50.
6. All options expire with a delta of 0 or 100.
7. For all practical purposes, a call and a put with the same strike and same month will have deltas with an absolute value of 100.

The Relationship between Volatility and Delta

One concept that often confuses new traders is the relationship between volatility and delta. They understand the basics of delta, and they understand the basics of volatility—yet setting them in concert results in confusion.

Volatility represents the level of uncertainty in the market and the degree to which the prices of the underlying asset are expected to change over time (see **Exhibit 6.2**). When there is more uncertainty or fear, people will pay more for options as a risk control instrument. In July 2008, for example, as the markets reflected the troubled economy, investors became fearful and bid up the prices of options or implied volatility. But when people feel more secure, they sell their options, causing the implied volatility to drop.

An increase in volatility causes all option deltas to move toward .50. The higher the spike in volatility, the more options converge toward .50. So for in-the-money options, the delta will decrease, and for out-of-the-money

EXHIBIT 6.2 Volatility and Delta, With Stock Price at $100

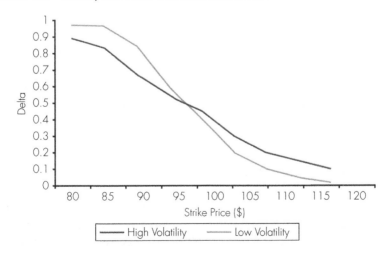

options, the delta will increase. This makes intuitive sense, for when uncertainty increases it becomes less clear where the underlying might end up at expiration. For example, an in-the-money call with a delta of .80 under normal volatility conditions might drop to .65 under a higher-volatility environment, reflecting less certainty that the call will finish in the money.

A more concise approach is to look at expiration. At expiry, volatility is 0; all deltas are either 0 or 1, finishing either out of the money or in the money. Any increase in volatility causes probabilities to move away from 0 and 1, reflecting a higher level of uncertainty.

Higher Volatility and Delta

Higher volatility suggests that the market anticipates a wider range of movement. Say, for example, that you own a stock which, for over one year, has consistently traded between $34 and $36 dollars per share. It makes sense that the option's volatility on this stock would be low and option deltas would be widely distributed between 0 and 1.00. If you held a stock that instead traded at a monthly range of $20 to $50, it would be safe to say that the option's volatility would be higher than that in the previous scenario, and you would notice a slight convergence in deltas toward 50. The deltas above 50 would tend to fall, and the deltas below 50 would tend to rise. The 50 delta option would always remain a 50 delta option. The call option, which previously had a 30 delta (with the corresponding put having a delta of $-.70$), would under the new scenario possibly show a delta of 35 (with the corresponding put having a delta of $-.65$).

As a commonsense approach to higher volatility and delta, assume you are watching a commodity, stock, or other asset that has experienced an average of 1 percent moves *per day*. Furthermore, assume that the asset is now experiencing moves of 10 percent or greater *per day*. Given the new assumption, in which the asset is moving at least 10 times greater per day than usual, an options model would logically assign deltas that converge toward .50 to the various strikes.

Lower Volatility and Delta

When options traders talk about volatility, the average investor assumes they are discussing *higher* volatility and/or uncertainty about their present investments. The effect of higher volatility on delta can be clarified by analyzing a lower-volatility environment. Lower volatility will have the opposite effect on option delta, but for a variety of reasons it is often easier to comprehend.

Assume that the government has created a firm policy of aggressive market intervention. A commodity that has experienced gyrations of 25 percent or more per day will now no longer be allowed to move more than 5 percent per day. With that information, traders would realize that the intervention increases the likelihood of the following two scenarios:

- A 100 delta call will remain a 100 delta call.
- A 20 delta put will remain a 20 delta put.

A sharp drop in volatility implies a tighter band of movement in the underlying, suggesting the following results:

- An option with a delta more than .50 will rise.
- An option with a delta less than .50 will drop.

Delta, Time, and Volatility

We know that at expiration option delta will be either 0 or 1.00, whether the option is in the money or out of the money. With that understood, it makes sense that the further out you go in term, the more difficult it becomes to estimate the direction or movement of the underlying asset. This commonsense approach to understanding how delta reacts by moving out along the term structure (i.e., days till expiration) is strongly correlated with higher volatility. The further out your option is (until expiry), the more your delta will compare similarly to an upward move in volatility. The closer you are to expiration, the easier it may be to quantify movement, which is the same principle as that behind a lower-volatility environment.

Because it gets more and more difficult to determine where XYZ will be months into the future, keep in mind that option delta will undergo the following changes:

- One hundred delta options decrease (slightly) as you go out in time.
- Fifty delta options remain essentially constant the further you go out in time.
- Ten delta options increase (slightly) as you go out in time.

Exhibit 6.3 illustrates the term structure of XYZ. It looks vaguely familiar to that of a volatility structure for a single month.

EXHIBIT 6.3 Time to Expiration and Delta, With Stock Price at $100

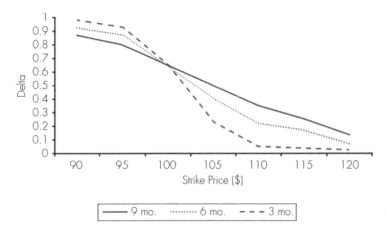

Delta, Position Delta, Volatility, and the Professional Trader

Professional traders are concerned with not only with the delta of an individual option, but also the delta of more complex trades and/or their net position delta. When dealing with a complex position that involves more than one option, the traders' "anguish" is their total exposure to the position's environment (e.g., time, underlying movement, volatility, interest rates), which is known as a "position delta." Position delta is computed as shown here:

Position Delta = option delta × shares per option × number of options

The table below shows how a trader can compute the position delta on a hypothetical stock/option position in XYZ. Recall that long stock, long calls, and short puts add positive delta, but short stock, short calls, and long puts introduce negative delta.

Position	Delta	Position Delta
Short 250 shares of XYZ	−1.00	−250
Short 10 XYZ August 25 calls	−0.80	−800
Long 5 XYZ August 30 calls	0.53	+265
Long 15 XYZ September 30 calls	0.56	+840
Position Delta		+55

Delta neutral, therefore, is the process of establishing a position in which negative deltas offset the positive deltas. The hypothetical trade in the table above has a position delta of +55 and is, therefore, approaching delta neutral. Obviously, the delta of the position will continually change as the price of the underlying stock rises and falls. Therefore, remaining completely delta neutral involves consistently adjusting the position as time passes. Although some professional traders will attempt to establish completely delta neutral positions (e.g., to hedge a portfolio, to profit from changes in volatility, or for some other reason), they rarely end up with a position delta of 0. Nevertheless, low-risk options trading involves lowering the delta associated with simply owning a stock or option, which can be done by using countless strategies discussed later in this book.

Volatility and Its Effect on Position Delta

Assessing a professional's position risk isn't overly complex, but it can be a bit difficult to visualize since it is multidimensional. The position risk can be measured by hypothetically adjusting price, time, and volatility and measuring the effects on position balance and value. Understanding each dimension individually helps to simplify the assessment, but actual market dynamics occur simultaneously.

Floor traders accumulate multiple positions of options. Most professionals hedge their portfolio with the associated underlying. Today's computer models can immediately provide the trader with the instant gratification of a net delta. Yet that net delta can and does change with variations in volatility.

Imagine you had specific orders to make trades and hedge them properly. In addition, you were told to manage your net delta if it approached a certain level. Assume you were unaware of the effect of volatility on your position and you went about your business. You could employ one of the following strategies:

- Hedge deltas that you really didn't have to hedge.
- Add more risk to your net position.
- Reverse hedge and, more likely than not, lose money.
- Get yourself fired.

The average investor needs to understand how volatility affects delta in order to be confident in his position. Investors hoping to add income to their portfolio or reduce risk will most likely not rehedge their original position. However, understanding this potential effect is worth noting.

Assume you are short a 50 delta call option against long stock. Furthermore, assume the option will expire in 10 to 90 days. It's safe to say that any type of volatility movement in your option will not affect your delta. An at-the-money option, no matter what the price, will always have a 50 delta.

Assume you are long a 30 delta put against stock that you own. If volatility should rise drastically, the delta of that put will rise as well (disregarding any other type of parameter change). Your net position will become more negative, inviting you to buy more stock (to remain hedged) against your position. The danger lies in two situations:

- The rising volatility will increase your delta—in this case, negative delta— but will the volatility continue to rise and continue to inflate your delta?
- All options expire with 0 or 100 delta. If you buy more stock (as the negative delta suggests) against your put, which has grown from a 30 to possibly a 45 delta due to volatility expansion, you may end up with a 0 delta and then be dealing with a bigger inventory of underlying than you anticipated.

Assume you are short a 30 delta call with stock that you own. If volatility should rise, it makes sense that your 30 delta call will rise in value as well (again excluding all other parameters). Your net position will become longer, meaning you could sell some of your underlying to be mathematically hedged. Or, more enticing still, you could sell more options—hoping to receive that already anticipated income!

CHAPTER 7

Smoke and Mirrors: Managing Gamma through Volatile Markets

Gamma is the rate of change of the delta of an option, with respect to the underlying asset: the "delta's delta." Gamma is also expressed as the curvature of an option, or the rapidity at which the delta of an option changes as the value of the underlying asset changes. Gamma is the chief characteristic of all financial instruments that have a nonlinear payoff stream, including options. Without curvature, the sphere of financial derivatives simply would not exist. Option gamma is typically articulated as delta gained or lost per one point change in the underlying asset (also known simply as "the underlying"), with delta increasing by the amount of gamma when the underlying increases, and falling by the same amount of gamma when the underlying decreases.

Gamma indicates how steady your delta is. A large gamma indicates an unsteady delta. When gamma is high, delta can begin changing dramatically from even a small move in the underlying. Long calls and long puts always have positive gamma. Short calls and short puts always have negative gamma. Stocks, or any underlying asset, possess 0.00 gamma because their delta is always 1.00—it never changes. Positive gamma indicates that the delta of a long call will become more positive and move toward -1.00 when the underlying rises and less positive and move toward 0.00 when the underlying price falls. The delta of a long put will become more negative and move toward -1.00 when the underlying price falls and will become less negative and move toward 0.00 when the underlying price rises (see **Exhibit 7.1**).

EXHIBIT 7.1 Delta and Gamma Composition

Position	Delta	Gamma
Long Underlying	Long	0
Short Underlying	Short	0
Long Call	Long	Long
Short Call	Short	Short
Long Put	Short	Long
Short Put	Long	Short

The reverse is true for negative gamma. Negative gamma indicates that the delta of a short call will become more negative and move toward −1.00 when the underlying rises and will become less negative and move toward 0.00 when the underlying price falls. The delta of a short put will become less negative and move toward 0.00 when the underlying rises and will become more negative and move toward −1.00 when the underlying falls.

For example, assume that the XYZ July 100 call has a delta of +.45, the July 100 put has a delta of −.55, and the price of XYZ is $96.00. The gamma for both the XYZ July 100 call and the corresponding put is .07. If XYZ moves up $1.00 to $97.00, the delta of the XYZ July 100 call becomes +.52 [+.45 + ($1.00 × .07)] and the delta of the XYZ July 100 put becomes −.48 [−.55 + ($1.00 × .07)]. If XYZ drops $1.00 to $95.00, the delta of the XYZ July 100 call becomes +.38 [+.45 + (−$1.00 × .07)] and the delta of the July 100 put becomes −.62 [−.55 = (−$1.00 × .07)].

Just as option delta changes, so does gamma. A graph of the strike prices of options would resemble a mountain, with the peak very close to the at-the-money strike. At-the-money options will always have the most gamma, whereas the rest of gamma spreads out at the foot of the mountain, flattening out as options are in the money or out of the money (see **Exhibit 7.2**).

Let's dig deeper. A deeply in-the-money call has a delta near 1.00, an at-the-money call has a delta of .50, and an out-of-the-money call has a delta of .10. If the underlying asset increases, the absolute value of the in-the-money call will increase the most, given that a deeply in-the-money 100 delta option imitates the underlying. Even though the in-the-money call has positive gamma, its delta really doesn't get much closer to 1.00 than it was before the

EXHIBIT 7.2 The Nature of Gamma: Gamma versus Underlying

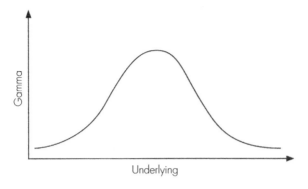

EXHIBIT 7.3 Total Delta and Gamma of Strike Prices

Exercise Price	Call Option Price	Call Option Delta	Call Option Gamma	Put Option Price	Put Option Delta	Put Option Gamma
90	10.41	91	1.9	0.3	−9	1.9
95	6.12	75	4	1.17	−25	4
100	3.1	50	5	3.1	−50	5
105	1.29	28	4.3	6.25	−72	4.3
110	0.44	13	2.5	10.35	−87	2.5

Underlying = $100
Time till expiry = 56 days
Implied volatility = 28%

underlying rose. The value of the out-of-the-money call will also grow, and its delta will probably increase as well, but it will still be a long way from 1.00. The value of the at-the-money option will increase, and its delta will change the most. That is, the delta of the at-the-money option will move toward 1.00 much more quickly than the delta of the out-of-the-money option. Practically speaking, the at-the-money call can provide a good balance of potential profit if the underlying rises versus potential loss if the underlying falls. The out-of-the-money call will not make as much money if the underlying asset rises, and the in-the-money call will lose more money if the underlying falls.

In **Exhibit 7.3** there are a couple issues to note. First, the absolute value of the delta (per strike) equals 100. Regardless of the strike price or month, adding the absolute value of a strike will equal 100. Therefore, buying a call and selling a put with the same strike and month would be, for all practical purposes, synthetically equivalent to buying the underlying asset. Inversely, selling a call and buying a put with the same strike and month would be virtually equivalent to selling the underlying asset.

Second, notice the gamma in Exhibit 7.3. Although we know calls and puts provide the investor with different rights and/or obligations, depending whether you are a buyer or seller, the gamma for each strike—whether it be a call or a put—is exactly the same. It may not seem logical that a 91 delta call (90 strike) would share the same exact gamma as the corresponding .09 delta put (90 strike), but the mathematics behind options shows no partiality to the call or put of the same strike and month. The mathematical logic relies solely on the relationship of a strike price and its distance from the underlying.

To Review:

- Option gamma is the rate of change of the delta of an option with respect to the underlying asset.
- When looking at the combination of a call and put of the same strike and month, the absolute delta value will equal 100.
- The gamma of a call and put combination of the same strike and month will always be identical.

Gamma and Volatility

Determining how gamma varies as volatility changes depends on whether the option is in the money, at the money, or out of the money. A *decrease in volatility* acts as if it is pulling up the top of the mountain on the graph of gamma and making the slope away from the top steeper. This steep slope indicates that the at-the-money gamma is increasing, but the in-the-money and out-of-the-money gamma is decreasing. The gamma of at-the-money options rises higher as the underlying volatility becomes less. With out-of-the-money or in-the-money options, however, the gamma declines with volatility.

A sharp *increase in volatility* has the opposite effect on gamma and depends particularly on whether the option is in the money, at the money, or out of the money. An increase in volatility acts to flatten out the gamma curve and make the slope from the peak more moderate. During a high-volatility environment, the at-the-money gamma decreases, whereas the in-the-money and out-of-the-money gamma increases. The gamma of at-the-money options decreases as volatility increases in the underlying asset. With out-of-the-money or in-the-money options, however, the gamma increases with volatility.

At this point, it may be helpful to think of the delta as the speed with which an option moves with respect to its underlying asset. The maximum speed is 100 percent for very deeply in-the-money options, and the minimum speed is 0 for very far out-of-the-money options. Continuing with this analogy, the gamma is the acceleration of the option—that is, how fast the option picks up or loses speed (deltas) as the price of the underlying contract rises or falls.

What this all means to an options trader is that a position with positive gamma is relatively safe; that is, it will generate the deltas that benefit from an up or down move in the underlying. But a position with negative gamma can be dangerous. It may generate deltas that will hurt you in an up or down move in the underlying. To make things even more complicated, a trader's position can potentially flip from long gamma to short gamma or from short gamma to long gamma. The reason(s) for this will be discussed in Part 3 of the book, and the subject is worthy of close attention from the new trader or investor.

Managing Positive Gamma during a High-Volatility Environment

When a portfolio contains long gamma, it is possible to profit on both sides of the movement of the underlying, every time it ebbs and flows. Simple, right? Just buy options—giving you a long gamma position—and sell underlying (for that's what the delta suggests you do) on any up move and buy it back on any down move, locking in a tidy profit. Unfortunately, the real world does not accommodate this scenario, and a successful trader must understand the risks lying beneath these assumptions.

Assume your portfolio consists of an equal number of 25 delta calls and 25 delta puts. Furthermore, assume both of these options (called a strangle, which will be discussed in Chapter 16) provide you with a net delta of 0 (long a 25 delta call against long a 25 delta put, providing you with a net 0 delta) and a positive gamma of 8.0 (4.0 gamma for the 25 delta call plus 4.0 gamma for a 25 delta put). Remember that options with the same delta will also have the same gamma because they are equally distant from the at-the-money strike.

Assume that volatility increases significantly. This is most likely a good thing—if not a great thing—because your position is net long delta. Also assume that as volatility explodes, the underlying (attached to these options) experiences a large downward move. Your once neutral delta position has now become a very short delta position. And there's better news yet: Because of the sharp rise in volatility, your gamma position is increasing as well. In other words, although you are accumulating negative deltas due to the downward move, you are getting all the more negative due to the out-of-the-money options' propensity to pick up more gamma as volatility increases.

The Bad News: There's Always More than Meets the Eye

There's always a catch. You have negative deltas in a falling market (that's a good thing). You accumulated even more negative deltas because volatility increases and the curvature of your slope "flattens," assigning more gamma than in a lower-volatility environment. A trader's natural propensity is to quickly hedge these deltas. It seems like free money and boy, is it ever hard to lay off. Yet you need to take the following points into consideration.

Point One

In the decision to buy back your deltas (which the model says you rightly deserve) you are, in effect, *taking an opinion on the market*. You are making a directional bet on the market. It's time to think hard about your position. Forget about the negative deltas for a moment! You are buying deltas against a long put that is presently out of the money. Sure, it's not as out of the money as it once was, but it's still out of the money.

What happens if you buy your "rightly deserved" negative deltas (according to what the model says), and the market, after a few days, returns to a state of normality? Even if volatility is sustained at these higher levels, if the market begins to creep lower, you have long deltas that now become part of your portfolio. The deltas you bought will lose money as the underlying drifts lower.

If you bought deltas and the market rebounds, you're a hero—but a lucky one! If you bought deltas and the market stagnates, those short deltas that you bought (making you theoretically delta neutral) will quickly become long deltas. Recall from Chapter 5 that options, at expiry, will have either a 0 or 1.00 delta. If, after the original down move and subsequent volatility spike, the underlying asset experiences a "sideways drift," it will take little time for your increase in net negative delta to become a flat delta. Since you bought deltas in, your position will quickly flip from short to flat to long delta.

Point Two

By buying in your deltas, you are also *stating an opinion about volatility.* As we've learned, the volatility spike has helped give your portfolio a larger gamma and thus a larger negative delta. Again, this is due to the flattening effect of gamma during a high-volatility environment.

If volatility is sustained, you and your newly bought deltas are in great shape. If volatility begins to soften after a few days, even slightly, those once short deltas will rapidly disappear, leaving you naked long delta. If volatility continues to go higher, and there is rapid movement, pat yourself on the back for making such an informed decision to buy those deltas. Yet chalk that profit up to randomness working in your favor, not skill.

Practical Considerations for Managing Long Gamma in a High-Volatility Environment

When in doubt, hedge half. With the position described above, it may make sense to buy half of your deltas. If the down move and volatility spike gave you a theoretical negative delta of −600, buy half (300). There's nothing wrong with being half right.

Try lowering the volatility of your model. If the down move and volatility spike gave you a theoretical negative delta of −600, it may make sense to readjust your model's volatility, perhaps to where it was before the tremendous volatility explosion, to give you a different read on your delta. This conservative approach is often applied by seasoned options professionals with multifaceted positions. Lowering volatility requires discipline since you are, in effect, accepting a lower theoretical profit and loss.

Reduce your position to a place where you can think straight. If you find your delta position (resulting from long gamma) eating away at you, consider reducing your position. Many traders make dumb decisions solely because of overtrading. This goes for a good position as well as a bad one! Options trading is about leverage. Make every possible effort to control your winners while reducing your losers.

Hedge options with options. Another common strategy is to hedge your negative deltas (resulting from long gamma) with options. Due to the volatility spike, after a sharp down move in the underlying asset, you may find yourself with a net short delta position. This position is the net result of the long 25 put increasing its negative delta faster than the original 25 call loses its positive delta. Some traders will sell a further out-of-the-money put naked against their short delta. The put you've sold (naked) will reduce the cost of the long portfolio you are holding.

What are the results? If the market stagnates, you've supplemented your portfolio with a short put, reducing the net cost of holding this position. If the market indeed rallies, not only have you reduced the cost of your position, but you may eventually find your position net long deltas with perhaps an opportunity to sell an out-of-the-money call in addition to the one on which you're currently long. This will further trim the cost of your position. If the market continues to drop and volatility continues to rise, you are, in effect, stopped out of your long gamma position. Once the underlying crosses below the long put strike of your position, you will find your position becoming flat to short gamma due to the naked out-of-the-money put you sold.

Managing Negative Gamma in a High-Volatility Environment

Experienced options traders encounter sleepless nights when there is an excessive amount of negative gamma on their books, and they are generally more relaxed when they run positive gamma. Years ago, a senior options trader would tell young traders, "The more the gamma you can buy, the greater your bonus will be!"

When selling, the chief dilemma for options traders is that their gamma becomes negative, and the best-case scenario is that the underlying does not move. Any movement in the underlying price from the initial level will multiply sleepless nights and magnify poor decision making. Add to that a volatility spike, and trading gets ugly. Yet with risk comes reward. Negative gamma can also work very well in your favor.

Assume you are deeply convinced that XYZ will drop in price. Acting on your hunch, you decide to sell short some 50 delta calls which will expire in 30 days. Further assume that this short 50 delta call position gives you a negative gamma position of -21. Lastly, you learn that XYZ options have been trading at approximately 10 percent volatility.

The next morning, volatility explodes in XYZ options. Your theoretical values suggest the options have jumped from 10 percent volatility to 20 percent overnight. This can't be good, you think to yourself. Or do you? There are two possible scenarios.

EXHIBIT 7.4 The Relationship of Volatility and Gamma With Underlying Price at $150

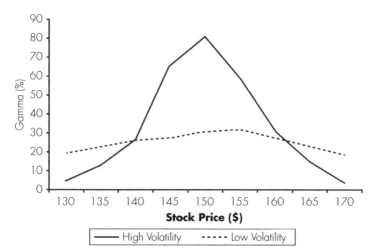

Scenario One

In the scenario in which volatility moves higher, and in this case doubles, without any substantial movement in the underlying, you are certainly in grave shape because you've sold premium which has gone up exponentially overnight. Your saving grace, if there is any, is that you're not double-whammed by both price and delta. Why? If volatility explodes, the gamma curve (see **Exhibit 7.4**) will flatten out. In this case, your position gamma (because it's a 50 delta) falls from −21 (at 10 percent volatility) to approximately −12 (at 20 percent volatility). This situation is highly theoretical and generally unlikely.

Scenario Two

You are short a 30-day 50 delta (at-the-money) call, which gives you a position gamma of −.21. Also, you happen to be wrong with your downside conviction in XYZ. The underlying rallies every day, although never by a lot, and volatility in the option continues to rise. As the days go by, you find your delta becoming more and more negative, because the underlying continues to rise and volatility is sustained. Usually this type of portfolio predicament undergoes a typical series of phases.

> *Phase One.* Your negative delta becomes more and more negative. If volatility keeps rising, your gamma will decrease, due to the

flattening effect. You are losing money (probably lots of it) as the premium in the option goes up with the volatility.

Phase Two. After a few days of this annoyance, you buy some underlying against your ever-increasing negative deltas. You are defeated, but all is not lost. You feel you did the right thing by neutralizing your delta.

Phase Three. As soon as you buy in your negative deltas, the underlying makes a sharp move to the downside. To further complicate things, option volatility remains high.

Phase Four. You are now in a whipsaw predicament. The underlying has relaxed, yet volatility has increased. You may have made some of your money back in the call's theoretical value due to the drop, but now you must deal with the long underlying that you bought at higher levels.

Practical Considerations of Negative Gamma in High Volatility

Be aware of the change in gamma with respect to the underlying. With a higher or lower value of the underlying asset, your gamma can be more or less negative depending on where your position is along the option curve.

Position your stops. Before entering any trade, especially a negative gamma trade, know your stops ahead of time. In general, traders place stops to minimize loss in case of violent movement in the underlying. But when you position your stops, it's also important to balance the amount of decay (or theta, which will be discussed in Chapter 9) and the level of volatility of the underlying asset.

Gamma bleed. With volatility (as well as other factors such as time decay), a negative gamma position can become more or less negative. This is what is better known as bleed. The gamma bleed results in corresponding delta bleed, and a portfolio might get shorter or longer delta depending on the underlying with respect to the short strike.

Negative gamma is highest for short-dated at-the-money options. However, the risk can be theoretically unlimited, as the underlying can move either up or down to any extent.

Being short short-dated at-the-money options. It is a fine balance to consistently operate negative gamma under different levels of volatility to provide you with various delta positions. Solely running negative gamma at higher implied volatility (higher than the market is trading) or lower implied volatility (lower than the market is trading) both carry consequences.

Gamma and Volatility with Respect to Time Structure

You may have learned, and correctly so, that *front-month options have "the gamma" while back-month options have "the volatility."* This is true in theory, but there's more to the story.

How gamma changes largely depends on whether your option is in the money, at the money, or out of the money. Also, volatility changes have the same effect on gamma as do changes in time. Therefore, time and volatility correlate accordingly.

More time can be equated to an increase in volatility. In this case, your gamma becomes more widely distributed among strike prices.

Less time can be compared to a decrease in volatility. In this case, your gamma becomes more heavily concentrated with your at-the-money strike prices, or strikes that are closer to the current price of the underlying.

The More Time You Have, the Less Gamma Your Option Will Have

This is a commonsense general principle. It's difficult enough to pinpoint where an underlying asset will be tomorrow. Imagine the difficulty of correctly guessing where it will be three, six, or even nine months in the future. There are simply too many unknowns. It's safe to say that the *time value of an option is closely linked to higher volatility.* The way gamma acts in high-volatility environments mimics how gamma acts with time. With time, as with high volatility, there is a softening effect of gamma along the slope. As you move out in time, the gamma curve flattens out.

The Less Time You Have, the More Gamma Your Options Will Have

The closer an underlying asset gets to its expiration date, the narrower the range in which it will settle becomes. Don't misunderstand—it's never crystal clear where things will finally come to rest; it just gets plainer to see with less time for the asset to move.

As an option gets closer to expiration, your gamma will react in a way that is very similar to how it behaves in a low-volatility environment, which implies a narrower range of movement of the underlying. If that is true, then a steep gamma slope should make sense. If you look at an option three days from expiration, which is attached to an underlying that moves perhaps 1 percent per day, wouldn't it make sense that the bulk of your gamma would be centered on the at-the-money strikes? In addition, the strikes that are now 5 percent out of the money or in the money would have a negligible amount of gamma. See **Exhibit 7.5** for an illustration of how gamma changes over time.

EXHIBIT 7.5   Difference in Gamma for Thirty-, Sixty-, and Ninety-Day Options

			XYZ 121	XYZ 123	XYZ 125
30 Day	121 Strike	Gamma	26	10	3
60 Day	121 Strike	Gamma	13	12	4
90 Day	121 Strike	Gamma	6	5	4

Summary

- Option gamma is one step above option delta. Option delta measures the slope of the price curve. Option gamma measures the curvature of the price curve.
- At-the-money options will always have the highest gamma. In-the-money and out-of-the-money options will have relatively less gamma depending on how far they are from the at-the-money strike.
- Short option positions are characterized by negative option gamma. This applies to both put and call options. Long option positions are characterized by positive option gamma. This applies to both put and call options.
- Options with a short time to expiration generally have higher option gamma than do long-term options.
- Option gamma increases (for at-the-money and near at-the-money strikes) as the option approaches its maturity.
- When option gamma is high, option delta changes rapidly. When option gamma is low, option delta changes relatively little.
- Stock and futures have a constant gamma equal to 0.
- A high-volatility environment will reduce your at-the-money gamma while raising your in-the-money and out-of-the-money gamma.
- A low-volatility environment will raise your at-the-money gamma while lowering your in-the-money and out-of-the-money gamma.

CHAPTER 8

Price Explosion: Volatility and Option Vega

Vega—the only greek that isn't represented by a real Greek letter—is an estimate of how much the theoretical value of an option changes when volatility changes 1 percent. Higher volatility means higher options prices. Why? Higher volatility results in a greater price swing in the underlying asset price, which translates into a greater likelihood for an option to be profitable by expiration. Lower volatility signifies lower options prices, for the inverse reason: Lower volatility implies a smaller swing in the underlying asset price, translating into less likelihood that the option will be profitable by its expiration date.

Long calls and long puts always have positive vega. Short calls and short puts always have negative vega. Stocks and futures have zero vega—their values are not affected by volatility. Positive vega means that the value of an option position increases when volatility increases and decreases when volatility decreases. Negative vega means that the value of an option position decreases when volatility increases, and it increases when volatility decreases (see **Exhibit 8.1**).

For example, look at the XYZ August 100 call. It has a value of $2.00 and a vega of 1.20 with the volatility of XYZ at 30 percent. If the volatility of XYZ rises to 31 percent, the value of the XYZ August 100 call will theoretically rise to $2.20. If the volatility of XYZ falls to 29 percent, the value of the XYZ August 100 call will drop to $1.80.

Vega is highest for at-the-money options and becomes progressively lower as options are in the money and out of the money (see **Exhibit 8.2**). This means the value of at-the-money options changes the most when the

EXHIBIT 8.1 Vega Composition

Position	Vega
Long Call	Long
Short Call	Short
Long Put	Long
Short Put	Short
Long Underlying	0
Short Underlying	0

EXHIBIT 8.2 Vega Curve

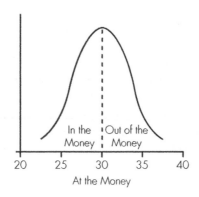

volatility changes. The vega of at-the-money options is higher when either volatility is higher or there are more days to expiration.

Position vega measures how much the value of a position changes when volatility changes 1 percent. Position vega is calculated by multiplying the vega of each option in your portfolio by the number of contracts and the dollar value of one point for the option contract, then adding them together.

The Relationship between Implied Volatility and Vega

If the volatility of an underlying asset changes, option vega changes as well. Option vega grows as the option moves from out of the money and closer to at the money, but it declines as the option moves toward deeply in the money. Option vega is greatest for options at the money, and it is smaller for options completely out of the money or very deeply in the money. This can be explained more easily by saying that if the option is worthless, it doesn't matter how volatile the underlying asset is, because the chance that the option will suddenly become in the money is relatively small. If the option is deeply in the money, the chance that the option will suddenly become worthless with increased volatility is also relatively slim. But if the option is at the money, which is on the verge of being worthless or valuable, then even a relatively small change in the volatility in the price of the underlying asset can change the position.

It is nearly impossible to understand why option vega is so important without first acquiring a basic understanding of implied volatility.

The more an underlying asset is expected to move due to an important news report or earnings release in the near future, the higher the implied volatility of that underlying asset becomes. Implied volatility has the tendency to escalate as the date of that important release approaches. This is due in part to the higher demand for the options of the underlying as speculative heat builds. In these circumstances, traders (market makers) hike implied volatility in order to charge a higher price for the higher demand, which suggests that implied volatility is largely at the mercy of option supply and demand, and its effect on the price of an option is measured by option vega.

Since implied volatility has a "tendency to rise" as important news releases approach, and since option vega makes certain the price of the option rises along with it, wouldn't the few days prior to such events be perfect for buying options and hoping that the underlying remains relatively stagnant so as to profit from the rise in implied volatility? Many options professionals take delta neutral and gamma neutral positions (e.g., short front-month at-the-money options versus longer dated options) a few days before important news releases so as to profit from the rise in implied volatility safely; they close the position just before the release.

Just as implied volatility can float an option's price through option vega, however, it can also slice a big chunk of value off the price very quickly if implied volatility falls dramatically, particularly after important news releases are made. This catastrophic drop is sometimes referred to as a *volatility crunch*. When implied volatility falls, options with positive option vega fall in value along with it. That's why it can be dangerous to buy options with a very high option vega just before an important news release if you plan to hold the position long term. In fact, the implied volatility could float the extrinsic value of those options so high that when the big move is eventually made, it barely covers the extrinsic value and results in a loss.

Implied Volatility: Price Analogy

Another way to look at implied volatility is to think of it as a price, not as a measure of future stock moves. Implied volatility is simply a more convenient way to communicate option prices than currency. Prices are different in nature from statistical quantities. We can estimate the volatility of future underlying returns using any of a large number of estimation methods; however, the number we get is not a price. A price requires two counterparts: a buyer and a seller. Prices are determined by supply and demand. Statistical estimates depend on the time series and the mathematical structure of the model used. It is a mistake to confuse a price, which implies a transaction, with the result of a statistical estimation, which is merely the result of a calculation. Implied volatilities are prices derived from actual transactions. Seen in this light, it should not be surprising that implied volatilities might not conform to what a particular statistical model would predict.

Option Vega and Time

The more time to expiration an underlying asset has, the more uncertainty there will be as to where it will end up by expiration, which translates into greater buyer opportunity and seller risk. This results in a higher vega for options with longer time to expiration in order to compensate for the additional risk assumed by the seller (see **Exhibit 8.3**).

EXHIBIT 8.3 Time till Expiration and Vega, With Stock Price at $30

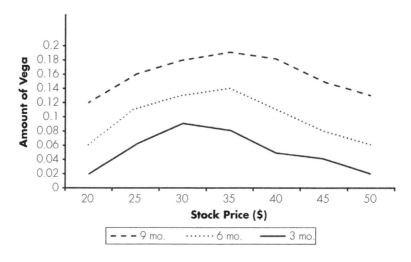

Option Vega and Its Greek Cousins

Again, higher reward comes with higher risk. Like option theta, option vega also shares a linear relationship with option gamma. When option gamma is highest, which is when options are at the money, option vega is also at its highest, subjecting the trading position to a high risk of volatility "crunch" along with the potential of exponential, explosive gains granted by gamma. With vega as well as theta working against an at-the-money position, options traders must ensure that the expected gain in the underlying asset more than covers the extrinsic value.

Option Vega Implications

1. Option vega is equal for both call and put options with the same month and strike price (e.g., if the August 50 call has a vega of .30, the August 50 put will also have a vega of .30).
2. Options with a short time to expiration have a lower option vega than those with a long time to expiration because the long-term options are exposed to a greater risk of ending out of the money than options with only a few days to expiration. The price of the underlying asset is more likely to move by 50 percent up or down in the long term than in the short term.
3. Options are most sensitive to changes in the volatility of the underlying asset when they are at the money.
4. Out-of-the-money and in-the-money options are not affected by volatility in the price of the underlying asset.
5. Option vega can be hedged with another option only.

Don't Underestimate the Relationship between Volatility and Option Vega

A professional trader has a good grasp on the theories of vega. To a market maker, the concept is very straightforward. Yet the market doesn't rely on theoretical knowledge, and over the years more than one wretched soul has lost a fortune due to volatility trades and/or the underestimation of what vega can do to a portfolio.

For all the academics behind it, along with the PhDs in financial engineering and the endless streams of models and modeling, vega ends up being the one greek that, in the end, defeats even the best and brightest. Vega, unlike the other greeks, is an expression of an unknown. Surely, you can work out what your option will be theoretically worth given a 1 percent move—that is all well and good for textbook study. The reality is that there are forces nearly impossible to quantify that influence the vega of an option.

All derivative traders know that option prices actually boil down to the market's expectation of the future volatility of the underlying instrument, because all the other determinants of an option's price—the underlying price, time to maturity, interest rate, and strike price—are objective. Volatility is the subjective X factor, and only rarely does an option's actual, realized volatility replicate the implied volatility reflected in its valuation.

Too often traders may simply focus on one variable and imagine, hope, or expect that all the action will involve that variable. For instance, a trader might want to bet on a change in implied volatility because he believes it will head higher or lower, or because he expects a shift in the implied volatility curve and wants her profit and loss to reflect the correctness of his view. But in many cases the position's profit and loss will respond to the change in implied volatility in a nonlinear way. Also, the trader may have to live with the fact that the underlying price movements of time decay (theta) might have a greater effect on his profit and loss than the accuracy of her view of implied volatility. In other words, he might want to bet on a change in implied volatility, but most of his profit and loss might depend on the actual volatility of the underlying.

Another oversimplification that traders sometimes make is to rely too much on greeks to manage options risk. Greeks are useful tools, but they have limitations.

1. *Greeks only focus on one variable at a time.* Delta and gamma are measures of an exposure to underlying price movements, assuming that none of the other variables is going to change. Theta and vega serve similar roles with respect to changes in time and implied volatility. Each greek offers a one-dimensional view of a three-dimensional puzzle.
2. *Greeks consider only incremental effects; they don't show your exposure to a discrete change in any of the variables.* In the real world, instead of a small change in a variable, we often wind up with a big change in perhaps more than one variable. Greeks don't even begin to address those exposures.

You may have heard a wise old trader say, "Volatility represents opportunity, but vega measures money." Pay attention. Many people use the terms vega and volatility interchangeably, but there is a distinction. *Implied volatility is one of the inputs that compose an option's price, whereas vega measures the actual dollar impact of any change in volatility.*

Sometimes the impact of a steep drop in implied volatility on an option's value is greater than the impact of a change in the underlying asset's price. This can lead to a situation in which an option fails to increase in value despite a significant price change. Knowing the vega of a position is especially crucial as the market proceeds into earnings season. Typically, implied volatility increases ahead of an earnings report or some other impending event, such as a court ruling or a government decision, as traders anticipate the news causing a change in price. This is referred to as "pricing in the move" and is often expressed in percentage terms to gauge market expectations.

But once the news is out, no matter what the underlying asset does, there's typically a large decline in implied volatility, which pressures the value of the option. Unless the change in price of the underlying asset is large enough to offset the decline in implied volatility, the value of both puts and calls could decline immediately following an earnings report.

It is amazing how often traders—even experienced traders—get hurt by sloppy thinking about volatility. For example, in January 1991 the Gulf War was looming. U.N. forces threatened to start bombing Iraq on January 15. As that date grew closer, financial instruments altered a bit, but implied volatility kept jumping higher because traders thought as soon as the bombs dropped—or didn't drop—there would be a lot of movement in financial commodity prices.

When the bombs finally dropped, the market saw momentous volatility. Some financial instruments moved a lot, but the implied volatilities of options collapsed quickly. *Some people thought they were betting on high actual volatility, when in fact they were really more exposed to implied volatility.* They were right on one count and painfully wrong on the other—and in most cases, they lost a great deal of money.

Volatility and Vega Insensitivity

Vega insensitivity represents a sophisticated and fundamental concept of derivatives pricing and trading. It means vega neutrality over a range of volatility levels. Volatility sensitivity means that rather than looking for an option's vega at a specific volatility level, traders (buyers and sellers) use the price variation over a wide variation of volatility to quantify vega.

Traders do not need to resort to exotic products to create volatility-insensitive structures. Vanilla options work just as well.

If you want your portfolio to be vega neutral—or volatility insensitive—you must buy and sell a specific ratio. Take the case of a simple call spread. If you sell a 120 call and buy a 110 call, you create a call spread. Since the 120 call and the 110 call will each have its own volatility-dependent vega, you must multiply the long option position with its corresponding vega and add the short option position with its corresponding vega to arrive at your overall position vega.

In theory, this is effective—you can flatten your vega risk. But although you do accomplish a flat vega position, you are adding different layers of risk by creating a ratio portfolio where your risk may not be predefined:

1. Your assumption (i.e., the risk) is that the underlying asset will remain basically unchanged.
2. You are potentially adding more greek risk by creating a ratio spread.

Important Concepts When Applying Option Vega in a Volatile Marketplace

The basic concept behind volatility trading is to buy volatility near the low of its trading range and selling it near the high. It sounds so simple: Buy low, sell high. But how you actually make that happen is a little abstruse.

The first consideration when buying volatility is the *current implied level of volatility* compared to the past level of implied volatility. An inexpensive option is one that is in a low percentile of its implied volatility over the last two to three years of volatility information. That type of historical data seems to supply a healthy distance and a credible foundation. Yet relying solely on history has severe drawbacks as well. The market is completely random: What happened in the past (meaning the tendency of volatility) doesn't in any way guarantee future results. Charts, graphs, moving averages, and volatility studies are all reasonable exercises—but they tend to give an investor a false sense of confidence about decision making. Volatility is influenced by so many factors—ones that math can't always quantify. Therefore, use historical data as a tool but not a crutch.

The market changes constantly, but options don't just suddenly become cheap. They tend to float into cheapness. In the equity world, if a takeover rumor surfaces, options can move from cheap to expensive overnight. But there aren't many news items—such as a confirmed news report of a takeover—that would change an option from expensive to cheap overnight. Many traders seek implied volatility near historic lows because it indicates buyer boredom and seller aggression.

Volatility trading is a distinct form of investing. It's like trading sentiment, which is why it's so difficult to accomplish successfully. Other people are making the options whatever price they are, and you're betting that they are going to be wrong at the major turning points. You really don't know why the options are cheap or why people are selling them. They may have a particular axe to grind. They may be selling calls against their position, or a hedge fund may be doing its arbitrage function or whatever.

There are two ways to trade volatility. You can be a short-term volatility trader and look for volatility that reverts quickly to some level of normalcy. In that case, you would want to hedge yourself with only vega risk so that you are exposed only to volatility. *There's nothing worse for a trader than to have the right idea and the right timing, but to have a position that doesn't pay off due to other risks!* Then you hope volatility will pop back up to a reasonable level so you can get out of your position, but this is not likely. More often than not, when options get cheap, they stay cheap, even when the underlying asset starts to move.

The other way to play volatility is to take a position to hold—for example, buying straddles (see Chapter 16), which gives you two ways to make money. Either volatility can revert to some higher level or the underlying asset can make a move and you can make money even if volatility doesn't help you out.

The chief difficulty when you take an intermediate- to long-term approach is that you start acquiring some delta risk right away. Of course, you are always taking on vega risk, the risk of volatility. One other important risk is time decay—theta (Chapter 9). Time decay will most likely not manifest right away. A six-month straddle (Chapter 16) is not going to decay much—at least not until the last month or so. The other important risk is the price risk. Say you buy a straddle for $10. If the underlying asset moves up five points and implied volatility moves up five points, implied volatility is still low and you haven't made any money yet. But you've acquired a positive delta. Your position is now delta long because the underlying moved up five points. If the stock moves down five points back to the starting point, you're definitely going to lose money because you're back where you were and some time will have passed. *The biggest risk to a vega trade is monitoring the price risk and deciding what to do with it.*

Floor traders look for volatility to regress to some sort of mean. They will see one order priced at the wrong volatility and try to snap it up. Suppose they know that a certain underlying generally trades at a volatility of 45 percent. If someone comes in looking to sell volatility at 43 percent, a volatility trader on the floor would buy that volatility immediately and then offer it back at 45 percent, because that was where it had been trading, and hopefully make a little bit of money. Yet this is a professional, non-commission-paying, floor-trading strategy. You can almost do it from upstairs except that it's harder to see everything that's going on.

People think that volatility selling is easy. It's the closest thing to free money! If you look at a chart of implied volatility, you often see that when it's trading near its lows, it is pretty well defined. But the highs are sometimes spiky peaks. If you could sell one of those spiky peaks in volatility and then buy it back later, in theory you'd have a nice trade. Yet in reality, traders often quip that invariably an overpriced option deserves to be overpriced. Eventually, you will find out why the buyer was bidding high for that option—he probably knew something you didn't. It's a tough game.

Some vega sellers have made small fortunes over the years. But anyone will tell you that the business of vega selling takes its toll on the stomach lining. What invariably happens to vega sellers—especially naked sellers who have no predefined risk—is that they make money for an extended period until they hit one bad month, day, or hour, which costs them their house, and they must start over again.

The biggest mistake traders and investors make is the tendency to think that selling options (selling vega) is a great moneymaker because the time decay of the contract will certainly outweigh any adverse move in the underlying. A portion of an option that is not of intrinsic value eventually does wear because of time, but the option is most heavily influenced by changes in volatility until it reaches the end of its life.

It's a common scenario. Someone tells you, "Implement this strategy because you collect time premium while you're waiting." Sure, but meanwhile you're at huge risk to volatility. If the market goes up and the trader has a covered write in place (see Chapter 12), he justifies his outcome by saying, "That's okay, I made money." In fact, he may have given away a small fortune in the process and would have made more money if he hadn't sold that option.

Correct valuation is only part of the game. One has to understand the dynamics of implied volatilities. If the market moves up or down, what happens to option prices? What happens to the vega implied by those option prices?

Consider the example of an at-the-money one-year option with a spot and strike of 900. If the market trades up 10 points, to the 910 strike, will the value of that option increase in proportion to its delta, which assumes that its implied volatility will remain constant? Or will it go up by more or by less on the basis of other factors? In relative terms, the at-the-money option's implied volatility will go down by the difference in volatilities between the two strikes.

A consistently successful trader must understand not only vega, but also the relationship of underlying movement and its effects on implied volatility and vega. Where are your strikes concentrated? If volatilities go up or down significantly, how is your long or short vega going to change? And by how much? What will happen if you're short a lot of out-of-the-money strikes and volatility suddenly goes up? You may be comfortably within your personal risk limits when the markets are quiet, but when things get a little more excited, you may find that you're suddenly short volatility—and all of those out-of-the-money options suddenly have loads of vega. Now you're short lots of volatility, more than you bargained for, and the risk managers want to know why—and what you're going to do about it.

Summary

Option vega is an estimate of how much the theoretical value of an option changes when implied volatility changes 1 percent.

1. At-the-money options will always have the highest vega.
2. Long options positions are generally characterized by long vega. This applies to both put and call options.
3. Short options positions are generally characterized by short vega. This applies to both put and call options.
4. Options with a short term to expiration generally have lower vega than long-term options. Options lose vega as they approach expiration.
5. As you move out in time, vega increases and is generally concentrated less on the at-the-money strike than a shorter-dated option.
6. Stock and futures contain zero vega.
7. A high implied volatility environment will smooth your vega among strikes around the at-the-money strike.
8. A low implied volatility environment will tend to concentrate a large proportion of your vega on your at-the-money strike.

CHAPTER 9

Sand in the Hourglass: Volatility and Option Theta

Theta, otherwise known as time decay, is an approximation that measures how quickly time value disappears from an option with the passing of one day without movement in either the underlying asset or implied volatility. Specifically, theta is used to approximate how much an option's extrinsic value is carved away by the passage of time. The theta for a call and put at the same strike price and the same time to expiration is generally similar but not exactly equal.

The difference in theta between calls and puts solely depends on the individual stock's cost of carry. Thus, an underlying asset without a dividend or a dividend yield that is implied (i.e., stock index future) will have call and put thetas that are equal. When the cost of carry for a stock is positive (i.e., dividend yield is less than the interest rate), theta for the call is higher than theta for the put. When the cost of carry for the stock is negative (i.e., dividend yield is greater than the interest rate), theta for the call is lower than that for the put (see **Exhibit 9.1**).

Long options always have negative theta. Short options always have positive theta. An underlying asset, whether you are long or short, has zero theta (see **Exhibit 9.2**). In other words, its value is not eroded by time. Theta causes an option with more time to expiration to have additional extrinsic value as compared with an option with fewer days remaining to expiry. Thus, it should make sense that long options contain negative theta, whereas short options have positive theta. If options, by their very nature, continuously lose

EXHIBIT 9.1 Cardinal Rules of Theta

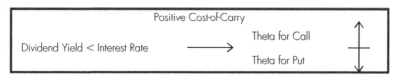

EXHIBIT 9.2 Theta Graph

Type	Theta Value	Effect of Time Decay
Long Call	Negative	Negative
Short Call	Positive	Positive
Long Put	Negative	Negative
Short Put	Positive	Positive
Underlying Asset	Zero	Zero

extrinsic value, a long option will lose money in part due to theta, whereas a short option will make money in part due to theta.

An option's rate of decay (theta) is mathematically sloped, insinuating that option theta will accelerate as expiration draws near. For example, the XYZ July 50 put is worth $4.00, has twenty days until expiration, and has a theta of −.20. The XYZ September 50 put is worth $5.75, has eighty days until expiration, and has a theta of −.05. If one day passes and the price of XYZ doesn't change, assuming there is no change in the implied volatility of either option, the value of the XYZ July 75 put will drop by $0.20 to $3.80, whereas the value of the XYZ September 75 put will drop by $.05 to $5.70.

Theta is at its highest point with at-the-money options and decreases as the strike moves either further in the money or out of the money (see **Exhibit 9.3**). This is because at-the-money options contain the highest amount of time value, having more to lose in comparison to in-the-money or out-of-the-money options.

EXHIBIT 9.3 Theta and Its Relationship to In-the-Money, At-the-Money, and Out-of-the-Money Options

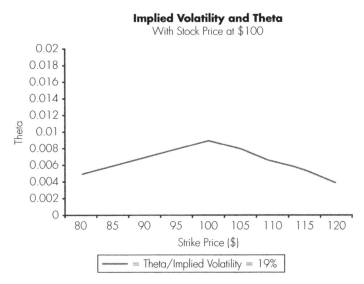

Implied Volatility and Theta
With Stock Price at $100

—— = Theta/Implied Volatility = 19%

Balancing Time Decay with Volatility: Mistakes Traders Make

In a perfect world, a beginning options trader can read a book about options, grapple with the terminology involved, and end with a tidy sum of information resulting in consistent profits. But in the real world, options trading is far different. Mastering options requires the development of a multidimensional instinct where one combines the entirety of theoretical information into one solid part. That part is then cobbled together with personal goals and risk allowance. Balancing theta with volatility—understanding them both collectively and separately—is a prime example of that multidimensional thinking.

Mistake #1: When Traders Don't Fully Understand the Effect of Time Decay

Many traders do not fully appreciate or understand the complete effect of time decay on an option's position. It's universally accepted that an option is a wasting asset and that theta is the term describing the rate of decay (see **Exhibit 9.4**). In simple terms, an options buyer is continuously racing against time. If you buy a call and the underlying rises, you should theoretically make money; however, the asset's appreciation must offset, among other things, the effect of time value decay in the specific option. If the

EXHIBIT 9.4   Theta Decay Curve: Theta and the Passage of Time

underlying asset does not go up in price, or not enough to offset the decay, this trade will most likely result in failure.

Match your options trading with your investment horizon. If you have a long-term perspective, *do not* buy short-term options (those with less than a thirty-day term) where theta dominates the very nature of your option.

Correctly forecasting market direction may not translate into a profitable options trade. Directional bias is great, but converting that into a quality options trade, with its myriad of complexities, is a whole different story.

From the very beginning, build the expected or worst-case dollar amount of decay into your overall investment decision. Human brains are subconsciously enticed by the thrill of unexpected returns; thus, we naturally gravitate toward options with dreadful profit probabilities.

Compare the actual dollar amount spent with the risk/reward provided. When contemplating the difference between owning a 30-day option for $1.00 versus a 200-day option for $4.00, think beyond the mere dollar amount. Consider that a 200-day option may be four times more expensive but will provide you with eleven times more benefit.

Mistake #2: When Traders Underestimate or Misinterpret Volatility and Its Effect on Theta

Every options trader understands—either from book learning or an excruciating trading experience—that options are a wasting asset and thus will lose money as time passes. What's more, theta isn't linear but exponential. With every other parameter held constant, options will show a predictably smaller amount of decay the further you go out in time. Once an option approaches thirty days to expiration, the decay moves rather quickly. For example, an August 50 call with four days till expiration will lose approximately $70 per day. The September 50 call with thirty-two days till expiration will lose $20 per day. The November 50 call with one hundred days till expiration will lose $7 per day.

Theta becomes more significant as expiration draws near, whereas volatility becomes proportionately less important. Professional traders recognize that the risk in short-dated options is more theta, whereas the risk in back-month options is chiefly volatility.

Traders who don't fully anticipate or comprehend the implications of theta (time) and vega (implied volatility) are subject to costly mistakes. Say you think XYZ will trade up from its current price of $37. You decide to buy a one-month call with a strike price of $40 for a premium of $2. As time passes, the price for XYZ moves up to $39, but the call option is now worth only $1. What happened?

Many unschooled options traders may not recognize that an option's price depends on much more than just the price of the underlying stock. An option's price is also affected by the combination of time (theta) and implied volatility (vega).

In this example, even though the stock went up, there is a low vega (i.e., correlation between the underlying's movement and the option's sensitivity to that movement). Although the underlying moves up $2, the option will not necessarily mimic that movement. Also, the option loses value as it nears expiration; it has less time to move toward being in the money. Both of these factors affect the movement of the option independently from its underlying. Many traders don't understand how important the greeks are; therefore, they are discouraged by the seemingly random movement of the option even though their predictions about the underlying were correct. *When you are trading options, you are trading derivatives. There are complexities at work that may reward you even though you were wrong about the movement or, more often, cause you suffering even when you were right about direction.*

Buying Options (Negative Theta) in a High-Volatility Environment

When you purchase a call, you become long deltas; for puts, you will be short deltas. Gamma and vega will also be long. With this long purchase, you will become short theta—you will be paying a "theoretical" amount per day for the privilege of providing the seller with the risk of the trade.

Your portfolio will be affected by how far the option is from the at-the-money strike and by time till expiration.

If You Happen to Be in the Fortunate Position of Owning Options during an Upward Movement in Volatility, This Is What You Should Expect to Happen

No matter how large the volatility movement is, if you're long a near 50 delta option, it will remain a 50 delta option. At the money is at the money is at the money! Your out-of-the-money deltas will converge ever so slightly toward 50. Case in point: If you're long a 30 delta put with volatility increasing, your delta tends to climb, becoming more negative. If you're long a 90 delta call during a sustained volatility upward move, your delta will be reduced. The math behind this is intuitive. Large upward volatility moves suggest a wider band of movement in the underlying. Thus, it becomes harder to pinpoint what exactly an at-the-money option will be.

An upward volatility move could, depending on the maturity of your option, affect your gamma position. If you are long a short-dated at-the-money option, your gamma will fall and will continue to do so as your volatility increases. A significantly out-of-the-money option will tend to pick up more gamma the higher volatility rises. This occurs all the way along the time structure of options, but its effect is lessened (because gamma is less of an issue) the further out you go along the curve.

An upward move in volatility will certainly affect the vega of your position. In a volatility upswing, all options will benefit from the increased vega. But if volatility makes an enormous, "once-in-ten-years" spike, all options will tend to have the same vega. Logically, a huge spike in volatility will cause your deltas to converge toward 50; therefore, your at-the-money vega will become closer to your out-of-the-money vega.

An increase in volatility will increase the value of an option's extrinsic value relative to the underlying price. Option value is a direct function of the probability of a price move upward or downward. The more time available for something to occur, the greater the probability of the price move. Likewise, as remaining time declines, so does the probability and thus the option value. As an option's extrinsic value increases, so will the theta. That theta will eventually bleed out of the position but, in a rising volatility level, it is masked.

Selling Options (Positive Theta) in a High-Volatility Environment
A short option will generally have a positive theta. With each passing day, that option loses value to time decay. In general, option sellers prefer selling at-the-money or near–out-of-the-money contracts with less than sixty days

until expiration. These types of options will have the most time premium to erode, relative to the expiration. The seller relies on the notion of the exponential time decay pattern.

If You Happen to Be in the Unfortunate Position of Being Short Options during an Upward Movement in Volatility, This Is What You Should Expect to Happen

The closer you are to expiry, along with your distance from the at-the-money strike, you will find the anticipation of your fat theta check could be possibly offset by your gamma and delta. As an option approaches expiration, delta can move at an alarming rate, which can be problematic for short-option sellers when short a call in a rising market, and vice versa for put sellers in a declining market. If you are short a deep in-the-money option or far out-of-the-money option, your delta risk, in general, will not outweigh the anticipated theta income. Yet it is a risk.

The closer you are to expiration, the more pronounced your gamma will become for at-the-money and near–at-the-money options. As if staying balanced and disciplined were not complicated enough, any short options position—especially one closing in on expiration in a rising volatility environment—is at risk in terms of gamma. In this scenario, the higher the volatility, the larger your anticipated theta will be. The higher the volatility, the more pronounced your gamma will be. If you are short a thirty-day at-the-money option and volatility rises, your gamma will become bigger. With any move in the underlying, you will find your delta moving at a faster rate. This is somewhat offset with your larger theta. But it can become a seesaw, where you ask yourself whether the large theta is worth the kinds of moves you are experiencing.

Selling options in a high-volatility environment will surely increase (but not ensure) your theta. Yet this can be quickly offset by the implied volatility of your option versus its rate of decay. The further out you go in time, the greater the effect of vega on your short option. Conversely, the shorter your option is dated, the more theta affects your position. Traders judge the cost/benefit of volatility and theta. Simply put, how much does volatility need to rise—hence creating greater vega—to offset theta? If a short option theoretically has a theta of $.20 per day and vega is .75 per point, the implications are obvious. If the underlying is stable and volatility moves up 1.00, the option will lose money.

As volatility increases, so will your option theta. Again, it depends on where the option is in time and location relative to the at-the-money strike. Theta is a direct reflection of the extra premium priced into the option due to the volatility's upward move. If volatility has made a sharp upward move, or even a gradual but sustained one, theta will become larger for all strikes. At-the-money options will always have the largest theta. *Yet the larger the volatility move, the greater the extrinsic value, and therefore the greater the theta per strike.* The problem here is for traders who are short the short-dated out-of-the-money strikes—the ones they've already counted as profit. If volatility goes up and up, the extrinsic value could follow to historic proportions. The theta they counted on has evaporated, and many will make the irrational decision to buy back something that is out of the money and quite inflated.

It is not uncommon for vega and theta to work against you. In a volatile market, you're short a call while the underlying goes down, and your option still loses money! You see vega beat theta! If you asked professional traders whether they make more money trading delta, direction, or vega, most of them would say that their money was made through vega.

Volatility and Theta: What Every Investor Needs to Know

Black and Scholes developed the first mathematical model for determining the fair value of an option. *Fair value, in this case, is a price at which no one makes any money over time by buying or selling.* That does not mean the frequency of making money for buying options is equal to selling them. In general, selling options is frequently more profitable than buying them, but the payoff for buying them is occasionally sufficiently greater to offset the loss frequency.

Regardless of the effect of implied volatility, theta remains the same for a call and a put of the same month and strike price. An at-the-money call or put (with the same month and strike price) will increase at the same rate. An out-of-the-money 5 delta call will experience the same theta increase as its corresponding in-the-money 95 delta put.

As volatility increases, so does theta. Theta is proportionate to the option's location along the time structure. Options are directly affected by many factors, including the passage of time. At expiration, options will be either in the money or out of the money. If volatility goes up, increasing the option's extrinsic value, it will eventually have to make tracks back toward being either in the money or worthless.

]In any option class there will eventually be a "crossover" effect wherein theta becomes more of an issue than vega. This effect can vary greatly depending on the implied volatility of your option combined with the time left until expiration. With higher volatility comes greater vega and theta. It is absolutely crucial to be able to delineate the difference, in your position, between vega and theta. To misinterpret this could cause you to underestimate the risk of your position and possibly lead to a need to rehedge or, worse yet, liquidate.

Theta is merely an estimate and is not necessarily guaranteed. If volatility continues up, day after day—even with little movement in the underlying—the estimated theta will rise, and it won't be necessarily realized. Implied volatility is just that—implied. The options are suggesting that the market will have a larger move than in the past. When buying options, think of yourself as the insurance company that charges more to take on more risk. As the seller, envision it as extra premium to be given to you—hopefully—for assuming that risk. With implied volatility at, say, 19 percent, your theta will be, say, $600. Compare that to implied volatility rising to 23 percent, and suddenly your theta will be $1,200 (see **Exhibit 9.5**).

Consider theta in a high-volatility market as an asset class in and of itself. From the negative theta (long option) point of view, consider the premium as an asset to help leverage yourself. From the positive theta (short option) point of view, theta can be seen as an asset class to deliver (hopefully) consistent returns even in an uncorrelated means. Positive theta can help cushion your decision, and even if you're directionally wrong, you can still win with the income of the theta. Especially with high volatility, theta can deliver a desirable return profile because it is one of the few asset classes that is not overly inflated.

The certainty of time value erosion. Aim to have as much time value/theta exposure as possible. You need to short options with high time value and high time value erosion per day and be very, very mindful of the associated risks

EXHIBIT 9.5   Theta Comparison: Low Volatility versus High Volatility, With Stock Price at $100

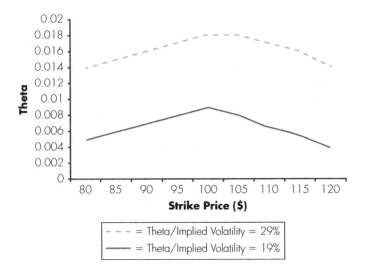

involved. The premium for out-of-the-money options with short maturities consists mainly of time value; intrinsic value is low and vega is negligible at this point in time, which limits the risk exposure. Shorting an option closer to the money would give more time value exposure, which is positive, but it is associated with a higher risk of being exercised and a very high greek exposure which (for your purpose) is negative.

Be disciplined and rigorous about the "risk creation" and risk management of theta positions in any market—but particularly in a volatile one. When you are not disciplined, one event is enough to wipe out all of your invested capital. As long as markets move within the band suggested by your current implied volatility, a strategy to be positive theta should deliver decent returns made of option time value. Sideways-moving markets are perfect, but up- or down-trending markets can also deliver good uncorrelated returns. Again, you can be slightly wrong on direction and still be profitable.

High volatility, theta, and a misunderstanding of strike supply and demand. A disciplined application of basic option theory is a good thing. Yet relying solely on theory could land you in a whole heap of trouble. For example, assume you have a long option position in a certain out-of-the-money strike. Volatility explodes, and your option valuation model shows your correct greek position at the current implied volatility level. But the strike you are long isn't keeping up with the rest of the options. It can happen for a variety of reasons, including simple supply and demand. Suppose that strike has a large open interest, where the professionals are stuck long. At any uptick in the underlying or volatility, they will do anything to reduce their inventory of that strike. Or perhaps the open interest is in a strike around it where, again, the crowd is very long. They are willing to sell the strike you are long with the intent of becoming vega neutral.

Theta as an asset class in a high-volatility environment boils down to carefully constructing the risk you will be managing. Extensive experience and a deep knowledge of trading in options markets can only help because theory, as everyone knows, has its pitfalls.

Recognize danger and react quickly. Theta and volatility are strange bedfellows. Unlike some other theoretical values, volatility is based solely on perception, fear, and supply and demand. Theta, however, is eventually certain—the certainty lies in that options are wasting assets and, if sufficiently out of the money, will lose value the closer they get to their expiry. If your strategy goes awry, don't make it worse by holding on. Don't let pride distract you from making competent decisions. Rolling can be expensive, but it is even more expensive to rely on theta in a volatile market.

CHAPTER 10

The Nuances of Volatility

Interpreting the Mix of Academics and the Study of Volatility

Whenever I find myself with the intellectual stamina required to read through an academic publication, I cannot help but occasionally take exception to the analysis. This catches my attention especially in many academic papers revolving around volatility and quantitative finance. These shortcomings include an incredible overfascination with statistical significance. The long established application of statistics in academia seems to be centered on determining whether a theory is, in fact, statistically significant. Academic-based publication bias seems predisposed toward the reporting of positive results, where the authors are able to demonstrate a statistically significant finding of their theory, even though in reality a null or even questionable conclusion can full well be of equal or even greater importance. This is mainly because the real marketplace—along with the real volatility associated with it—is far too complex to reduce to individual sets of data points.

Academic studies often seem to be intent on showing whether a specific variable matters for the data set they have selected. They tend to neglect analysis that shows whether the same study really matters and fail to show how the authors arrived at the premise in the first place. How much conjecture is built into the model? Does the professor have a theory that needs to be proved as a matter of professional honor or reputation? How much data mining is required to find enough statistics to demonstrate that an idea is statistically significant? It's important to recognize that the authors of academic studies can influence the precise terms of the data set and the circumstances of the test in order to arrive at a result with a strong statistically significant outcome. This doesn't mean that the result is invalid. But the markets are better presented as a jigsaw puzzle than as a chart or graph—a complex mix of numerous patterns of inputs, time series, evaluation periods, and variables. When taken together, these complex sets of interlocking values could suggest that a statistically significant result for a single set of data points or variable is irrelevant. Other sets of data might be shown to support an inconclusive or null hypothesis instead.

By and large, academic studies tend to do such a methodical job of data mining to show statistical significance that any special case offered in an academic study should be viewed skeptically. Does the model work in real life without being adjusted? Researchers have an incentive to find "important" results. Due to this bias, an author might not recognize that a statistically significant result might still be unlikely, and for the trader or investor this uncertainty waters down the conclusions offered as a result of the research.

Also, even a hypothesis that looks radical on the surface can simply be window dressing for conclusions that can be arrived at in more simple, straightforward ways. Though these particular types of back tests or hypotheses are clearly not directly applicable to use, we should constantly balance our investigation looking for the common threads between volatility and any supposed correlative effects.

When studying volatility through a quantitative lens and looking for data that matters, it is far more important to consider *why* that data matters, and if the reason why that data matters is conveniently consistent with what the researcher considers important. In other words, traders need to keep up with academic research in their field, but they also need to balance statistical significance with common sense. Finding the balance between statistical analysis and instinct is one of the most significant trading decisions you will ever make.

The Complication Surrounding Vega Risk in an Option Position

Option positions are susceptible to a variety of market risks. Most traders think of delta and gamma risks as the key exposures of an options position to change in the price of the underlying asset. That initial reaction makes sense because when an option position loses money it typically means that the trader was burned by the gamma, and ultimately the delta, of a position. While most of us agree that there is something called vega risk, the concept is somewhat fuzzy as it is complicated by factors that sometimes can't be explained, modeled, or predicted.

Vega risk is unique. Vega can be and is complicated by the predominance of volatility skew (Chapter 4) and term structure (Chapter 20) in most option markets. Both of these factors—which can have potentially devastating effects on option positions—are scrutinized by traders and risk managers alike, all the time. But there is little practical advice available to guide them. In real life, implied volatility for a given underlying asset at a given time is not an identical constant for all options on a given underlying asset observed at a given time. Rather, implied volatility differs for options with different strike prices and days to expiration, and this leads to both implied volatility skew and term structure.

What is the best measure of skew? How should one compare skew for a 12 percent volatility stock index with skew for a 28 percent volatility stock index? Is there any clairvoyance suggesting what cheap or expensive skew would be? What is the best measure of an implied options term structure? How should a trader interpret a flat term structure compared with one that is rising or falling? Is an options term structure predictive?

Think of pure vega risk as the ownership of price risk for an option position. Implied volatility can be used as a yardstick of option prices and, most importantly, helps to interpret the markets' perceived (collective) future variance of returns. Therefore, option markets should be viewed as markets for the volatility of the price of the underlying asset. Clearly, traders are trading exposure to volatility. In the end, the options markets provide volatility of price discovery.

Implied Volatility Skew + Term Structure = Volatility Surface

It's important to stress that option positions are not just exposed to changes in the level of the option's implied volatility but to changes relative to the difference in the curvature or skew of the implied volatility option's curve or to direct changes in the implied volatility along the curve itself.

Since Black Monday 1987 the implied volatility curve observed by the market in stock index and equity options has taken the general form as seen in **Exhibit 10.1**. Looking at this exhibit you will notice that the implied volatility decreases as the strike price increases. In other words, the implied volatility of a lower strike option (whether it be a deep in-the-money call or a deep out-of-the-money put) is significantly higher than that used to price a higher strike option (no matter if it's a deep in-the-money put or far out-of-the-money call). This "implied volatility skew" corresponds directly to the implied probability distribution shown by the dotted line in **Exhibit 10.2**. A typical lognormal distribution—the one we learned about in college—is represented

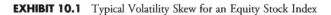

EXHIBIT 10.1   Typical Volatility Skew for an Equity Stock Index

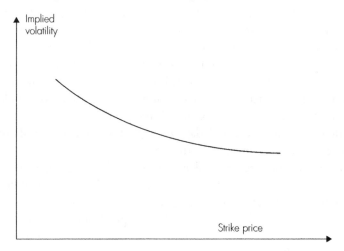

EXHIBIT 10.2   Implied Distribution and Lognormal Distribution for a Typical Stock Index Option

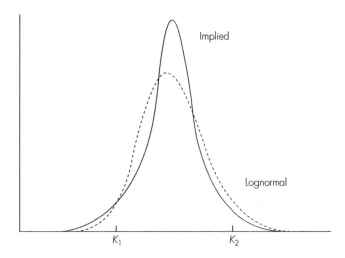

with the solid line. Hopefully, you can see that the implied distribution (real-life) has a somewhat heavier left tail and a less heavy right tail compared with the standard (theoretical) lognormal distribution.

The lesson in all of this can be seen in **Exhibit 10.3** where, in practice, skews are fluid things steepening or collapsing depending on a variety of things such as: supply and demand, market sentiment, where the market is relative to

EXHIBIT 10.3 SPX 1M Skew Structure

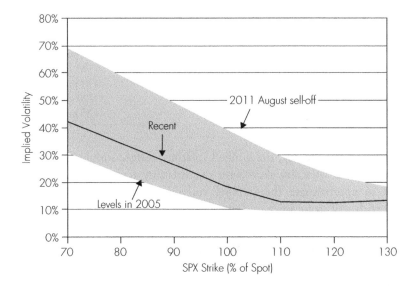

recent history, and so on. If skew steepens, the implied volatility of the deep in-the-money calls and far out-of-the-money puts will consequently rise relative to the out-of-the-money calls and in-the-money puts. Conversely, if skew should drop or flatten, an opposite effect would occur whereas the implied volatility of the in-the-money calls and out-of-the-money puts would drop relative to the out-of-the-money calls and in-the-money puts.

See the following table to get a firm idea on what happens to Greek values with a significant change in skew.

The Effect of Skew on Greek Values

Higher Skew			
Delta	ITM calls less positive		OTM calls less positive
	OTM puts more negative		ITM puts more negative
Gamma	ITM calls up	OTM calls down	
	OTM puts up	ITM puts down	
Theta	ITM calls higher	OTM calls lower	
	OTM puts higher	ITM puts lower	

(*Continued*)

Lower Skew

Delta	ITM calls more positive	OTM calls more
	OTM puts less negative	positive
		ITM puts less negative
Gamma	ITM calls down	OTM calls up
	OTM puts down	ITM puts up
Theta	ITM calls lower	OTM calls higher
	OTM puts lower	ITM puts higher

At the end of the day, the implied volatility surface simply combines the current implied volatility skew with the volatility term structure (days till expiry) to approximate the implied volatility appropriate for pricing an option with any strike price and any interval.

Implied Volatility Term Structure

Besides the fluctuation of implied volatility options skew, term structure can also vacillate. This makes the potential vega risk all the more difficult to calculate. An implied options term structure is the implied volatility difference between various maturities along the underlying assets available at the money option contracts. Note that under the benchmark Black-Scholes option pricing model, term structure should not exist, or more precisely, it should be boring, a flat line. See **Exhibit 10.4.**

EXHIBIT 10.4   Volatility Term Structure (2y-3y)

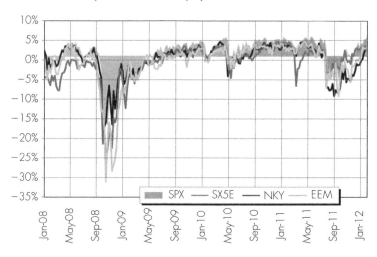

Source: CS Derivatives Strategy

EXHIBIT 10.5 S&P 500 ATM Implied Volatility Term Structure

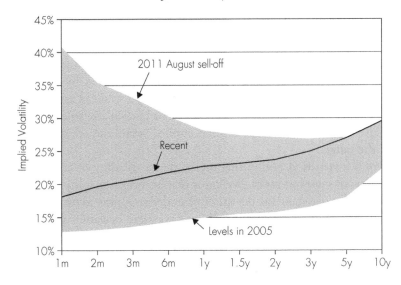

However, in real life, the term structure can and does slope upward or downward. But like skew, the underlying causes of why the term structure slopes one way or another are not always obvious. An econometrician may theorize that the fair value of an options term structure can be boiled down to terms of overreaction, and consequently the mispricing of asset values is predictable. Option modelers rest assured that the slope of the curve can be described by a complicated, overreaching stochastic volatility model. The rest of us are left to lean on supply and demand and leave it at that. See **Exhibit 10.5**.

Whatever the factors for causing the implied volatility term structure to slope—whether it be supply and demand, macroeconomic risk expectations, or a built-in jump fear component—it is important to know how it can and does affect the vega of your options position. Term structure—like implied volatility skew—is hard to predict and harder still to manage.

Did You Know Your Volatility Has Volatility?

One of the more troublesome issues in the derivatives world is the phenomenon of the "volatility of volatility" or Vvol for short. Every options trader's volatility estimate includes volatility and the trader should be aware that this is exactly what, in the end, produces what the industry calls "fat tails." A fat tail is another name for the fourth moment of a probability distribution (Chapter 4). The Vvol embedded is premium of a shock or rare event, such as a specific stock moving 20 percent in one day. It's the market's best guess at a random event occurring. The fat tail can also be considered to be a mathematical phenomenon of sorts as these rare events seem to occur far more frequently than what is predicted by the normal probability distribution. A fat tail can also occur even when an asset has a low volatility but a very high Vvol. This tends to be particularly true for very far out-of-the-money S&P 500 puts when implied volatilities are on the lower end of the range.

Vvol is a statistical notion that means that a volatility of arbitrary variables is not constant but varies. We know that historical volatility (Chapter 3) is measured by the standard deviation of underlying price returns around a mean. If this standard deviation itself has a standard deviation (and it does) we say that the underlying prices have a volatility of volatility. Mathematicians call this by a terrible sounding name, "heteroskedasticity." Heteroskedasticity is related to the fourth moment, kurtosis, of a normal probability distribution. Heteroskedasticity (I won't use this term again!) in a Gaussian or normal distribution makes a normal probability distribution display the fourth moment, when according to the math, there should be none. Recall that in Chapter 4 I discussed the probability distribution and how this makes sense for circumstances with a finite set of outcomes, such as card games. When looking at the financial markets—especially when pricing options— varying volatility makes complete sense due to the large difference in the sheer size of observations in a time series. Vvol flies in the face of common statistics. One practical way to think of Vvol is through the lens of a risk manager who quickly transitions from asking, "How bad can things get?" to asking, "How much can I expect to lose?" That is Vvol plain and simple!

In the financial marketplace, the whole idea of variable volatility— standard deviation of underlying returns have their own standard deviation— has given rise to what is known as "stochastic volatility." Still, the only way the volatility of an asset can have its own volatility is if that volatility behaves randomly, just like the underlying asset itself. In the old days (directly after Black Monday 1987), traders used to talk about how certain strike prices had "personalities." Those traders had discovered Vvol without knowing it! In the end, stochastic volatility is the rationale and is intricately related to another high-octane concept in trading derivatives called "vega convexity."

Since Black Monday 1987, traders have come to terms with the reasons for the higher price of out-of-the-money puts than what is implied by the Black-Scholes model. However, what many traders find absolutely infuriating is that volatility of volatility is never known in advance and nobody really knows how to quantify this correctly. In recent years there have been financial engineering models that attempt to calibrate Vvol from option prices employing a stochastic volatility model. However, I'm very skeptical as to whether this—or any model—will reflect the actual Vvol.

The Normal Value of Volatility

Traders are trained to differentiate between the market value of volatility and the normal value of volatility; market value being the value at any particular point in time, as shown by the implied volatility ruling at the moment, and normal value being a somewhat indefinite thing that the market value tends to obey. Market circumstances may be such at a given point that the value of volatility is higher or lower than one would naturally expect, as compared with the value yesterday, and we all feel that this won't continue very long—that the volatility value is unusual, that there is a normal value toward which it will drift. In these last few years, when everything has been upset by the confusion of the Great Recession, that feeling is not as clear-cut as it used to be, but in normal times there is a fairly confident feeling about normal values.

You may ask, "What is the foundation for that feeling?" The tailor or barber certainly has the same feelings as the trader, but the tailor or barber can give no tangible reason for having it. The normal value, to these people, is simply the price that they have become familiar with; any other value is atypical basically because it is abnormal. If only the market value for implied volatility could ever be normal!

PART III

Ten Proven Strategies to Employ in Uncertain Times

CHAPTER 11

Preparing for Trading Using Volatility Strategies

The writing and re-reading of this chapter reminds me of Jon Krakauer's book, *Into Thin Air: A Personal Account of the Mt. Everest Disaster* (First Anchor Books Edition, May 1998), in which the author recounts a disastrous attempt to climb Mt. Everest. The weather at the summit tends to get violent and thus very dangerous in the early afternoon. The mix of profound emotion, physical strain, and especially low oxygen levels can derail even the best of climbers.

Krakauer wrote that at the summit of Mt. Everest, you no longer pay attention to your emotions or your brain; rather, you solely rely on your clock. At 2:00 P.M. you get out of there! If a member of a climbing group has not reached the summit by that point, he turns around and heads back to the base camp. No argument, no discussion, no matter what. When a pair of climbing groups ignored this wisdom and pressed on to the summit regardless of the time, they were trapped by a storm, and nearly every member of those two climbing groups died.

The parallels between climbing Mt. Everest and options trading are significant and worth paying attention to. Being keenly aware of your risk limits, getting out of a trade no matter what, and relying solely on ironclad discipline rather than heartfelt emotion are the things that separate a lucky trader from a consistent one. Like Mt. Everest, options trading can also be violent and dangerous. But you can learn to take the danger out of your personal trading.

The Elements of a Sound Trading Decision

The typical trading decision, if based on a sound investment and trading plan, includes four elements:

1. *Time horizon.* What time span do you employ in your options trading? Do you plan to buy and hold contracts until they expire or trade them regularly, even daily?
2. *Goals.* What are your plans and intentions with options trading? Do you seek to use options to protect larger stock positions? Or are you trading options for their own potential for profit? What profit levels are you content with, and how much time do you want to devote both to monitoring your portfolios and to research and education?
3. *Financial stability.* This refers to your personal financial state and how it affects your trading style and approach. It comprises your assets, liabilities, net worth, and the extent to which you will use your income from trading for living expenses.
4. *Personal risk tolerance.* This describes how well you are able or willing to withstand the ups and (especially) the downs with regard to options trading. Risk tolerance describes the trader's emotional stability and willingness to accept losses in portfolio value while consistently pursuing investment objectives.

The first three items—time, goals, and financial stability—tend to be straightforward, impartial, and fairly easy to measure. The fourth, risk tolerance, is based on personal attitude and emotional tolerance, and it's harder to quantify.

Risk Tolerance

Risk tolerance refers to your own level of comfort with trading risk. Two people may agree on the riskiness of a certain options strategy but nevertheless prefer different approaches. A trader with a high level of risk tolerance would be expected to accept a higher exposure to risk in the sense of taking sole responsibility for decisions, acting with less information, and requiring less control than would someone with a low level of risk tolerance.

Your risk tolerance for options trading can grow over time as you learn more about how options work and develop discipline in staying with your plan when rolling, exiting, or adding to a trade.

The investment community spends a lot of time researching investor risk tolerance. Their models suggest variables such as gender, age, marital status, income, and education all contribute to an individual's risk tolerance level. This is valid but it misses the point, especially when dealing with risk tolerance as it relates to options strategy. First, risk tolerance will grow. When you as a trader come to fully understand the implications of an options strategy, you will be willing to take more calculated risk. Second, risk tolerance will also grow when you develop an ironclad discipline in pursuing that strategy. This involves taking emotion out of your trading decisions and developing an escape plan, and then staying with that escape plan when things go awry.

Developing an Approach to Options Trading

An often overlooked feature of risk tolerance is discovering your own style. There are three distinct options-trading approaches. Each one differs in emotion, time commitment, trading horizon, analytical tools, and intensity. An options trader fits into one of these styles according to individual personality, objectives, and lifestyle.

The Day Trader

Day trading is the buying and selling of options and/or options strategies multiple times during a one-day trading period. The intention of the day trader is to find discrepancies in the market, such as over- or undervalued volatility, mispriced spreads, and directional bias trades, and then to take advantage of them. Furthermore, the day trader is predisposed toward making a large number of wagers with very small reward.

Day trading with options used to be extremely unprofitable in the days before brokerage firms started to offer deep discounts for options trading. The situation is different today for several reasons. First, the cost to execute trades for the retail trader has dropped to the extent to which the day trader can now be marginally profitable and still realize a profit. Second, the advent of cheap access in the form of low brokerage fees has served to add an enormous amount of liquidity to the options market. Bid/ask spreads are generally much narrower than in the past. In some cases, bid/ask spreads are so tight that the result is a margin market that almost becomes a "choice" market where you can buy or sell at nearly the same price.

Effective day trading requires technology, from specialized brokering platforms to software trading systems and even a live streaming data feed. Because so many factors and events can move an underlying asset price by the minute, effective day trading demands a heavy investment in tools in order to level the playing field with professional market makers.

Day trading can also be time consuming. To be effective you will need to be in front of your computer all day, every day. It is impossible to act as a part-time day trader, because it is impossible to achieve analysis and proper decision making on the fly when variables are constantly moving. Also, profitable day trading demands high levels of discipline and skill. It requires great analytical skills and an ability to execute trades mechanically.

Day trading can be extremely risky for two simple reasons. Day trading is expensive, and most traders lack the discipline needed to succeed. Beginning traders (and some veterans) generally do not have the emotional control required. Most aspiring day traders find themselves doing all the wrong things, breaking the rules, and spoiling every trade, especially during volatile market conditions. Volatile markets are normally the most profitable conditions for market makers. But watching profit and loss profiles fluctuate in big waves and being bombarded by news every second results in one of the most emotionally challenging environments in the world of investing.

Also, because day trading is an approach that depends on a high volume of trades, the commissions add up even with the deep discount brokers available today. But a solid day trader cannot factor in costs when making a disciplined decision to exit a trade, even if the commissions make that trade unprofitable. Losing money on day trades because of the cost structure is common.

The Short-Term Trend Trader

A short-term trend trader tries to take advantage of price swings that commonly last from five to twenty trading days. The short-term trader believes that when prices move for most underlying assets (stocks or commodities), the prices have momentum in one direction, otherwise known as swing. The asset typically pulls back to more reasonable levels in the near future. The goal of a short-term trader is to anticipate momentum changes and to get out profitably before the swing ends.

Short-term trading is best for those who cannot afford or don't want to monitor the markets continuously throughout the day. After a trader identifies the beginning of a pattern, he or she implements an options strategy with a sensible and predefined stop-loss order in place. After that, all the trader needs to do is check how the position is doing at the end of each day. This style does not require the rigors of technology or expense of hardware, and because this strategy doesn't involve multiple trading decisions, your cost structure is less of a concern.

Short-term trend trading requires sound analytical skills both in fundamental economics and in options strategy. A solid trend trader understands the importance of identifying a trend but equally knows how to benefit from that trend with the appropriate options strategy. For example, if a trader perceives a trend to be bullish, yet the implied volatilities are high, the short-term trend follower would identify the trend and then execute an options strategy that would coincide with his volatility opinion. The trend-following trader does not, under any circumstances, want to be right on direction and wrong with volatility.

The Position Trader

Position trading with options is the use of options-trading strategies in order to profit from the unique opportunities presented by options. Traders use elements such as time decay, volatility, and even arbitrage to make relatively safe and fixed, if lower, profits from options trading. Position trading is the realm where professional traders work.

The notion behind position trading is to profit with as little risk as possible even if it means making much less profit. Position trading involves complex mathematical calculations, software applications, and a lot of patience to identify the right opportunities. Position trading profits not only from momentum in price changes for the underlying assets, but also from environments that are downright stagnant. In fact, most position traders hope to use hedges to eliminate risk from their portfolios and seek to profit from time decay, volatility, or options arbitrage. As such, traders usually need to hold their positions until the options contracts expire in order to realize their maximum profit potential. The holding periods for trades for a position trader are generally longer than those for the short-term trend trader.

Note that a hedge is an investment strategy used to reduce the risk of another investment. The idea is to buy one security to offset or cancel the risk of another. A trader could buy one thousand shares of stock and then hedge that investment by also buying ten put contracts (one hundred shares each) to give that trader the right to sell those shares to another trader at a specific share price. That would work to limit the trader's loss if the share prices start to fall. Arbitrage refers to taking advantage of varying prices for the same financial asset or security offered on different markets. Commonly, the same stock or bond or contract offered on two different exchanges around the world could appear for two different bid/ask prices, so a trader who can move fast and in sufficient volume can make a profit with a series of buys and sells.

Position trading is also the options-trading style that demands the most understanding and mastery of options as a financial instrument. Intimate knowledge of the mechanics that drive options, such as the greek values (i.e., delta, gamma, vega, theta) as well as the aggregate effects of combining different options through synthetic positions, is a must for any aspiring position trader. Complete understanding of all the different options strategies and their advantages and disadvantages is also essential. Finally, as the returns from position trading can be small, the trader must pay close attention to cost structure too.

The Mind of a Successful Trader

Most traders have been in this familiar spot. You've done all the research and everything points to a specific plan. You know that the trading process may not happen exactly as you intend, but you know deep in your soul that this will be a winning trade. You set your stop-loss just in case, but this is merely a formality, an indicator of your disciplined approach to trading.

The first few days go by and the price of your trade makes a few upticks, just as you expected, but then without explanation, the price starts to turn. You feel that pit in your stomach, that feeling of denial, as the price starts a hasty and unremitting spiral to your stop-loss price. Your confidence all but disappears. Frantically, you try to figure out what has gone wrong with your careful examination. To give yourself some time to evaluate, you decide to loosen your stop-loss order.

You can guess the rest of this story. After reducing your stop-loss price, you comfort yourself that there is *not anything out there to warrant such a move,* and your strategy should adjust itself shortly. But as you confirm the current price, you double over like someone just punched you in the stomach. You've been stopped out! How could this happen? It's not fair! You did everything according to plan. On some level, way deep down, you don't feel necessarily wrong. Rather, you feel like an incompetent loser.

Preparing to Win Big by Losing Well

Most traders are not in tune with the importance of the emotional facets of trading and how a disciplined mental awareness is just as important as owning a reliable software trading system. The ability to deal with losing money in trades is what ultimately separates successful traders from ex-traders. Developing a disciplined mental approach to trading mixes knowledge, self-awareness, and experience. But the markets thrive on chaos or the variable of the unknown. So no matter how well-prepared a trader is, even the best traders will experience losses. A good trader must learn how to be a good loser.

A Deer in the Headlights

You need to be able to remove yourself from the situation and analyze what is actually happening. First, you likely have a general fear of losing money that prompts you to make irrational decisions concerning your entry and exit points to a trade. Second, while trading you might hear internal whispers taunting your ego, pointing to a losing trade as yet another example of how you just aren't that smart. In fact, you're probably better off to continue skimming off your yearly bonus from the company's balance sheet.

We are conditioned to equate losing with shame. We are inclined to avoid it at all costs. Sometimes losing stimulates a reaction to fight back. But for most of us, we permit losing trades to cause us to deny responsibility, avoid situations, and think irrationally. The result may well be a foolish decision to remove a stop in an options trade.

Making mistakes and losing trades no doubt have varying effects on individuals. But if you can understand and appreciate that traders will lose money, and sometimes lose money on a consistent basis, you will be well on the road to successful trade management.

The Making of a First-Class Loser

Trading is not instinctive; we must learn trading from scratch and learn how to endure trading in a very complex environment. Still, many aspiring traders seem to jump in when starting to trade with little knowledge, planning, or structure. The average beginning trader does more research when planning a vacation than in establishing a trading plan.

One of the foundations of trading is to *develop and stick to a trading plan.* That means you have a system in place for a high-probability strategy, unwavering entry and exit points, staunch guidelines on the amount of capital risked, and the application of the same criteria and procedures on every trade, all with absolutely no exceptions. Successful planning will help mitigate the emotions of losing money and being wrong.

Gaining insight on how to correctly evaluate risk and reward is, as a rule, a blend of knowledge and experience. However, since chaos and grand mystery are always part of the market, even the best-prepared and brightest trader will lose money at times. The best trader in the world, someone who has a 70 percent or better chance of winning on a given trade, still needs to address the 30 percent of trades that fail.

That said, the process to *take the confusion out of losing* is a personal and intentional attack on two fronts. The first step is education. Continually studying strategies and their implications and constantly reviewing how to best apply them is key to relieving the stress of losing. Most professional traders have spent many years to get where they are today and in the process have lost large sums of money on costly mistakes. It is foolhardy to believe you can become a successful trader without knowledge and experience.

The second step is to develop the emotional conditioning necessary to submerge the disgrace of losing. You only see what you know; besides all of the information unavailable to us in the marketplace and the unpredictability of the markets, your emotional makeup allows you to create a world that makes some sort of sense to you. We perceive the world according to what we want to see. This relates to trading in that we develop an opinion, a bias, on what we see. And there is so much going on around us, things our finite minds can't possibly translate into consistent trading decisions.

Decision Making, Options versus Everything Else

Ideally, traders should imitate a robot and just initiate the buys and sells. But the features that make us human are sometimes tricky to restrain. Learning how to make good decisions is an essential skill. Whether you are a current options trader or an equity trader who wants to use the benefits of options trading, pay careful attention to both the similarities and differences in the trading decision processes between stocks and options.

1. In both options and equities, you want to define your goals and also define what you need to reach those goals.
2. Determine the amount of funding you can dedicate to trading and whether that funding is realistic for the goals you set.
3. Learn everything possible about what you will be trading. Commit yourself to an ongoing education about anything pertaining to the business or industry where you trade.
4. Before making any trade, set up rock-solid entry and exit points with absolutely no room for discussion.
5. Institute clear, concise money management rules regarding maximum trade risk amounts and account drawdown limits.

Determining your personal risk tolerance, figuring out your trading style and comfort level, developing rock-solid discipline, and cultivating a stable emotional attitude toward failure are the same for trading options and trading equities. The difference—one often overlooked by the equity turned options trader—is the overall analysis of the options trade.

Consider this problem. Two companies in the same industry issue non-dividend-paying stocks, Company XYZ and Company ZYX. Prices for both stocks are currently at $40 a share. Over the course of the last week, the share price for XYZ has been rising by 2 percent each day, whereas the price for ZYX has been dropping by 2 percent.

Lacking any other information about the two stocks or the economy in general, if you ask an equity-only trader which stock he would buy, he would say XYZ because its value has been climbing. But if you ask an options trader which stock he would prefer to have a call option strategy on (provided he can hedge the trade with shares of the underlying stock), he would reply, "It really doesn't matter."

The stock trader will buy XYZ, given its direction. The options trader will stay apathetic between the calls on either stock. This illustrates the divide between the way equities and options are analyzed.

CHAPTER 12

The Buy-Write, or the Covered Call

The covered call strategy naturally extends from buying common stock. Using covered calls offers the possibility for immediate income and tends to be a safe investment, from the perspective of both a brokerage house and the investor who is eager to generate additional income for his portfolio. Thus, the covered call is a popular strategy for the individual investor. The concept is also easy to explain. Even so, it is one of the most misunderstood and perhaps overused option tactics available.

The Buy-Write (Covered Call) Defined

In its most basic form, an investor who owns (long) stock sells (writes) a near–at-the-money call or slightly out-of-the-money call. This strategy is called *covered* if the investor writes enough call options to cover the stock position (usually one option contract equals one hundred shares of stock). For example, if an investor owns one thousand shares of stock, he or she will write ten call options to cover those thousand shares. If the party who buys the call contracts exercises them, requiring the original investor to sell the thousand shares underlying the options, the investor has the shares in hand to complete the trade.

Although the terms *buy-write* and *covered call* are often used synonymously, they differ in implementation. Generally speaking, a *covered call* applies to an investor who simply sells call option contracts against his existing long stock position. *Buy-write* applies when the investor buys the underlying stock at the same time as writing the call option contract. Either way, the investor normally holds the stock in the same brokerage account

131

from which she writes the call. The shares of stock provide collateral for the investor's obligation when writing a call option contract, as described above.

An Example of the Covered Call Strategy

An investor buys one thousand shares of XYZ common stock for $28 per share. He wants to sell a call option that offers him a satisfactory amount of premium within his investment time horizon. He finds a two-month $30 call option which is actively trading at $1.50 per share. The investor decides to sell ten of these $30 two-month call options and receives a $1.50 premium or $1,500 for the ten contracts sold:

$$\$1.50 \text{ premium per underlying stock share} \times$$
$$100 \text{ shares per contract} \times 10 \text{ contracts} = \$1,500$$

This position is considered covered in that the investor sold ten option contracts against the thousand shares of stock that he holds. The premium received for the option sale ($1.50 per share) effectively lowers the investor's cost basis (purchase price) of the stock from $28 to $26.50 per share.

Three Possible Outcomes

1. At expiration the stock closes above $30 per share. The party buying the contracts will exercise them, and the investor will need to sell the shares (the stock will be called away). The investor's maximum profit in this situation calculated as follows:

$$\text{Strike price} - \text{purchase price} + \text{option premium received, or}$$
$$\$30.00 - \$28.00 + \$1.50 = \$3.50$$

2. At expiration the stock closes at $30 per share. The party buying the contracts will let them expire as worthless. This leaves the investor with his original stock investment and $1,500 in realized premium profit.
3. At expiration the stock closes below $30 per share. The party buying the contracts will let them expire as worthless. The investor enjoys $1,500 of realized premium profit. However, this strategy will offer the investor no protection below the original cost basis of $26.50 per share—that is, the $28 original purchase price minus the $1.50 in premium received (see **Exhibit** 12.1 and **Table** 12.1).

EXHIBIT 12.1   The Buy-Write

Investor's Position
* Long 1,000 Shares of XYZ at $28 per share
* Short 10 2-month XYZ $30 calls receiving $1.50 per share

Investor's Cost Basis
Long 1,000 Shares of XYZ at $28 per share $28,000
Short 10 2-month XYZ $30 calls receiving $1.50 per share $1,500
                                                            = $26,500

                    $26,500
                    1,000 Shares

TABLE 12.1   Buy-Write Profit and Loss Example at Expiration (Long 1,000 Shares of XYZ @ $28 per Share; Short 10 XYZ $30 Calls @ $1.50 per Share)

Stock Price at Expiry	Profit/Loss XYZ Stock	Profit/Loss $30 Call	Net
$56.00	$28,000	($24,500)	$ 3,500
$40.00	$12,000	($8,500)	$ 3,500
$29.50	$ 1,500	$ 1,500	$ 3,000
$28.00	$ 0.00	$ 1,500	$ 1,500
$26.50	($ 1,500)	$ 1,500	$ 0.00
$16.00	($12,000)	$ 1,500	($10,500)
$ 0.00	($28,000)	$ 1,500	($26,500)

The Theory and Reality of the Covered Call

If the stock price does not move, or even goes down slightly, the option will expire as worthless, and the investor gets to keep both the option premium and the stock. Then the investor can start all over again by selling another option for the next month out, collecting even more premium. If, on the other hand, the stock goes up, the short call will be exercised by the owner, and the investor will be *assigned* for the strike price of the option sold. When a contract is assigned, it means that the holder of an options contract has decided to exercise it. The Options Clearing Corporation (OCC) manages options trading; when investors write contracts for the same strike price for the same underlying stock with the same expiration date, the OCC collects these contracts and places them in a pool. If an investor who holds contracts in this pool decides to exercise them, the OCC randomly selects a party that issued some of the contracts and assigns the exercised contracts to that party to satisfy the conditions of the contract. This is the only practical way to manage options contracts when they expire because the amount of contracts written is so vast and because investors rapidly trade contracts in large volumes until they expire if they are close to being in the money.

The investor might see the assignment of contracts as a good thing if he is compelled to sell the stock to another investor at a share price slightly higher than that he had originally paid for the shares. The investor would also have the premium earned on selling the options contracts.

The Realities of the Covered Call

If you were to review a risk graph for a covered call, you would find that the calculated risk looks a lot like selling a naked put or selling a put contract without buying shares of the underlying stock to hedge your risk if the contracts are exercised against you. The only difference in risk profiles between a covered call and a naked short put is that the stock (in the covered call example) will not expire. So as the share price begins to nosedive, it will prolong your agony and increase your losses.

In the covered call example (**Exhibit** 12.2a), the maximum profit—in this case, $100—is reached when the stock price closes at or above the strike price of the call that was sold. The loss continues to spread as the stock price falls all the way to zero. In the naked short put example (**Exhibit** 12.2b), the maximum profit—again $100 in this case—is reached when the stock price closes at or above the strike price of the put that was sold. The loss continues to grow as the stock price falls to zero.

The reasons the investing public persists in using the covered call are likely twofold. The first is the lure of generating cash each month. If an investor owns the stock, selling calls against those shares could be a channel for short-term cash, in the form of premiums for the options contracts sold. This is particularly true if the stock price does not move very much. Second, it is a strategy that is safe for the brokerage house to promote, because they hold the investor's stock and have the authority to deliver the shares if the contracts are exercised against the investor.

EXHIBITS 12.2a, 12.2b   Buy-Write Graph in Comparison with Naked Put Graph

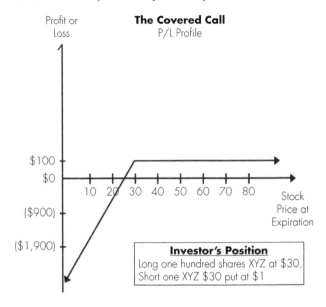

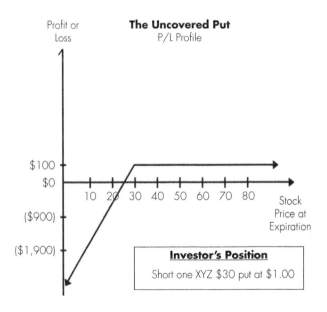

Reality #1

Using covered call writing as a long-term trading approach usually results in a portfolio of stocks that perform poorly. An investor buys a variety of stocks and then sells call contracts against them. After several months, some of the stocks have gone up, some have gone down, and some have not changed. The stocks that went up were called away. The ones that have gone down are often well below the original strike price that was sold. What remains is a portfolio that is worth far less than before the covered call writing strategy was attempted, because you are forced to sell the best stocks. Covered call writing can be a painfully effective way of sorting out the good from the bad—and keeping the bad.

Reality #2

Don't expect that you can consistently pick stocks that have both a high amount of option premium and a stable price. In actuality the opposite is generally true. Only stocks with share prices that are highly volatile relative to the market are likely to have large option premiums. The truly safe, stable, established, high-dividend-paying, blue-chip issues that tend to track the market and not fluctuate are the stocks that generally offer the lowest option premiums. If a stock has a high option premium, there is probably a good reason for it. The high premium suggests the stock price is or will soon be extremely volatile and therefore risky for a short-term investment strategy.

Reality #3

Covered call writing is not as simple as it seems. The complexity is not so much in the strategy itself but rather in addressing the two primary challenges the strategy presents. For the first, the downside risk is only reduced, not eliminated. For the second, the profit potential is capped. With those challenges, it would appear this strategy could potentially violate the fundamentals of conservative options trading. The primary objectives are maximizing income while using leverage to limit portfolio risk. There are stocks and various circumstances where the covered call makes good sense, but the investor must apply the strategy correctly and be fully aware of all the risks involved.

Reality #4

Covered call writing in a bull market is not necessarily intrinsically safe. First, diagnosing exactly what the market is doing sometimes involves pure guesswork. For example, when a bear market ends and a new bull market (or at least a new upward trend) begins, it takes time before it clearly is considered a bull market. And who exactly decides that a bull market is a bull market? It can take a lifetime for everyone to confirm a long-term market trend, and by the time unanimity is achieved, the upward move has long been over. Second, there will always be stocks underperforming in a rising market and vice versa. To base your covered writing strategy solely on broad market sentiment is nothing short of false assurance.

Covered Call Writing and Implied Volatility

Higher option premiums imply that the underlying share price is about to become more volatile than usual; low premiums suggest the opposite. The higher the premium—or rather, the more overvalued the premium— the more volatility is implied. Implied volatility is just another way of saying that the market believes the price of the underlying stock is about to move more than it has in the past. Implied volatility is not a forecast and certainly not a guarantee of actual volatility.

Below are some of the main causes of high implied volatility:

- Significant news is pending on an individual stock.
- Significant news is pending on a larger company in the same industry that the underlying stock follows.
- The underlying stock is currently volatile.
- There is a shift in market sentiment.
- A rare event (e.g., the Russian ruble crisis, the collapse of Long-Term Capital Management, 9/11) takes place.

So what does a high level of implied volatility really suggest, since it's not a failsafe forecast of actual volatility? The answer to this is rather straightforward—it means that both investors and traders are willing to pay more for option contracts on underlying stocks for which there is a perceived chance that the share price for that stock will move. This is simple supply and demand. When a hurricane is predicted to hit the eastern seaboard of the United States, plywood gets expensive because more people are likely to buy plywood to board up their windows. When thinking about implied volatility as it translates to option premium, think of it less in theoretical terms and more in terms of practical application. The market's implied volatility is nothing more than a speculation tax on the fear and greed of the investing public.

Implied Volatility in Practice

Witnessing the constant ebb and flow of implied volatility can be both exciting and excruciating. Implied volatility differs from most option theoreticals in that its definition cannot be stowed away in a tidy box. Implied volatility is the end result of supply and demand or fear and greed. Before proceeding into the nuts and bolts of implied volatility and how it can be applied to the covered call, consider the following points:

- Over time, neither the fact of implied volatility nor the level of implied volatility reached is a reliable predictor of actual volatility.
- Implied volatility does not predict the direction in which an asset's value will move.
- Implied volatility is a direct result of the supply and demand for an option.
- Some investors wrongly believe that the strike price with the highest implied volatility for a series of options contracts for a particular month predicts where the asset value is heading.
- Option premium (implied volatility) is high or low for a reason. The market is willing to pay more for an option if it thinks the asset is more likely than others to move on impending news or after an event.
- Implied volatility in and of itself does not necessarily mean that the underlying asset will actually be more volatile. Rather, implied volatility means that the market suggests it might.

Writing Covered Calls

If you are confident about an underlying stock's inherent value, you use covered call contracts to cash in on your expected profits. If you plan to sell the stock after the share price moves past what you view as its intrinsic value, you are effectively using the call contracts to build a return on investment while you wait. If the stock takes longer than expected to reach your selling point, the covered call strategy will provide you with some extra return via the premium earned on selling the options contracts.

Choosing Which Strike to Write

Your first and most important decision when you write call contracts for an underlying stock is choosing the right strike price. The strike price you select will vary depending on your investment strategy—whether you are motivated by limiting the risk of loss or by increasing your profits. Your choice is based on two interrelated factors:

1. Where do you believe the share price for the stock is heading?
2. How much do you want to protect the value of your stock position?

Remember that the maximum profit occurs if the share price of the underlying stock you bought is at or above the strike price for the same shares on the call contract when the contract expires. This is also true if another investor holding your contracts decides to exercise them. But you risk financial loss if the underlying shares continue to decline in price as the call contracts expire. The loss accrued from a decline in stock price, however, is at least partly offset by the premium you received from the initial sale of the call contracts.

In-the-Money Call

Writing an in-the-money call is the best strategy to protect your stock position from loss. In a market with high implied volatility, writing an in-the-money call contract allows you to benefit from the increased premium, though not as much compared with an at-the-money contract. More important, it will provide the investor with increased downside protection. Volatility generally increases when the market fears a decline in value. This is especially true for index options.

But there are tradeoffs. First, the premium received for an in-the-money covered call contract is marginal in comparison with other strike prices. The further the option is out of the money, the higher the earned premium will be from selling the options contracts. Second, writing an in-the-money call provides additional protection in case the share price of your stock loses value, and the deeper you write the strike, the more downside protection you gain from the options contracts.

In the table below, compare the differences across strikes in both the premium received (extrinsic value) and the range of protection offered. The example is based on a long XYZ position at $92 per share.

Strike Price	Call Value	Intrinsic Amount	Extrinsic Amount	Downside Price
$60	$32.10	$32.00	$0.10	$59.90
$70	$22.20	$22.00	$0.20	$69.80
$80	$12.60	$12.00	$0.60	$79.40
$90	$5.00	$2.00	$3.00	$87.00
$100	$0.70	$0.00	$0.70	$91.30

XYZ ninety-day options; XYZ = $92 per share.

Yet with that security you reduce the upside potential for the same stock position. After all, if you sell a call contract and it goes into the money, the party holding the contract is likely to exercise it. You might sell the shares at an agreeable profit, not to mention the option premium. But what if the share price soars? You make a nice profit for part of the increase, but you turn the shares over to another investor to benefit from the rest of the increase of the share price. Using covered calls is a balancing act that requires you to consider carefully what you want, whether it is greater downside protection or additional upside potential.

The table below shows both the downside protection price and the corresponding upside potential of various strike prices. The example is based on a long XYZ position at $92 per share.

Strike Price	Call Value	Intrinsic Amount	Extrinsic Amount	Downside Protection	Upside Cap
$ 60	$32.10	$32.00	$0.10	$59.90	$92.10
$ 70	$22.20	$22.00	$0.20	$69.80	$92.20
$ 80	$12.60	$12.00	$0.60	$79.40	$92.60
$ 90	$ 5.00	$ 2.00	$3.00	$87.00	$95.00
$100	$0.70	$ 0.00	$ 0.70	$91.30	$92.70

XYZ ninety-day options; XYZ = $92 per share.

At-the-Money Call

Writing at-the-money calls generally offers the highest return and provides some degree of downside protection while preserving a little upside potential. Just how much an in-the-money call reduces your risk depends solely on how much extrinsic value you receive upon implementation of the trade. In a high implied volatility environment, the at-the-money option will increase the most on an actual dollar basis.

Yet even with the at-the-money call there are tradeoffs. First, you are making the bet that the underlying will not move beyond the amount received in premium. Second, you are shorting volatility at the highest point along the implied volatility curve. Being short volatility—even when covered and the investor's risk/reward is predefined—is risky in that the investor simply doesn't know the direction of future volatility and probably isn't receiving enough compensation (premium) for taking on the risk.

Out-of-the-Money Call

Writing out-of-the-money calls is the best strategy if you are confident you have an excellent underlying stock. In an environment with high implied volatility, out-of-the-money option contracts will gain from the volatility increase. Writing an out-of-the-money call will increase the investor's upside potential. The further out of the money the strike price is, the higher the upside cap will be placed.

The table below lists out-of-the-money options with a nineteen-month expiration. It is obvious that the higher you go out of the money, the higher your upside potential will be. The higher strike will consequently lower your downside protection price. The example is based on a long XYZ position at $153.50 per share.

Strike Price	Call Value	Intrinsic Amount	Extrinsic Amount	Upside Cap Price
$160	$28.00	$0.00	$28.00	$181.50
$170	$24.00	$0.00	$24.00	$177.50
$180	$20.50	$0.00	$20.50	$174.00
$190	$17.20	$0.00	$17.20	$170.70
$200	$14.40	$0.00	$14.40	$167.90
$210	$12.20	$0.00	$12.20	$165.70
$220	$10.20	$0.00	$10.20	$163.70
$230	$8.50	$0.00	$8.50	$162.00
$240	$7.00	$0.00	$7.00	$160.50
$250	$6.00	$0.00	$6.00	$159.50
$260	$4.90	$0.00	$4.90	$158.40

XYZ nineteen-month options; XYZ = $153.50 per share.

With the out-of-the-money call there are two main tradeoffs. First, writing an out-of-the-money call dampens downside protection. Like a seesaw, the higher the strike price you choose, the less downside protection you will have. If the share price falls, the call contracts you issue won't help limit your losses. Second, even in a high-volatility environment, the additional premium received for an out-of-the-money strike needs to be weighed against the potential you may receive from it. The example in the table that follows is based on a long XYZ position at $153.50 per share.

Strike Price	Call Value	Intrinsic Amount	Extrinsic Amount	Upside Cap Price	Downside Break-Even
$160	$28.00	$0.00	$28.00	$181.50	$125.50
$170	$24.00	$0.00	$24.00	$177.50	$129.50
$180	$20.50	$0.00	$20.50	$174.00	$133.00
$190	$17.20	$0.00	$17.20	$170.70	$136.30
$200	$14.40	$0.00	$14.40	$167.90	$139.10
$210	$12.20	$0.00	$12.20	$165.70	$141.30
$220	$10.20	$0.00	$10.20	$163.70	$143.30
$230	$ 8.50	$0.00	$ 8.50	$162.00	$145.00
$240	$ 7.00	$0.00	$ 7.00	$160.50	$146.50
$250	$ 6.00	$0.00	$ 6.00	$159.50	$147.50
$260	$ 4.90	$0.00	$ 4.90	$158.40	$148.60

XYZ nineteen-month options; XYZ = $153.50 per share.

Managing Contracts in a Time of High Volatility or a Falling Market

A market correction or an individual stock losing much of its value are likely risks when you write covered call contracts for a stock position. On the other hand, if the market values skyrocket and you lose money on the covered call contract, it won't hurt as badly because you already own the underlying shares and will benefit from the increased share price. Where you place the covered write contract is the chief factor of the investor's downside risk. Consider the following alternatives when the market corrects.

Rolling Down the Strike

Inexperienced investors who issue covered call contracts tend to freeze when either the market drops or prices become volatile. A solid alternative to freezing would be the prospect of rolling down. Rolling down simply means to buy back the short calls (the calls you originally sold) and replace them by selling new call contracts with a lower strike price.

Assume an investor sold XYZ $20.00 calls when the stock was trading at $21.00 per share. If the stock drops to $19.00 per share, the trader might want to buy back the $20.00 call contracts and sell $17.50 calls. As the stock drops, even if implied volatility rises, the short calls ($20.00 calls) may become cheaper, making it possible for the investor to buy them back for less than they originally sold for.

Rolling down your strike will provide you with more downside protection and provide you with a new short strike with more value. At this point it's important to recognize that doing nothing is a decision as well. Allowing your short strike to go from in the money to out of the money with no recourse is in effect taking the opinion that the stock will, before expiry, bounce back up to your original short strike. If that is not true, the investor shouldn't stay short a strike that contains no residual value.

If volatility has risen to the extent to which rolling down has no monetary benefit, the investor might consider rolling out to another month where volatility may be higher still. Generally speaking, volatility affects options proportionately the further out they move in time.

Doing Nothing

Another alternative when facing a market sell-off or violent swings in value is to simply do nothing. If you re-examine your trade while the market is falling and decide the stock is fundamentally sound, there are good reasons to wait. First, you don't have to go through the trouble of rolling down or closing out the trade; you can merely buy back the short calls you sold originally as the stock falls, and thus get them out of the way. Second, if the market recovers, you can be hit with the volatility if you've sold call contracts for a lower strike price and the stock bounces back. Third, sometimes the moment for acting passes, and there is really nothing left you can do.

If you waited too long to roll down, or if no roll down or out in time appears satisfactory, and if you have faith in the stock and don't want to close your position for a loss, the thing to do is wait it out.

Instant action is not the same as contemplative action. Exercising both together is ideal, but acting too hastily may hurt you more than acting too slowly.

Effective Call Writing in a Volatile Market

To get the kind of returns covered call investors are looking for, an investor needs volatile stocks with high premiums on the options. But therein lies the fundamental problem. To make this strategy call work from a cash flow perspective, you need a low-priced stock that is highly volatile. These stocks, however, tend to see their share prices go up and down quickly, sometimes with stunning swings. The problem is that when they do rise, you lose out on most of the potential increase in the share price because you capped out at the strike price of the options contracts you sold. If the price rises quickly, the party holding the call contracts will exercise them, and you will be forced to sell the shares at the strike price and lose out on any future increases. But when the share price falls, it generally drops very quickly and often doesn't recover for a long time.

Why would an investor place a covered call on a lower-priced stock? There are two reasons. The basic reason is the greater return on investment opportunities with the lower-priced stocks. The return on the lower-priced stock would obviously be better than that on the higher-priced stock if the option prices were identical. For example, if the premium on both options is $1, the return on a $100 stock would be 1 percent, whereas the return on the $10 stock would be 10 percent. The second reason for choosing lower-priced stocks is that they tend to be more volatile by their very nature, so they have higher option prices. Except for the high-flying dot-com stocks of the late 1990s, higher-priced stocks tend to be blue-chip, low-risk concerns. Lower-priced stocks tend to be issued by firms that are higher risk, and stocks from these firms tend to have much higher percentage price moves in any given time period.

CHAPTER 13

Covering the Naked Put

Pricing an exchange-traded option requires the use of a complex mathematical formula. The mathematical model is driven by six basic factors:

1. Current price of the underlying
2. Strike price of the option
3. Time till expiry
4. Dividends
5. Interest rates
6. Volatility

Looking at the six components, you can know with near certainty what most of the inputs ought to be. You know, for example, exactly what the current price of the underlying is. The strike price of the option is an element of the option contract. You know specifically when the option contract is set to expire (exchange-traded options in general expire on the Saturday following the third Friday of the expiration month). You also have a high degree of certainty as to where interest rates are and what dividend, if any, will be paid on the underlying stock.

What an options price really boils down to is volatility, which is simply the model's evaluation of risk. In terms of the math, volatility is merely a measure of how much the underlying asset is expected to diverge from its current price. The input into the option pricing formula is the annual standard deviation of the stock's price.

Most option traders overlook volatility when making an investment decision. Traders will simply buy calls if they are bullish on the outlook of the underlying, or buy puts if they are bearish. The majority of options traders (probably) lose money over time, which speaks to the importance of understanding volatility. Many investors don't have a clear understanding of when volatility is over- or understated. For example, if options on the XYZ index are implying a volatility of 28 percent, is that good or bad? Without a frame of reference, it is impossible to know.

Option premium, for all intents and purposes, handicaps the underlying market, much like the spread handicaps the wager in a football game. For example, assume you placed a bet on the outcome of a football game. Team X, with a record of twelve wins and one loss, is playing Team Z with a one-and-twelve win–loss record. Most of us would expect Team X to win, based on past performance. However, if the bet is given a spread of fifty points, it could dramatically change the way we would view the outcome. Although Team X might win the game, it is highly improbable that they would win by more than fifty points. We instinctively realize that a fifty-point handicap in a football game is, on the whole, too high.

When making investment and/or trading decisions, traders follow a similar process. One trader may decide to buy or sell XYZ based on its history. Another may choose to look at specific price patterns, or perhaps use fundamental analysis, or an earnings estimate to make a decision. But the final decision to buy or sell is based, in large part, on how the underlying has historically acted, provided a specific set of circumstances.

For example, if you were using fundamental analysis, you would buy XYZ if your earnings expectations were greater than those of the market. Theoretically, you would sell if your earnings estimates were lower than those of the market. Without using options, your decision to trade is complete. However, once options are introduced into the equation, you need to understand how much vigorish the options market requires you to pay in order to trade. *The handicap is implied volatility.*

Unlike the football handicap, for which you may have an intuitive feel, you most likely do not have the same instinct about implied volatility. Is a 28 percent implied volatility assumption on XYZ too high or too low? One solution is to put implied volatility into perspective by defining it as an implied trading range.

To deal with this, consider the following approach. Assume that XYZ is trading at $50. If you buy the XYZ June 50 call at $3 and the XYZ June 50 put at $3, you have a total expense of $6. At this point, being long a call and a put on XYZ of the same strike price and month, you really don't care which direction the underlying goes. You're concern is that XYZ will move far enough so that you can earn back more than your $6 outlay (see **Exhibit 13.1**).

Adding a $6 cost, the upside break-even is $56, and the downside break-even is $44. *Six dollars is the trading range that the options market is implying*

EXHIBIT 13.1   Straddle Break-Even Graph

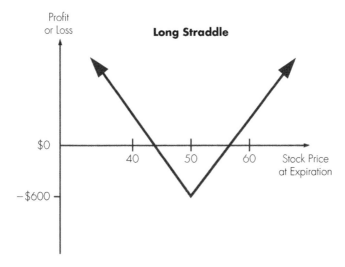

for XYZ between now and expiration. That is the amount of premium needed by the seller to assume that risk.

The next question is whether you think XYZ is likely to breach either end of that trading range between now and the June expiration. If you believe that XYZ is likely to be above or below the outer boundaries of that implied trading range, then you are in effect stating that either the options on XYZ are cheap or that the volatility implied by XYZ options understates future volatility. Similarly, if you think that XYZ will not likely infringe either end of that trading range between now and the June expiration, you are effectively stating that the options on XYZ are expensive.

You are now on your way to making a proper decision using options. Your first step is to decide whether you are bullish or bearish on XYZ. Regardless, you have a lot of choices to leverage your opinion.

Contemplating the Cash-Secured Put

When the topic of put selling comes up, there are two common yet utterly opposed groups. The first faction asserts confidently, "I never sell puts, because it is simply too risky!" The second group states with equal self-confidence, "I always sell puts, because it is so conservative!" Which group is right depends on how you look at it. An investor with a cash-secured put position has the ultimate obligation to buy the underlying stock. If you want to buy the shares *and* have the money to do so, then this commitment is no more risky than buying the shares outright. If assignment occurs, then stock is "put" to you, one hundred shares for each short put. The effective price of the purchased shares is the strike price of the put less the premium received. Now suppose that the assumptions above are not completely correct. Suppose that the investor with the short put position does not want to buy the stock, changes his investment decision, and furthermore, does not have the sufficient cash to bear the risk of the initial investment. In that case, this position, like any position, is both risky and ill advised.

Who Should Consider a Cash-Secured Put?

- An investor who is completely determined to buy a particular stock.
- An investor who is willing to give up short-term gains in the stock by selling the put, providing him with very limited upside benefit.
- An investor who is willing to buy a stock that is below current market levels yet has (consequently) continued to be dramatically lower than the put strike at which it was originally sold.
- An investor who perceives the cash-secured put trade as payment for entering a stock limit order.

Definition of the Cash-Secured Put

Investors who make use of a cash-secured put sell a put contract and at the same time deposit in a brokerage account the full cash amount for a potential purchase of underlying shares. The point of depositing this cash is to ensure that it's obtainable should the investor be assigned on the short put position and be required to purchase shares at the put's strike price. While the cash is on deposit it may generally be invested in short-term, interest-bearing instruments.

The net price paid for the underlying shares on assignment is equivalent to the put's strike price minus the premium received for selling the put in the first place. For this reason, the strike price selected, less the premium amount, should replicate the investor's target price for purchasing underlying shares. Regardless of the course the stock price takes after the put is sold, or whether assignment is received or not, the put seller keeps the premium. Bear in mind, the option seller is assuming the risk and therefore receives a justifiable amount of premium to assume that risk.

The break-even point for this strategy is an underlying stock price equal to the put's strike price less the premium received for selling it. If the stock declines considerably below the strike price by expiration, on assignment the

EXHIBIT 13.2 Cash-Secured Put Break-Even Graph

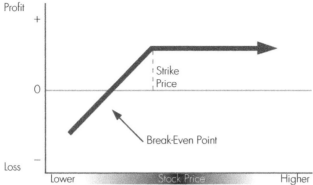

investor may be required to purchase shares well above their present price level. Stock bought under this condition may therefore show a loss when compared with its present trading price. However, this loss will be unrealized as long as the investor holds the shares. Any investor whose motivation in writing a cash-secured put is to buy underlying stock should therefore be committed in advance to a target price for a possible purchase and select a strike price accordingly.

The chief risk is that of opportunity loss. After selling the put, the stock price can go up and remain above the put's strike price. In this set of circumstances, neither a put seller who is not assigned, nor an investor who originally entered a low limit order for the stock instead, will buy the stock. The put seller, however, keeps the put sale premium received (see **Exhibit 13.2**).

Utilizing the Cash-Secured Put in a High-Volatility Environment

Cash-secured puts are typically viewed as a means to capture income in a neutral market. Yet when implied volatility is higher, it can also function as a channel to capture steep premium while waiting to buy a stock that you genuinely wish to own. It is a conservative means to harness volatility in that your risk is predefined and limited. In addition, options give you the opportunity to close out or roll up your obligation if your personal sentiment should change. Of course, closing out or rolling your position could prove to be costly; however, your decision to do so may be beneficial to your long-term financial health.

Cash-secured puts profit by the amount of premium collected if the stock is above the strike price at expiration. The maximum profit is your credit. For example, assume you sold the $50 put for $2 with the underlying stock at $50. You are entitled to keep your $2 credit if at expiration the stock is anywhere above $50. If the stock is at $49 at expiration, you will make $1, but you also will be assigned and will have the stock "put" to you at an effective share price of $48. In this example, the cash-secured put trade is actually profitable down to $48, since you received a $2 credit.

Example of a Profitable Cash-Secured Put Trade

XYZ's price continually bounces off your personal resistance area of $30 at the same time that implied volatility spikes. You definitely would rather sell puts on stocks with high implied volatility, if for no other reason than because there is more theta (time decay) on your side. There is a wider range—given the premium you collected—before you start to lose money and are most likely (via assignment) obligated to buy the underlying shares. See **Exhibit 13.3** for an example of a profitable cash-secured put trade.

- Time decay is the highest in the last thirty days of the expiration cycle. With that knowledge, you sell a thirty-day $27.50 put for $1.00.
- If the underlying price rises and implied volatility drops, it is best to buy back the put at some predetermined price. If the stock stays above $27.50

EXHIBIT 13.3   Example of Profitable Cash-Secured Put Trade

XYZ = $30.00; Position = short one thirty-day $27.50 put at $1.00; Effective Purchase Price = $26.50.	
XYZ Stock Price at Expiration	27.50 Put Value at Expiration
$60.00	$0.00
$35.00	$0.00
$32.50	$0.00
$30.00	$0.00
$27.50	$0.00
$25.00	$2.50
$0.00	$27.50

but the put does not quickly drop in value, you could allow theta to work for you and patiently wait for expiration to draw nigh.

- If the underlying falls and implied volatility remains constant, you will be profitable until the stock drops below $26.50. This is because you sold a $27.50 put for $1.00, giving you the potential obligation to buy stock at $27.50 minus the premium that you received.

Example of an Unprofitable Cash-Secured Put Trade

According to your perception and insight, the price of XYZ seems to have bottomed out, while implied volatility soars to unprecedented levels. The price breaks back above $30, so you decide to sell a twenty-day 29 put for $1. This trade, in effect, could obligate you to buy XYZ at $28 per share ($29 strike price – premium collected [$1.00] = effective purchase price of $28). See **Exhibit 13.4** for an example of an unprofitable cash-secured put trade.

- You sell a twenty-day 29 put for $1. After a few days, XYZ's price dives to $25 and implied volatility increases over 50 percent.
- You could buy the put back for a loss—a loss that was *specific* and *predetermined* (by you) prior to entering the trade. As with any options strategy, you must have an ironclad exit plan calculated before you make the trade.

EXHIBIT 13.4 Example of an Unprofitable Cash-Secured Put Trade

XYZ = $30.00; Position = short one twenty-day $29.00 put at $1.00; Effective Purchase Price = $28.00.	
XYZ Stock Price at Expiration	29.00 Put Value at Expiration
$60.00	$0.00
$32.00	$0.00
$31.00	$0.00
$30.00	$0.00
$29.00	$0.00
$28.00	$1.00
$0.00	$29.00

- As a spread you could roll your loss. You could buy back your short 29 put and sell a new out-of-the-money put against it. For example, you could buy the 29 put and sell the 24 put. This would not necessarily eliminate your loss. Rather, it would subsidize your loss (by creating a fresh sale in the 24 put) and re-establish your intention of buying the stock at a lower price.
- You could hold the position and be assigned the stock at expiration. At expiry, if the stock is at $25, the stock will be "put" to you at that price. Yet, considering the $1 put premium you originally collected, your actual purchase price will be $28 per share.

Cash-Secured Put and Volatility: Risks and Consequences

You have decided to invest in XYZ stock and furthermore have been intrigued by the large premiums attached to its options. How badly you want to buy XYZ should dictate which put strike you should sell. You most likely have learned that an increase in implied volatility generally means that the premiums for out-of-the-money options will be much higher (in percentage terms) than premiums for at-the-money options. This observation suggests that the investor should sell out-of-the-money puts only to capture a potentially higher rate of return. However, if your primary goal is to capture a high rate of return, you should probably not engage in cash-secured put selling at all! The protective put is considered a conservative strategy because your ultimate loss is predefined. Yet that predefined loss can amount to a worthless stock. You sold a put to generate a very small amount of premium. Although the potential return on investment (in percentage terms) is desirable, the downside risk is simply not worth it. See **Exhibit 13.5** for an example.

Think about it in pure percentage terms. Say XYZ is trading at $38 per share. To capture that (potential) high percentage return, you sell five thirty-

EXHIBIT 13.5 Return on Investment Table

XYZ = $38.00 per share
Sell five thirty-day $32.50 puts for $.40 each (× 100) = $200.00
Collateral requirement =   [100% × $38.00 + .40 − ($38.00 − $32.50)] × 500 = $16,450
Return on investment = $200.00/$16,450 = .01%

day $32.50 puts (100 percent secured with cash) for $40. If your $32.50 puts expire as worthless—XYZ would need to drop over 15 percent in thirty days before being in the money—you would collect the $200 and make a 1 percent return on your investment. In effect, you are saying that a 1 percent return is worth risking a minimum 15 percent downside risk. Fifteen percent should be your minimum, because the stock could go to zero, in which case you would give up 100 percent downside and 100 percent upside for a thirty-day 1 percent return. Many traders are comfortable with that. Furthermore, a potential 1 percent monthly return on a compounded basis is nothing to be ashamed of. Yet it needs to be weighed against the potential risks, such as missing out on an enormous buying opportunity or a 50 to 100 percent correction in the stock.

Think about it in pure dollar terms. In the above example, you would hypothetically receive $200 dollars to give away the entire upside on this stock. Additionally, for $200, you are stating that you are comfortable with XYZ remaining within that 15 percent downside range. In fact, you are so comfortable that you are willing to risk buying it there if it trades below $32.50. Better yet, for $200 you are willing to buy the stock at an effective price of $32.10 even if the price should fall to $0. Again, you may think it's worth that risk, especially in a high-volatility environment.

Many investors avoid selling puts because of the large downside risk; a stock can always fall to zero. However, these same investors are usually willing to buy stock and hold it through a lengthy decline, far beyond the point at which it should have been sold in the name of prudent risk management. The key to success with this procedure is to understand its unique drawbacks and to implement the strategy correctly in the appropriate market conditions. Despite the mathematically high success rate, this technique is not for everyone.

From a risk versus reward standpoint, the decision to write deep out-of-the-money options is based on a high probability of achieving a limited profit. But as with any "premium-selling" strategy, there will always be a few unexpected losers that create drawdowns far in excess of the profits from winning trades. With that truth in mind, one requirement for success is to prevent the majority of losing positions from being catastrophic to your portfolio. The best way to accomplish that goal is through diversity, both in the number of contracts per position and in the market sectors or industry groups selected for each position. Another requirement in achieving consistent profits with this type of (high-probability/low-profit) approach is to understand the statistical nature of the strategy, which suggests that careful trade selection and diligent position management can produce (over time) a reasonable return on investment.

EXHIBIT 13.6 Break-Even Graph—Covered Call

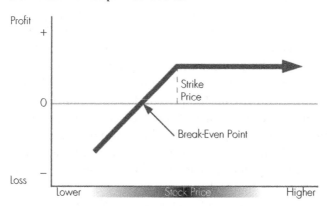

Income Strategy: Volatility as an Asset Class and Cash-Secured Puts

Many professional options traders will point out that cash-secured puts and covered calls have a nearly identical risk profile. The strategies are synthetically equivalent. Indeed, they are both effective strategies for stocks that are range bound, and they both offer about the same limited downside protection. However, the premium returns may differ on a percentage basis, especially if dividends are involved. The higher the dividend, the less the premium will be for an out-the-money call as compared with an out-of-the-money put (see **Exhibit 13.6** and **Exhibit 13.7**).

The example in Exhibit 13.3 may seem less metaphoric and more literal than some of the other strategies. For a long time, certain investors viewed writing puts, or naked puts, as a version of being an insurance company. You essentially choose a strike price at which you're willing to purchase a stock if it moves lower. It is, after all, the other side of the long put trade.

If you only write puts on stocks you really want to own, how do you define success? Is it when the stock goes up and you keep the premium but miss out on ownership? Or is it when the stock takes a dive and you're there to catch it? Most likely, you'll end up selecting stocks not because you want to own them (or wouldn't mind owning them) but because you don't think the share price will drop below the strike price between now and expiration. That's a great way to assemble a pretty lousy portfolio of formerly hot stocks you may or may not believe in or understand.

However, if you view writing naked puts primarily as a mechanism to acquire shares in companies you really want to own at substantial discounts,

EXHIBIT 13.7 Break-Even Graph—Cash-Secured Put

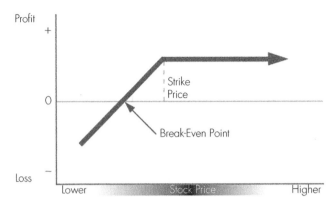

not only will your selection improve, but arguably so will your returns. This is a reasonable consolation to keep in mind if the stock rebounds strongly and you miss out on a big move upward. As with covered calls, frequently the greatest risk with naked puts is that of missed opportunity.

Position Management

Like all option-trading techniques, when dealing with cash-secured puts you need to have some type of exit strategy in case the market, stock, and/or sector or industry group moves in the opposite direction from that which is expected. In fact, learning when to initiate a closing transaction is probably the most important aspect of becoming a successful trader. Also, the success of a high-probability/low-profit strategy such as writing cash-secured puts depends on keeping losses at a minimum. There are never any big winners to offset the big losers, so there simply can't be any big losers. Obviously, a gapping issue will occasionally wipe out a portion of previous gains, and there is nothing you can do about it. At the same time, you must manage the remaining positions effectively or there will be no profits to offset the catastrophic losers.

A put writer has many different alternatives when the underlying issue moves below the strike price before expiration, but in most cases appropriate action should be put in place in advance. One outstanding principle that new investors fail to adhere to is the need to outline a basic exit strategy before initiating any position, to eliminate emotional decisions. This plan must be simple enough to implement while monitoring a portfolio of plays in a volatile market. In addition, these exit/adjustment rules should apply across a range of situations and be designed to compensate for one's weaknesses and inadequacies. Also, to be effective in the long term, they must be formulated to help maintain discipline on a general basis and, at the same time, offer a timely memory aid for difficult situations.

One of the great things about options trading is that once you become experienced with the various adjustment techniques, you can turn many losing plays into winning ones with the effective use of stops and by rolling out of or into new positions when the stock moves against you. When you do lose (and you will), at least you have reduced your losses by leveraging against another position. In all cases when attempting to recover a losing position, you must be prepared for further drawdowns and have a thorough knowledge of the strategy.

For the Investor

There are two key motivations for employing this strategy. It works as an attempt either to purchase underlying shares below current market price or to collect and keep premium from the sale of puts which expire out of the money and with no value. An investor should write a cash-secured put only when she is comfortable owning underlying shares, because assignment is always possible at any time before the put expires. In addition, she should be satisfied that the net cost for the shares will be at a satisfactory entry point if she is assigned an exercise. The number of put contracts written should correspond to the number of shares the investor is comfortable with and financially capable of purchasing. Although assignment may not be the objective at times, it should not be a financial burden. This strategy can become speculative when more puts are written than the equivalent number of shares you wish to own.

CHAPTER 14

The Married Put: Protecting Your Profit

An investor friend was managing a small hedge fund with $200 million in assets. When the markets plunged in 2008, the hedge fund blew up and he lost 35 percent of his trading capital in the span of a few days. He had nonchalantly placed stop-losses of around eight hundred points on a couple of index futures (thinking they would never, ever be hit) with large wagers, and all his stops got hit! He stated, "There was nothing in the history of the markets over the last year or so to warn that such a debacle was coming!" This notion was patently ridiculous. He had also gone long on most of the equity markets and consequently became a casualty of a strong positive correlation, a rare event.

Rare events are an oddity and a paradox; yet in the financial markets, there is actually no such thing as a rare event. No set of statistics can uncover the rare event, nor can any time series help in predicting a rare event. It could be a twenty standard deviation event—something that is likely to come about only once in more than a billion years—and yet it seems to occur every ten years or so. Traders make money more often and lose money less often, but when they lose, they lose big time. They may make money for a while, maybe even for quite long time, and then take a big hit; they eventually go down in flames!

Volatility, Downside Risk, and the Case for Portfolio Insurance

In the world of investment theory, any unpredictability is defined as risk as such. In estimating the risk of an asset return, both positive and negative returns from the mean return of the asset are just as relevant. But in the mind of the typical investor, *risk always boils down to losing money.* If there is changeability of the return on the positive side of the return distribution (i.e., the investor is profitable since the asset has moved favorably), he doesn't readily construe this as risk. Every investor or trader makes money in the financial markets because of volatility, but no one considers that as a part of risk. Therefore, even though the calculation of volatility, or standard deviation, takes into account both positive and negative variations around the mean, to an investor, *volatility connotes loss from investment.*

Risk, to an investor, means the loss of wealth in an absolute or a relative sense. A loss is continuously benchmarked or initialized to an absolute or relative value. If you have $10,000 to play with, then the loss of your wealth is benchmarked to $10,000. If you buy a stock for $40, then the loss of wealth affects values below $40.

Why Buy High Volatility?

We've been taught to buy low and sell high. Derivative traders follow a natural extension to this long-held premise. Buying options with a high implied volatility is stacking the odds against you, so the story goes. You have so many things working against you, the biggest being time decay. Yet some of the best buying (volatility) opportunities exist during periods of high implied volatility. In contrast, and with an appropriate amount of hindsight, some of the best-selling opportunities have existed during low levels of implied volatility. The markets are random; but remember, implied volatility is high or low for a definite reason.

Put away your charts, formulas, and logical deduction, and review your situation. Would one of the following reasons cause you to consider buying option premium, even during periods of high volatility?

1. You own a stock that you don't want to part with.
2. You agree that picking a stock's bottom is extremely difficult at best.
3. The price movement of a given option is not always directly proportional to the price movement of the underlying asset. As a result, even if you pick the precise low point for a given stock or future and buy a call option, it is still possible that the call option may not generate much profit and in fact might lose money.
4. You use options as a leverage tool, rather than as a means to strategically keep your portfolio within a given dollar range.

5. You have no interest in applying a complex strategy or one which requires constant monitoring.
6. Failure to manage your portfolio without options may lead to one huge loss that wipes out many small gains or even erases the portfolio completely.
7. You have a predetermined dollar amount that you're willing to lose on any trade.
8. You're willing to make smaller trades than you're accustomed to handling, providing you with capital to insure downside risk.

Buying options and watching them decay day after day is quite difficult. Yet when you consider the potential impact of implied volatility on your portfolio, take a moment to reflect on your objectives. It is true that the odds are in your favor (over time) if you sell implied volatility over the asset's historical volatility. It may seem foolhardy to think of utilizing an option-buying strategy during high volatility, but if you want to survive for the long haul, it's wise to take another look.

The Married Put

One option strategy that limits loss, alleviates fear, and allows you to get a peaceful night's sleep no matter how volatile the market gets is known by the old-timers as a *married put*. The term refers to a combination of two different purchases—an underlying stock and a put option on the same stock. It's also known as a *protective put*.

This is definitely *not* a strategy for short-term and day traders, but it is effective if you plan to hold the stock for the intermediate to long term, despite any short-term volatility.

The married put investor retains all benefits of stock ownership, he has insured his shares against an unacceptable decrease in value during the lifetime of the put, and he has a limited, predefined, downside market risk. *The premium paid for the put option is equivalent to the premium paid for an insurance policy.* No matter how much the underlying stock decreases in value during the lifetime of the option, the investor has a guaranteed selling price for the shares at the put's strike price. If there is a sudden, significant decrease in the market price of the underlying stock, a put owner has the luxury of time to react.

Buying a married, or protective, put involves buying one put contract for every one hundred shares of underlying stock already owned or simultaneously purchased. This put guarantees the owner the right, but not the obligation, to sell the shares at the strike price at any time until the option expires, no matter how low the stock declines in value. Just as with other forms of insurance, the investor pays a premium for this protection—the premium paid for the put.

The upside profit potential of the protective put is unlimited as long as the price of the underlying stock continues to rise. *However, purchasing a protective put in effect increases the net purchase price of the stock by the premium paid for the options contract.* When the underlying shares are ultimately sold, whether by exercising the put after a stock price declines or by simply selling the shares after a stock increases, the net price received will be the sales price less the put premium paid. The break-even point for this strategy at expiration can be calculated in advance as the stock's purchase price plus the put premium paid.

Another benefit of the protective put is that the investor is in total control of the sale of the protected shares. The protection provided is a long option position, so it is entirely up to the investor whether the put is exercised and the underlying shares are sold. If the underlying stock has declined below the put's strike price before it expires and the put is in the money with intrinsic value, the put may be sold instead of exercised and the shares retained. Regardless of the investor's decision at option expiration, during the lifetime of the put contract the investor continues to receive any dividends paid to stockholders as long as they own the underlying shares (see **Exhibit 14.1**).

EXHIBIT 14.1 Married Put Break-Even Graph

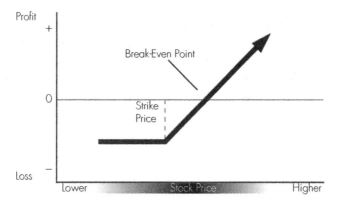

How and When to Use a Married Put

The motivations for utilizing a married put trade ultimately revolve around concerns about the unknown, near-term, downside risk of a portfolio. More specifically, a protective put may help in the following cases:

• When making a new stock purchase.
• To retain the benefits of stock ownership without complete downside exposure.
• To tie together unrealized profits from a previous purchase.
• To create an ultimate stop-loss in regard to shares that have already declined in value.

In the first case, an investor might be quite bullish on a given stock but justifiably concerned over the myriad of factors that could wrinkle his investment evaluation. Thus, the investor wisely buys a put in tandem with the original stock purchase, offering the specific downside protection he needs from the very start.

In the second scenario, an investor has a long-standing relationship with a stock, is long-term bullish, specifically desires to retain voting rights, and hopes to receive large dividend checks from now till eternity. However, after recently witnessing several economic catastrophes, the investor decides to protect his favorite stock from the risk of a once-in-a-lifetime event.

In the third example, an investor is the recipient of good fortune. Years ago, she purchased shares that have since enjoyed a steady increase in value over the initial cost and so have unrealized profits. She considers the stock to be a wise investment, has a positive outlook over the long haul, and wishes to continue owning the shares. However, the investor is concerned with an increasingly bearish sentiment in the broad market. She wishes to make a put purchase to help protect her unrealized profits.

In the last case, an investor owns stocks that have fallen into the flames. This investor's portfolio has declined in value and so has unrealized losses. He still has a long-term optimistic outlook and does not wish to sell. Rather, he wants to protect himself from additional loss. The investor is willing to hand over a relatively small amount of cash rather than lose his portfolio, and so he buys a protective put.

It's essential to note that in all of these cases, the amount of security provided by the long put depends on choosing both a strike price and an expiration month that mirrors the investor's timeframe for potential downside risk.

Example of When to Use a Married Put

An investor purchases one thousand shares of XYZ at $32 per share. If a protective put isn't purchased, then as soon as the stock drops below the purchase price the investor will begin to lose money, effectively leaving the entire $32,000 purchase price at risk. On the other hand, if the stock price rises, the investor profits from the entire increase without incurring the "insurance cost" of the put premium.

Consider the two scenarios for purchasing insurance on this $32,000 investment decision.

- The underlying stock has increased in value and protection for unrealized profits is purchased.
- The stock has decreased in value and protection from further loss is desired.

XYZ Shares Increase from $32 to $42 per Share, and an XYZ Put Is Purchased to Protect Unrealized Profits

In this scenario the investor has unrealized XYZ profits of $10,000 ($42 current price − $32 purchase price = $10 per share × 1,000 shares = $10,000). Safeguarding these unrealized profits, especially over the next several months, is of utmost importance to the investor. So the investor considers the purchase of ten three-month XYZ puts. She currently has a choice between buying an XYZ 40 put for $3 and an XYZ 35 put for $1. Both put options offer insurance on profits, but to different extents, by guaranteeing a stock sale price no matter how low XYZ actually declines.

Choice One: Ten XYZ 40 puts are purchased. With the purchase of ten XYZ 40 puts, the net cost is $3 × 100 × 10, or $3,000 total. If the price of XYZ declines below the $40 strike and the put is exercised at expiration, the thousand shares would be sold at the price of $40 per share. As shown in **Table 14.1**, the realized net profit on the stock purchase would be as follows: $40 (strike price) − $32 (stock's original purchase price) = $8 per share, or $8,000 total, less the $3,000 cost of the put. As a result, a premium of $3,000 would be spent to provide three-month protection of $8,000 in unrealized gains, not to mention the protection of the original investment against further or total loss.

Note that although there are $10,000 in unrealized profits, insurance in the form of a 40 put was purchased while the stock was trading at $42. The difference of $2 ($42 current stock price − $40 strike price) per share is given up due to the decline in the XYZ stock price. This $2, or $2,000 total

TABLE 14.1 Married Put Profit and Loss at Expiration (Long 1,000 XYZ @ $32 per Share; Long 10 XYZ $40 Puts @ $3 per Share)

Stock Price at Expiration	Stock Gain/Loss (from $32 per share)	40 Put Gain/Loss (40 put at $3)	Net Position Gain/Loss
$100	$68,000	($3,000)	$65,000
$ 45	$13,000	($3,000)	$10,000
$ 40	$8,000	($3,000)	$ 5,000
$ 30	($2,000)	$7,000	$ 5,000
$ 25	($7,000)	$12,000	$ 5,000
$ 0	($32,000)	$37,000	$ 5,000

XYZ increases from $32 to $42 per share; position = long 1,000 shares from $32 per share ($32,000); action = buy ten three-month 40 puts at $3.00 ($3,000).

TABLE 14.2 Married Put Profit and Loss at Expiration (Long 1000 Shares XYZ @ $32 per Share; Long 10 $35 Puts at $1 per Share)

Stock Price at Expiration	Stock Gain/Loss (from $32 per share)	35 Put Gain/Loss (35 put at $1)	Net Position Gain/Loss
$100	$68,000	($1,000)	$67,000
$45	$13,000	($1,000)	$12,000
$40	$8,000	($1,000)	$7,000
$30	($2,000)	$4,000	$2,000
$25	($7,000)	$9,000	$2,000
$0	($32,000)	$34,000	$2,000

XYZ increases from $32 to $42 per share; position = long one thousand shares at $32 per share ($32,000); action = buy ten three-month 35 puts at $1 ($1,000).

for one thousand shares, could be considered the deductible or personal risk taken for the price of this insurance policy.

Choice Two: Ten XYZ 35 puts are purchased. With the purchase of ten XYZ 35 puts, the net cost is $1 × 100 × 10, or $1,000. If XYZ declines below the $35 strike price and the put is exercised at expiration, the thousand XYZ shares would be sold at the $35 strike per share. As shown in **Table 14.2**, the realized net profit on the stock would be as follows: $35 (strike price) − $32 (stock's original purchase price) = $3 per share, or $3,000 total, less the $1,000 cost of the put. As a result, a premium of $1,000 would be spent to provide three-month protection of $3,000 in unrealized gains, not to mention the protection of the original investment against further or total loss.

Note that although there are $10,000 in unrealized profits, insurance in the form of a 35 put was purchased while the stock was trading at $42. The difference of $7 ($42 current stock price − $35 strike price) per share is given up due to the decline in the XYZ stock price. This $7, or $7,000 total for one thousand shares, could be considered the deductible or personal risk taken for the price of this insurance policy.

XYZ Shares Decrease from $50 to $35, and an XYZ Put Is Purchased to Protect from Further Decline

The investor in this scenario has fallen victim to a major decline in unprotected stock value, from $50 to $35, but for whatever reason she is determined to hold on to her one thousand shares. However, she is willing to commit a small amount of cash to this losing position for defense from further decline and decides to buy a protective XYZ 35 put. Checking the option screen, she finds an XYZ three-month 35 put for $2.20. The investor decides that buying the three-month put for $2,200 ($2.20 × 100 × 10) best fits her tolerance for further cash commitment, provides her with the downside protection she wants, and best fits her time frame for possible further decline in the underlying stock.

The $2,200 paid for insurance will protect the one thousand shares previously bought for $50 below the guaranteed sale price of the $35 strike. The investor has already experienced an unrealized loss of $15,000 from the steep stock price drop. But as shown in **Table 14.3**, no matter how much more XYZ continues to decline in price, further downside loss is limited as follows: $35 current stock price − $35 strike price + the $2.20 put premium paid, or $2,200. In other words, by purchasing put protection the investor has stopped her loss at a $32.80 per share price.

TABLE 14.3 Married Put Profit and Loss at Expiration (Long 1,000 Shares of XYZ @ $50 per Share; Long 10 XYZ $35 Puts @ $2.20 per Share)

Stock Price at Expiration	Stock Gain/Loss (from $50 per share)	35 Put Gain/Loss (35 Put at $2.20)	Net Position Gain/Loss
$100	$50,000	($2,200)	$47,800
$50	$0	($2,200)	($2,200)
$35	($15,000)	($2,200)	($17,200)
$20	($30,000)	$12,800	($17,200)
$0	($50,000)	$32,800	($17,200)

XYZ decreases from $50 to $35 per share; position = long one thousand shares from $50 per share ($50,000); action = buy ten three-month 35 puts at $2.20 ($2,200).

If at expiration XYZ has declined well below the put's 35 strike price, the investor may exercise the put and sell the thousand shares for a net price of $32.80 ($35 strike price − $2.20 cost of the put = $32.80). Alternatively, if the investor decides against further downside protection, she could sell the put to recoup some of its original cost.

The Married Put: Limiting Loss, Neutralizing Volatility, and Unleashing Upside Potential

The precariousness of the market can present great risk to investors. Lifetime events can occur with regularity and without notice. The inherent dangers to your portfolio can only be quantified with the benefit of hindsight. However, hindsight will add nothing but remorse and self-pity to your portfolio.

A married put strategy can potentially provide the investor with the comfort level necessary to stave off the various and sundry risks of any equity portfolio. This strategy may be considered more conservative than an outright stock purchase since as long as a put is held against an underlying stock position there is limited and predefined risk. The chief advantage of this strategy is that it provides a downside guaranteed selling price. Specifically, an investor has full knowledge regarding at what price shares can be sold no matter how low the stock drops. On the other hand, the protective put does not place a barrier on how high the stock can be sold. The married put strategy enjoys unlimited upside profit potential as the price of the underlying continues to rise, and as long as the shares are held the investor continues to receive any dividends paid.

Like any long option position, an investor pays a premium for the put and its protective benefits. However, consider the premium paid as merely a deductible to a short-term insurance policy on the shares held, resulting in an increased break-even point for the underlying owned.

Using at-the-money puts or out-of-the-money puts have assorted advantages and risks. In the majority of circumstances, there will be a put contract with a strike price and expiry term that optimally fits the balance of risk versus reward versus money spent that an investor is looking for. Alternatively, this strategy offers the freedom to roll a current protective put position by selling an existing long put position and purchasing another put with a different month, year, and possibly a different strike price.

Married Put: A Real-Life Illustration

Married put = Long stock position and long puts in equal quantity

Protective puts are often referred to as an insurance policy. Like most insurance contracts, options have established terms, appointed life spans, and possibly even a deductible. To illustrate the parallels between the protective put strategy and insurance, consider the following example.

Assume you purchase a very nice automobile for $100,000. If you wreck the car beyond repair and have no insurance, you would incur a loss of $100,000 (less the automobile's salvage value, if any). This is a significant risk—most people wouldn't own such an expensive car without some kind of insurance policy.

Next, apply this line of thinking to protective puts. Bear in mind that most options represent one hundred shares of the underlying stock, and prices must be multiplied by one hundred to calculate the cost when options are traded or exercised. Assume you own two thousand shares of XYZ stock at a purchase price of $52, costing you $104,000. If you are in a "buy and hold" mode, doing nothing, and the stock drops to $25 per share, you have an unrealized loss of $54,000.

To help reduce this risk, you could buy insurance on your stock. If you decide to buy twenty six-month XYZ put options (20 options × 100 shares = 2,000) with a strike price of $50, at a price of $4 ($4 × 2,000 shares = $8,000 total cost), you have the right to exercise your puts at any time prior to the six-month expiration and sell your stock at $50 per share, a full twenty-five points above the current market price, or sell your puts to offset most of the loss on your stock.

If you indeed decide to sell your stock at $50 per share by exercising your puts, the price you paid for your put options ($8,000) would be your insurance premium, and the two points you lose on your stock (purchased at $52 per share, sold at $50 per share) would be your insurance deductible. Overall, your loss would be $10,000—that is, $2,000 (stock deductible of $52 per share − $50 per share sell price) and $8,000 of put premium.

On the other hand, if XYZ remained above $50 by expiry, your put position would expire as worthless, and the $8,000 you paid for the protection would be lost—just like the insurance premium you paid on your car.

This brings up the question, "How much insurance should I have?" Depending on your risk tolerance and objectives, spending $8,000 (in the above example) to protect $100,000 of stock for six months' time may not make sense. You might consider protecting part of your initial investment by purchasing a fractional amount of the twenty puts necessary to be considered fully hedged. Or you might consider purchasing disaster insurance—buying twenty out-of-the-money puts, providing you with protection against an enormous downside move.

Summary of the Married Put

What if you could go back the day *before* that once-in-a-century rare event when your portfolio went bust? What would you do differently? What if you could have bought insurance on the performance of the stocks in your portfolio?

The married put strategy allows you to limit your loss while keeping your investment open to unlimited profit potential. It works the same way as an insurance policy—you pay a little over time for protection against loss, but at the same time you can capture the upside benefit without a cap.

CHAPTER 15

The Collar: Sleep at Night

I have worked the markets for decades as both a trader and an investor. As a professional trader, I stepped onto the floor eager for volatility. Then, trends changed quickly, spreads between bid and ask prices were wide, and orders flowed into the pit driven by irrational decision making and fear. In those days of low costs for trading and rapid changes in position, traders loved markets with volatile price changes because those kinds of markets made collecting profits easy for a savvy trader.

As a typical personal investor, however, I loathe volatility. Investors need to work through brokers and other professionals, adding costly commissions to trades. Investors generally can't access market data as quickly as traders, and they often don't have large amounts of cash available to gamble on short-term profits with small margins. As an investor, the game often feels rigged; I was constantly playing the fool.

The goal of this book is to help investors learn how to use options trading to an advantage. Personal investors must balance theoretical knowledge about derivatives against the practical need to manage risk, and they must protect savings and investments against unnecessary loss when market values for stocks begin to swing wildly up and down. One options strategy often used to control risk is the collar strategy.

Collar Strategy

As an investor, you probably seek to build up a varied portfolio of stocks, bonds, cash instruments, and other investments over time. Your goal is not to profit quickly but to grow your portfolio over time. Thus, you need a strategy that protects you if the markets fall sharply. At the same time, you need to design your strategy so that it doesn't protect against potential loss to the point that you end up missing out on profits if market values abruptly climb instead. In the meantime, you want to shield your portfolio against severe market volatility. Normal markets feature some volatility, but in recent years, severe swings upward and downward have become more common, making the application of investment strategies extremely difficult. One of the worst examples in American history occurred in October 2008 when the Dow Jones Industrial Average repeatedly endured days of staggering point swings of 700 or 800 points, or even more. On October 10, 2008, the Dow hit a low of 7882.51 and a high of 8901.28—a swing of over 1018 points—in a single trading session!

Most investors respond to high volatility with intense research—except during October 2008, when most investors watched in mute terror. The average investor tries to anticipate whether the market will move up or down for a given security and plan accordingly. Yet no matter how prudent the strategy may be, the best research won't help you plan for market divergences and random uncertainties. The outcome is not just difficult to discern—it is, in fact, unknowable. The market always faces both the substantial likelihood of a decline and the distinct likelihood of continued appreciation. You can't tell what is going to happen, and this uncertainty weakens the value of your research. Many experienced traders recommend a sophisticated method of risk management called a *collar*.

What Is a Collar?

A collar combines a *covered call* and a *protective put*. Both the covered call and the protective put are discussed in preceding chapters. As an investor, you would set up a collar primarily to protect your positions against loss if market values fall. But you can also use the collar to allow for growth in market values, and all of this protection comes at a modest cost. The money you earn from selling a covered call can be used to cover most or all of the costs to buy the protective put. The collar allows an investor to cap potential profits on a position in order to limit potential losses at little or no expense. If you have thousands or tens of thousands of shares in a single stock and you can't or don't want to sell some of them to reduce your risk, this strategy could help protect your position.

To create a collar, you buy a put option (a married put) and sell or write a call option (a covered call) at the same time. Both are based on the same underlying stock, both are out of the money, and both expire on the same date. Generally, you buy the puts and sell the calls for a stock position that you already own to completely cover that position.

Suppose you have one thousand shares of XYZ common stock, currently trading at $30 per share. You are familiar with using married put contracts to protect this stock if the share price falls, but you don't want to spend the money to buy the ten put contracts you would need to cover those thousand shares. This would be especially true if you want to protect the shares of XYZ for two or three years, which would require you to buy new contracts every three months as the old contracts expire, or if share prices are particularly volatile, which would drive up the cost of the option's contract premiums. For example, a six-month $27.50 put option on XYZ stock might sell for $3 a contract.

To lower the net cost of your risk strategy, you could buy ten six-month $27.50 put contracts for $3 each, and at the same time sell ten six-month $35 calls for $2.50 each. Your net cost is 50 cents per contract.

1. You own one thousand shares of XYZ common stock at $30 per share.
2. You buy ten six-month $27.50 puts at $3 per share.
3. You sell ten six-month $35.00 calls at $2.50 per share.
4. Net premium paid for collar = $0.50 per share.

Consider Three Potential Scenarios at Expiration

- XYZ common shares close above the short call strike of $35.
- XYZ common shares close below the long put strike of $27.50.
- XYZ common shares close between the collared strikes of $27.50 and $35.00.

XYZ Is above the Short Call Strike of $35 at Expiration

If XYZ is trading above $35 at expiration, the call options contracts you sold will probably be exercised against you, forcing you to sell the thousand shares of stock to the other investor at $35 a share. Keep in mind, though, that the other investor is not required to exercise the call contracts. However, we assume that he will, and if he does you must sell the shares to the other investor. So in this example you are selling the stock at $35 a share, making a profit of $5 a share over your original purchase price, but less the 50 cents per share cost for the collar. So your profit is $4.50 a share.

XYZ Is below the Long Put Strike of $27.50 at Expiration

If XYZ is trading below $27.50 when the contracts expire, you can (if you want) exercise the put contracts you bought and force the other investor who sold you the contracts to buy the shares from you at $27.50 a share. You end up losing $3 a share. You originally bought the shares for $30 each, so you lose $2.50 per share in the sale, plus the net cost of the collar, 50 cents per share. But in this case you limit your total loss to $3 per share. If the share price falls to $20, you would have lost $10 per share without the collar strategy.

Note that you can also decide to hold on to the shares and sell the put contracts rather than exercise them. The money you make from selling these contracts helps offset the loss on the stock.

XYZ Is Trading between $27.50 and $35 at Expiration

If the price of a share of XYZ is between $27.50 and $35 when the contracts expire, both the put and call options will be out of the money and will expire as worthless. You get to keep your shares of XYZ, you protected yourself against excessive loss, and the only cost to you is the 50 cents per share in insurance premiums in the form of the put and call contracts.

Table 15.1 shows the likely results of your investment strategy based on the price of a share of XYZ stock at the put and call contracts' expiration date.

TABLE 15.1   Collar Strategy Profit and Loss Table at Expiration (Long 1,000 Shares XYZ @ $30 per Share; Long 10 XYZ $27.50 Puts; Short 10 XYZ $35 Calls)

XYZ Price Expiry	Collar P/L	Stock P/L	Net P/L
$50.00	($15,500)	$20,000	$4,500
$36.00	($1,500)	$6,000	$4,500
$35.50	($1,000)	$5,500	$4,500
$35.00	($ 500)	$5,000	$4,500
$34.00	($500)	$4,000	$3,500
$33.00	($500)	$3,000	$2,500
$32.00	($500)	$2,000	$1,500
$31.00	($500.00)	$1,000	$500
$30.00	($500.00)	$0.00	($500)
$29.00	($500.00)	($1,000)	($1,500)
$28.00	($500.00)	($2,000)	($2,500)
$27.50	($500.00)	($2,500)	($3,000)
$27.00	$0.00	($3,000)	($3,000)
$26.00	$1,000	($4,000)	($3,000)
$25.00	$2,000	($5,000)	($3,000)
$10.00	$17,000	($20,000)	($3,000)

Summary

An equity collar pairs two basic strategies, the *covered call* and the *married put*, and it is a very common strategy. For a single stock, it protects the share price from loss with a set of put contracts in return for a cap on the amount of profit you can make per share with a set of call contracts. The advantage of using both put and call contracts for the same underlying stock is that the money you make in selling call contracts offsets the money you need to spend to buy the matching put contracts. If you are lucky you might be able to buy your insurance for free, if you can bring in as much money for the call contracts as you pay for the puts, or possibly even turn a modest profit on the contracts themselves. This strategy is particularly useful if you have a large position in a given stock, which makes up a large percentage of the net worth of your investments.

Types of Collars

In a collar, if the underlying stock declines below the strike price on the put contract (in our example, below $27.50 per share), you can exercise the put and limit your loss if the share prices fall even further.

If the stock price goes higher, you can profit up to the strike price on the call contract ($35 per share), plus the net cost to buy the call contracts. But you run the risk that the other investor will exercise the contracts against you. If the share price climbs to $50, you are out of luck—you must sell the shares for $35 each. So you make $4.50 per share, but without the call contracts you would have made $20 per share (see **Exhibit 15.1**).

EXHIBIT 15.1 Collar Strategy: Long Put Strike and Short Call Strike

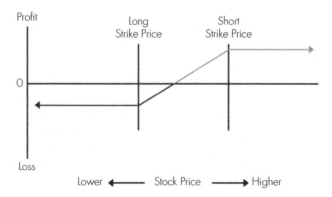

This example illustrates that you need to be careful in selecting the strike prices for the call and put contracts. It is very subjective and largely depends on your goals and needs. Strikes can be implemented close to at the money or far out of the money. If you are a long-term investor, you probably want to hold on to these shares, so you want the stock price to stay within the range you set—the strike price for the put contracts you plan to buy and the call contracts you plan to sell. But you can adjust your strategy on the basis of how much risk you can tolerate, the cost for the premiums over time, and how volatile the share prices are likely to be in the months to come.

To allow for differing strategies, you can use three different types of collars:

1. Protective collar
2. Appreciating collar
3. Flexible collar

The Protective Collar

Use the *protective collar* strategy if you already own shares of stock and either don't want to sell them or can't, even if you are pessimistic about the company that issued the stock or about the stock market in the near future. The protective strategy involves buying an at-the-money or near–at-the-money put contract while also selling an at-the-money or near–at-the-money call contract. This strictly limits on your risk and reward profile. The tighter you make the collar—that is, the closer the put and call contracts are to being in the money—the more restricted your profit or loss will become.

Suppose you work for a small technology company and have received as a benefit over three or four years several thousand shares of your firm's common stock. You are convinced your employer enjoys excellent prospects for the next several years, but you have friends who worked at similar high-tech firms in the 1990s that also looked great—until the Internet bubble burst in 2001. Most of these friends lost nearly all of their savings, and you don't want history repeating itself with you as the victim. Also, most of your personal net worth is tied up in this stock, and you simply don't want to add to your personal risk by holding your stock without any protection.

You consider your personal financial situation and decide that you cannot afford to sell your stock for less than $38 per share. To protect against loss, you decide to set up a protective collar. As a result, you are paying to make sure that the value of your stock will be safe no matter what happens to the market, but you are giving up a chance to make profit on the stock if the share prices climb in value.

EXHIBIT 15.2 The Protective Collar

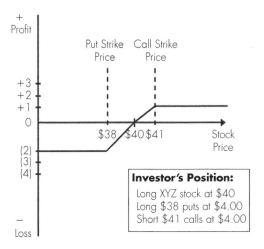

You decide to buy six-month $38 put contracts for $4 per share. Then, to pay for these put options, you sell six-month call option contracts trading at the same price. With that, you sell a six-month $41 call for $4 per share. With this trade, you now know that no matter what happens over the course of the next six months, you will receive an amount between $38 and $41 per share.

As seen in **Exhibit 15.2**, your total profit or loss from the combinations of these positions is limited to $3 per share. This means that if your stock explodes to $100 per share, the most you will receive is $41. Conversely, if your stock tanks to $1 per share, the least you will receive is $38.

The Appreciating Collar

An *appreciating collar* is used as a milder risk-management technique to provide downside protection yet upside potential as well. A standard appreciating collar is the simultaneous purchase of an out-of-the-money put against the sale of a further out-of-the-money call. Normally, the appreciating collar strikes are not equidistant (where the call strike is further out of the money than the put strike) from the underlying stock price. The wider the collar strikes chosen, the wider your profit/loss profile will be.

To illustrate this strategy, suppose that about a year ago you bought XYZ during the midst of a selling panic at $30 per share, and since then the stock has risen to about $40 per share. You may be either neutral or optimistic about the long-term prospects for this company's stock, but in the short term you're concerned about overall market volatility. More important, you have substantial unrealized gains in the stock ($10 per share), and you don't want to lose that. So you need to consider your strategy before setting up a collar trade on the stock.

1. Pick a time period for which you need the collar trade insurance to last.
2. Decide on the strike price of the put option for the time period you have chosen.
3. Attempt to reduce the cost of the put option by selling a call with the same expiration date.
4. Analyze the total cost of the trade.
5. Evaluate the *maximum risk* of the trade.
6. Consider the *maximum gain* of the trade.

As seen in **Table 15.2**, because you have a $10 per share unrealized gain in your stock, you may be willing to risk losing a few dollars per share if values fall, but you want to be protected against anything worse. Essentially, you just want to hold steady, spending as little as possible, without selling your stock and without losing too much money. In addition, you choose a six-month time frame for your collar strategy.

You decide to buy six-month $37 put contracts for $3.15 per share. This ensures an effective XYZ sale price of $33.85 per share:

$37.00 strike price − $3.15 per share put premium = $33.85

To help pay for the put contracts and increase your potential sale price per share, you choose to sell a six-month $45 call for $1.80 per share. This

TABLE 15.2 Collar—Sampling of Strikes and Strike Prices for 120-day Options Surrounding XYZ @ $40 per Share

Call Strikes	Price	Put Strikes	Price
$41.00	$3.30	$39.00	$4.05
$42.00	$2.90	$38.00	$3.60
$43.00	$2.50	$37.00	$3.15
$44.00	$2.15	$36.00	$2.75
$45.00	$1.80	$35.00	$2.35
$46.00	$1.55	$34.00	$2.05
$47.00	$1.35	$33.00	$1.80
$48.00	$1.10	$32.00	$1.50
$49.00	$0.95	$31.00	$1.30
$50.00	$0.80	$30.00	$1.10

XYZ = $40.00; 120-day options.

sale will obligate you to sell the stock at $45 if the contracts are exercised against you, but the sale also reduces your put premium cost. Your total collar cost is as follows:

Long six month $37 put − short six − month $45 call

or $3.15 per share − $1.80 per share = $1.35 per share

The $1.35 net purchase price of the six-month $37/$45 collar provides you with the following results:

1. If the share price falls, your effective sale price will be $35.65 per share, or $37 per share strike price on the put contract minus $1.35 per share net cost to set up the collar. No matter how low the stock goes, you know you will be able to sell the shares for the next six months for $35.65 per share.
2. If the share price climbs, your effective sale price will be $43.65 per share, or $45 per share strike price on the call contract minus $1.35 per share net cost to set up the collar. No matter how high the stock goes over the next six months, you know that you will not be able to sell your stock for more than $43.65 per share.

Summary

As previously noted, choosing the correct strike prices for your matching put and call contracts for your collar trade is highly subjective. In the example of the $37/$45 collar, a few issues become clear:

1. With a $1.35 per share cost, this collar apparently does provide insurance but at a hefty price. According to **Table 15.3**, you are risking $4.35 to make, at the most, $3.65. In the long run, this may not be a good gamble.
2. Notice in Table 15.3 that the prices are not equal in terms of call and put as well as the distance to the strike. For instance, with the stock at $40 per share, the $5 out-of-the-money call contract trades at 55 cents less per share than the $5 out-of-the-money put. This disparity between call and put prices is common, and the cause is directly caused by volatility, skew, dividends, and supply and demand.
3. Weigh the cost/benefit of the strike prices you choose for an appreciation collar. As the old adage says, "You get what you pay for."
4. You may decide that this $37 put/$45 call collar is too expensive for the amount of security it provides. Yet, consider the alternatives shown in **Table 15.4**.

TABLE 15.3   Collar—Profit and Loss Table at Expiration (Long XYZ Stock @ $40 per Share; Long XYZ $37.00 Puts; Short XYZ $45.00 Calls at a Net Debit of $1.35 per Share)

Stock Price at Expiry	Stock P/L at $40 per Share	Long $37 Put Value	Short $45 Call Value	Collar Debit	Net P/L per Share
$100.00	$60.00	$ 0.00	($55.00)	($1.35)	$3.65
$ 50.00	$10.00	$ 0.00	($ 5.00)	($1.35)	$3.65
$ 45.00	$ 5.00	$ 0.00	$ 0.00	($1.35)	$3.65
$ 43.65	$ 3.65	$ 0.00	$ 0.00	($1.35)	$2.30
$ 40.00	$ 0.00	$ 0.00	$ 0.00	($1.35)	($1.35)
$ 37.00	($ 3.00)	$ 0.00	$ 0.00	($1.35)	($4.35)
$ 35.65	($ 4.35)	$ 1.35	$ 0.00	($1.35)	($4.35)
$ 30.00	($10.00)	$ 7.00	$ 0.00	($1.35)	($4.35)
$ 15.00	($25.00)	$22.00	$ 0.00	($1.35)	($4.35)
$ 0.00	($40.00)	$37.00	$ 0.00	($1.35)	($4.35)

TABLE 15.4   Collar—Range of Protection Implementing Various Strike Prices

Collar	Strikes	Net Cost	Collar	Protected	Range
43 call	39 put	$1.55	$41.45	$37.45	$ 4.00
44 call	38 put	$1.45	$42.55	$36.55	$ 6.00
45 call	37 put	$1.35	$43.65	$35.65	$ 8.00
46 call	37 put	$1.20	$44.80	$34.80	$10.00
47 call	35 put	$1.00	$46.00	$34.00	$12.00

In Table 15.4 you can see a sample of collars that could be implemented against the long XYZ position. The suggested collar strikes are all, for practical purposes, a mathematical extension from the original $45 call/$37 put example. A collar can be chosen with any combination of strikes, but note the following:

1. You really do get what you pay for. Choosing the collar with the least cost or with no net cost at all may not provide you with the protection you want.
2. Weigh the factors that matter most to you. Are you simply trying to avoid a loss if the market falls? Or do you have a wider tolerance for risk if you can also gain more opportunity for profit if share prices rise?

The Flexible Collar

The *flexible collar* allows you to account for volatility in the marketplace. Volatility refers to the rate of change in the price of a security or market over a defined period of time. Implied volatility is the likely amount of volatility in the future. It is just another way of saying that the market believes the value of the share price of the underlying stock is about to change more than it has in the past. If the price of an underlying share of stock is likely to change, the premium price for an options contract based on that stock will probably change with it. But implied volatility is not a forecast and certainly not a guarantee of actual volatility.

If a market or share price is volatile, it makes it more expensive to hedge against risk, because the premiums for the options contracts based on these stocks tend to go up. Also, options contracts with lower strike prices have higher implied volatility than contracts with higher strike prices because they are more likely to be exercised. So if you are looking at a collar strategy, keep in mind that a standard collar means selling call option contracts with low levels of implied volatility (higher strike prices) and buying put option contracts with high levels of implied volatility (lower strike prices). This can make your strategy riskier.

Volatility is an essential factor to consider when creating a collar. If implied volatility is high, the put contracts you buy will most likely have a much higher implied volatility than will the call contract you sell. This fact, better known as the *skew*, was first noticed after the 1987 stock market crash that took the market down 25 percent in a single day. Over time, the market has shown that share prices for a stock tend to become more volatile as their share prices decline.

This effect causes out-of-the-money put contracts to be more expensive than traditional options pricing theory would predict. Also, when you set up a collar, you want the relationship between strike price and implied volatility to be the same for both the put contracts you buy and the call contracts you sell for the same stock. That is, you need to adjust the strike prices for the put and call contracts separately to account for the implied volatility for each. This means that in-the-money call contracts would be more expensive than in-the-money put contracts.

As an example, look at the differences in implied volatilities for prices of various options contracts based on the stock XYZ before and after the market crash of 2008. All of the contracts in this example were due to expire within twenty days.

Table 15.5 lists implied volatilities for options contracts below and above the stock price in May 2008, shortly before the market crash, with XYZ trading at $170 a share.

Table 15.6 lists implied volatilities for options contracts based on XYZ in February 2009, six months after the 2008 financial crisis began, with XYZ trading at $85 a share. These contracts also have twenty days remaining until they expire.

Note the prominent differences between **Table 15.5** and **Table 15.6**. Before the large market decline in May 2008, at-the-money implied volatilities were consistently around 40 percent. In the period after the market crashed, however, implied volatility for at-the-money options swelled to 90 percent. In pure percentage terms, the skew between at-the-money and out-of-the-money options was basically flat between the two volatility comparisons. In the first table, put volatility grew 30 percent from 40 percent to 57 percent across six strikes. Similarly, in Table 15.6, put volatility expanded by approximately the same amount, across six strikes, from 90 percent to 127 percent. Yet in absolute terms, implied volatility increased much more dramatically in **Table 15.6**. This absolute change in implied volatility suggested

TABLE 15.5 List of Implied Volatilities per Various Strike Prices in May 2008 with XYZ @ $170 per Share

Call Strike	Implied Volatility Percentage	Put Strike	Implied Volatility Percentage
170	40	140	57
175	38	145	53
180	36	150	50
185	34	155	48
190	33	160	45
195	32	165	42
		170	40

TABLE 15.6 List of Implied Volatilities per Various Strike Prices in February 2009 with XYZ @ $85 per Share

Call Strike	Implied Volatility Percentage	Put Strike	Implied Volatility Percentage
85	90	50	137
90	85	55	127
95	80	60	119
100	77	65	110
105	74	70	103
110	70	75	97
		80	93
		85	90

TABLE 15.7 Collar—Comparison of Volatility between Strike Prices for Both the Standard and Appreciating Collar

Time Difference	Type	Call Strike	Volatility	Put Strike	Volatility	Volatility
XYZ = $170	Standard Collar	180 Call	36%	160 Put	45%	9%
XYZ = $170	Appreciating Collar	190 Call	33%	160 Put	45%	12%
XYZ = $85	Standard Collar	95 Call	80%	75 Put	97%	17%
XYZ = $85	Appreciating Collar	105 Call	74%	75 Put	97%	23%

that share prices would fluctuate wildly in the near future. This in turn would lead to a much steeper price curve for options contracts based on these underlying stocks, and as a result would make setting up a collar trade for a stock much more expensive.

Table 15.7 compares the differences in volatility between strike prices for both the standard collar and appreciating collar.

The difference in net volatility becomes obvious when comparing collars in two different volatility environments. In both the standard and appreciating collars, the net volatility between the long put and short call strikes nearly doubles. The added volatility difference directly affects how much premium you will need to pay for the collar to protect your shares of stock. The greater the volatility difference, the more you need to pay for a collar.

Conclusions on the Collar Strategy

The Flexible Collar Strategy

A flexible collar strategy involves buying put contracts and selling call contracts as usual, but in a carefully managed way. If you use the typical standard or appreciation collar, you will find the strategy effective if the market declines before the options contracts expire. But if the market does not decline, or if you face high implied volatility in the market, you may find that using a collar to protect a position becomes expensive over time. Even if you break even on the contracts, in that you can sell the call contracts and make as much as you need to spend to buy the put contracts, you risk giving up the gains beyond the strike price of the call contract if the market advances high enough. Also, if during the life of the collar strategy the market advances and then declines, the gains from the advance will not be protected. Furthermore, if the market declines and then recovers, the protection would not cover what you lose in the decline.

Another negative aspect is the risk/reward profile in terms of the volatility skew between the short call and long put. Even when market volatility is low, you find yourself selling low volatility in your call contracts and buying higher volatility in put contracts. In effect, the marketplace is forcing you to pay an extra, artificial premium for your collar.

This means that although a collar protects a stock position in a market decline, and therefore could be a solid tactical defensive *strategy*, they are not the best defensive *trades*, especially in a volatile market. So instead of using a standard or appreciation collar, you can use the flexible collar strategy to respond directly to this dilemma. The flexible collar can protect you against losses if the market declines sharply, allow you to participate sufficiently if share prices appreciate, and at the same time respond well in a volatile market. Finally, this strategy allows you to maintain a collar for a stock over the long term without spending a lot of money on net premiums or losing a lot in opportunity costs.

The Reset Collar

You own one thousand shares of XYZ stock and want to use a collar strategy for one year. Currently, implied volatility is high, and so a standard collar trade costs too much.

- Buy ten twelve-month put contracts to cover the thousand shares of stock, 3 to 5 percent out of the money.
- Sell ten three-month call contracts, 8 to 10 percent out of the money.
- Sell ten three-month put contracts, 15 to 20 percent out of the money.
- After three months, as the options contracts that you sold expire, sell the twelve-month put contracts (they will now be at nine months to expiry) and set up a new collar to reflect the latest market share prices and volatility. The preferable strike prices for the options contracts you buy and sell for the new collar should depend solely on the current volatility of the market. Don't try to account for the net amount you paid to set up the last collar or adjust to limit the net amount you will need to spend to set up the next round.

Benefits

1. The put contracts you buy protect your stock investment while the three-month puts and calls that you sell help limit the cost for the collar strategy.
2. By resetting your position every quarter you can protect your long-term position more easily. You can adjust the collar so that your protection against falling share prices and the amount of profit available to you if share prices rise both move appropriately to keep up with the latest market values.
3. The rolling adjustments you make every three months tend to allow the collar to capture a much better opportunity to profit if share prices climb than you would get from a standard collar. This also allows you to protect the gains you accumulate each quarter.
4. In a high-volatility environment, the reset collar typically requires a net initial investment that is less than the standard or appreciation collar.

Costs

1. A flexible collar requires a more active management approach because you need to reset the trade every ninety days.
2. Like any collar, the reset collar is a defensive approach to investing. This strategy is not designed to allow you to capture profits if your stock share prices climb quickly and to levels you had not anticipated.
3. Except for a drastic market correction, the reset collar will tend to behave more put-like on the downside and more as a short-term collar on the upside, given that the position gives you net long volatility and long theta.
4. The actual cost or return of the strategy does not simply depend on the return on the market but is also influenced by the path the market took to get there. This is because you are adjusting your collar every three months in response to changes in the market.

The Revised Collar

You own one thousand shares of XYZ currently trading at $50 per share. You'd like to apply the collar strategy for the intermediate future to protect your investment, but at the moment, implied volatility is very high.

1. Buy a three-month out-of-the-money put option in an amount equal to the number of shares of the stock you want to protect—in this example, ten contracts. Choose the strike price *based entirely on the amount of*

protection you want in case the share values fall. In this example, you choose to buy a three-month $30 put contract, 20 percent out of the money.

2. Sell ten six-month call options contracts, out of the money. The strike price you choose for these contracts should fit the profile you want for potential profit if share prices increase and also provide you with enough revenue, in the form of premium, to cover your costs for this type of collar. So you decide to sell a six-month $70 call contract, which would be 20 percent out of the money.

3. After two months, assuming the put options contracts you bought are about to expire (they haven't been exercised already), sell the put contracts and set up a new collar at the new market level. The put contracts will now be one month from expiration. The preferable strike prices for the options contracts you buy and sell for the new collar should depend solely on the current volatility of the market. Don't try to account for the net amount you paid to set up the last collar or adjust to limit the net amount you will need to spend to set up the next round.

4. Alternatively, if volatility at any time during this trade period relaxes back down to historical levels, you may want to buy back the contracts you sold earlier and set up a new collar which would either have both legs expiring in the same month or readjusted so that the strike prices on the contracts you buy and sell are closer to the current at-the-money strikes.

Benefits

1. You have more flexibility in participating in the potential increase in the value of the underlying stock.

2. Buying put contracts protects the stock from losing value, while selling the calls helps to reduce the cost of the trade.

3. Buying an intermediate-term option against selling a longer-term option provides you with a short volatility position. This could prove to be an added benefit, in that you may be able to capture short volatility while protecting your underlying asset.

4. Regularly resetting the position allows you to protect your stock position indefinitely. At the same time you can adjust to match the current market both the protection against loss and the opportunity to capture profits (if share prices increase).

5. The "revising effect" will tend to capture a much better opportunity to profit if share prices increase, and it will also help you continuously create current protection against loss.

Costs

1. This strategy requires ironclad discipline. You revise your collar regularly, but you may be tempted to wait rather than revise your collar strategy on schedule. In particular, if you are losing share value, you may be tempted to hold on to a near-term worthless put against the call contracts you sold. You would do better to continue with your existing strategy.
2. Except for a very slow decline in the market, the revised collar will tend to behave more put-like on the downside and more as a short-term collar on the upside, given that the position gives you net short volatility.
3. The actual cost or return of the strategy does not simply depend on the return on the market but is also influenced by the path the market took to get there. This is because you are adjusting your collar every three months in response to changes in the market in the meantime.

CHAPTER 16

The Straddle and Strangle: The Risks and Rewards of Volatility-Sensitive Strategies

Traders and investors who trade straddles and strangles make these dicey choices because they believe that the volatility of the underlying asset does not correspond to the implied volatility embedded in the option price. When you buy or sell a strangle or straddle, you are on one level stating that the market is wrong, that the market is not correctly pricing the implied volatility of the options contracts involved. There is often substantial risk, however, in options strategies set up to exploit a perceived mispricing in the implied volatility of the underlying asset. The risk is that the asset could abruptly change after the straddle or strangle is in place.

Yet traders love to buy and sell volatility-sensitive options, even though these strategies typically carry significant risk. After placing these trades, two primary factors impact the value of the options:

1. The future volatility expected to prevail over the life of the options contract
2. How the share price of the underlying stock moves over time

You can create an options strategy sensitive to the *volatility* of the underlying stock but not particularly sensitive to *price changes* of that same asset. Likewise, you can form a strategy sensitive to the underlying price changes while being only minimally sensitive to its volatility. Finally, you can create a strategy that will provide you with a balance, so that you limit exposure to both volatility and movement of the underlying asset.

The Buying or Selling of Premium

When discussing volatility-sensitive strategies—straddle and strangle strategies—you must first understand buying and selling of premium.

- *Buyers* of premium are counting on the market to move.
- *Sellers* of premium are hoping for the market to remain within a tight range.

In this context, "buying premium" refers to buying options contracts. The buyer pays a premium to the party issuing or selling the contracts to gain the right to exercise the contracts in the future and thus to buy or sell the underlying at a predetermined price.

The purchaser pays the premium to buy options contracts because she expects that the implied volatility of the contract will increase or because she expects a substantial increase or decrease in the underlying asset. The ultimate reward to the buyer is a long gamma position, in which the buyer will gain longer deltas as the market increases and shorter deltas as the market sells off. The tradeoff to the long gamma is negative theta, where the long option position's value can be whittled away with the passage of time.

The seller receives premium for selling options contracts, and thus for assuming the risks of both an implied volatility increase and/or a substantial change in the share price of the underlying asset. The seller will have a short gamma position, which will be balanced with a long theta position. The seller has time working to his advantage, as the options contract position tends to lose value with time. Many professional traders make money consistently by selling premium. However, when a trader loses on this strategy, it is normally by a much greater amount than his average gain. In fact, a seller can make money consistently for months or even years until that one rare event occurs that could wipe out all of the trader's gains and more.

Properties of Straddles and Strangles

With a *straddle*, the trader buys or sells an equal number of call and put contracts for the same underlying asset at the same time, and with an identical strike price and expiration date.

With a *strangle*, the trader buys or sells an equal number of call and put contracts for the same underlying asset with the same expiration date at the same time, but with differing strike prices. Typically, both the call and the put will be out of the money; for the call, the strike price will be above the underlying asset price, whereas for the put the strike price will be below the current underlying asset price.

When a trader creates the straddle or strangle, the value of that straddle or strangle—that is, the value of all of the contracts considered together as a single investment—does not change much in response to subtle changes in the price of the underlying asset. Also, it appears that the higher the volatility of the underlying asset until the options contracts expire, the higher the potential payoff from a long position. The lower the volatility of the stock, the higher the potential payoff for a short position. In this case, a short position refers to forming the straddle or strangle by *selling* options contracts.

A trader might sell a straddle or strangle if he expects the share price of the underlying stock to remain stable until the options contracts included in the investment strategy expire. On the other hand, a trader might buy a straddle or strangle if he expects high volatility for the share price of the same underlying asset.

The table below summarizes the characteristics of both the long and short side of the straddle and strangle.

	Long Straddle	Short Straddle	Long Strangle	Short Strangle
Delta	Dependent on strike price	Dependent on strike price	Dependent on strike price	Dependent on strike price
Gamma	Long gamma	Short gamma	Long gamma	Short gamma
Vega	Long vega	Short vega	Long vega	Short vega
Theta	Short theta	Long theta	Short theta	Long theta
Maximum Profit	No limit	Limited to premium collected from both options	No limit	Limited to premium collected from both options
Maximum Risk	Limited to premium paid from both options	No limit	Limited to premium paid from both options	No limit

Comparing Straddles and Strangles

Straddles and strangles have similar properties. The only real distinction is how the trader places the strike prices. The strangle buyer is willing to give up profits the straddle buyer might realize on more ordinary moves in exchange for the potential of a larger profit if the market makes a very large move. The strangle seller is willing to forgo bigger gains on smaller moves in return for having more flexibility that would keep the short options out of the money.

The Short Straddle

For example, suppose stock XYZ is currently trading at $50 per share. Assume that the ninety-day $50 call and $50 put contracts are both trading for $4. A seller would earn a net credit of $8 for each straddle (pair of contracts) sold. The seller wants the share price of XYZ to remain as close to the $50 strike as possible. At expiration, the seller profits if XYZ remains between $42 and $58 dollars per share, or less than the $8 credit earned for selling the call and put contracts. **Exhibit 16.1** illustrates the possible outcomes of this short position at expiration.

Note in Exhibit 16.1 that the maximum possible profit (A) is the combined premium received for each pair of put and call contracts sold, or $8 ($4 for each contract). The break-even points (B and C) are $42 ($50 − $8) and $58 ($50 + $8). Thus, this short position will be profitable if the share price for XYZ remains within that bounded range, or an increase or decrease in price of 16 percent from the initial price of $50 per share.

EXHIBIT 16.1   Short Straddle Break-Even at Expiration

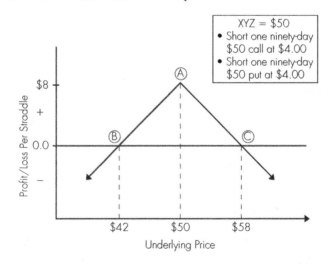

The Short Strangle

Now, suppose for XYZ, currently trading at $50 per share, the XYZ ninety-day $55 call contracts are currently trading at $1.80 and the $45 puts are trading at $2.20. Selling this strangle would net the seller $4 in option premium ($1.80 + $2.20). The seller wants the share price for XYZ to remain as close to the $50 strike as possible. At expiration, the seller profits if XYZ remains between $41 and $59 per share. Anything below or above that price results in a loss. **Exhibit 16.2** illustrates the possible outcomes of this short position at expiration.

As seen in Exhibit 16.2, the maximum profit at expiration for this short strangle position occurs between XYZ prices of $45 (A) and $55 (B), as both the put and call will expire as worthless within this range. Above $55, the call will be in the money, thus lowering the profit for the seller. Below $45, the put will become in the money. The break-even points are calculated by subtracting the premium received ($4) from the strike price of the put and adding it to the strike price of the call. In other words, this position will break even if the put or call is in the money by an amount equal to the premium received for both options. In this scenario, the lower break-even point (C) is $41 ($45 − $4), and the upper break-even point (D) is $59 ($55 + $4). In this case, XYZ would have to move plus or minus 18 percent for this position to lose money at expiration.

EXHIBIT 16.2   Short Strangle Break-Even at Expiration

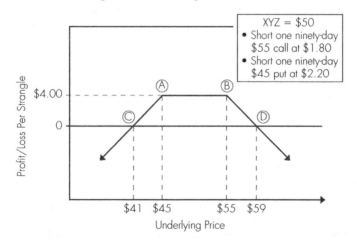

The table below illustrates the profit and loss of each strategy over a range of possible XYZ prices at expiration. This comparison demonstrates that one strategy is not necessarily superior to the other. You need to consider tradeoffs. Note how the maximum profit of the straddle ($8) is greater than that of the strangle ($4). The strangle, however, enjoys a maximum profit over a $10 range, whereas the straddle achieves maximum profitability only at the $50 strike price. Also note how the strangle is profitable over a wider range and how its losses will always be one point less than the straddle's. As with all options strategies, use your own opinion of how far and how fast you expect the underlying asset to move to determine the strategy you use.

XYZ Expiration Price	$0	$20	$45	$50	$55	$80	$100
Straddle: Short $50 Strike at $8	($42)	($22)	$3	$8	$3	($22)	($42)
Strangle: Short $45 put/$55 call at $4	($41)	($21)	$4	$4	$4	($21)	($41)

The main problem with this strategy is its unlimited risk from the standpoint of both volatility exposure and the movement of the share price of the underlying asset. On the other hand, the chief advantage of this strategy is that you don't need to be absolutely correct in your opinion on the underlying; you merely need to be confident about the future price range of the underlying asset.

How to Compare Historical and Implied Volatility

To better understand how a straddle or strangle is a wager on volatility, assume that the implied volatility is 50 percent on an annualized basis for a straddle on an options contract that expires in thirty days. This is based on the Black-Scholes model. Assume that the maximum historical volatility of the underlying asset for one month is 40 percent on an annualized basis. The implied volatility appears to be too high. Would you therefore sell the straddle or strangle?

If you believe that volatility is constant—that is, that the mathematical assumptions of the Black-Scholes model hold true—you may be tempted to sell the straddle or strangle. But most volatility traders believe that in most asset markets volatility evolves randomly through time. Even if volatility were constant or predictable, the price of the underlying asset could periodically see an abrupt level shift, referred to as a jump in the price process. In other words, expect the unexpected. It is very difficult for any options valuation model to account for rare events with any degree of accuracy.

Therefore, you need to include a risk premium to account for random changes in volatility or unpredictable changes in asset prices when pricing an options contract, even though this safety factor will probably contaminate your pricing model. Your pricing model, with a risk premium, will still provide an implied volatility, but comparing this implied volatility with historical volatility for the same asset will be problematic at best.

If you are convinced that volatility is random, and the returns on an underlying asset price and its volatility are negatively correlated, then it should begin to make sense that the implied volatility from options prices could be higher than the observed historical volatility from the underlying stock. Since implied volatility tends to reflect the expected value of an asset embedded with the ever-pending risk of that rare event, it is quite possible—normal—for the implied volatility to be higher than the historical volatility.

The Impact of Correlation and Implied Volatility Skew

Although it is quite possible to be successful selling a straddle or strangle based on an incorrect comparison of volatilities, the larger risk from these strategies often arises from the correlation between returns and volatility as well as large changes in the underlying asset price over time. In many markets, especially equity markets, returns and volatility tend to be negatively correlated. Volatility tends to go up if the market goes down, and volatility tends to go down when the market goes up.

Possible Impact #1: Implied Volatility Spike

If a trader sells volatility through straddle or strangle and the market goes down, the value of the short position in the straddle or strangle could lose more, and in some cases a lot more, than the drop in the share price of the underlying asset itself. The loss incurred largely depends on the strike price (or prices, in the case of the strangle) sold and the resulting implied volatility of the strike price involved. In a rare event, it would not be uncommon for the implied volatility to spike two to three times higher than the drop in the underlying asset itself.

On the other hand, a sharp upswing in the asset price could similarly impact the value of the straddle. As the underlying share price increases, don't expect to see the implied volatility of the options decrease at a much greater pace than that of the underlying asset.

Possible Impact #2: Skew of Implied Volatility

Another feature of implied volatility that could adversely impact the seller of the straddle if the price of the underlying asset changes is the so-called skew in implied volatility. Markets consistently exhibit a skew in implied volatility for equities, especially equity index options.

The lower the strike price of an option, the higher the implied volatility, and vice versa. If the price of an equity index rises sharply, the at-the-money call option of the straddle becomes an in-the-money call. As a result, the short call position loses value on a relative basis due to skew. Besides the impact of the change in the value of the index itself, the skew in implied volatility also alters the value of the straddle. This is because an in-the-money call contract will have a higher implied volatility than an at-the-money call, simply because the in-the-money contract is more likely to be exercised.

Possible Impact #3: Winning Small and Losing Big

Over time, the probability of losses from selling straddles and strangles far exceeds the probability of profit, and the probability of large losses far exceeds the probability of large returns. This is not to say that selling volatility through straddles and strangles is altogether bad. Selling volatility can be very lucrative; yet it is quite risky over time. You must understand that when selling a straddle or strangle, you expose yourself to three risk factors you can't control: a change in the implied volatility, a drastic change in the level of the market, and a rare event that can disrupt both the volatility and the value of the underlying asset very quickly.

An Alternative to the Naked Volatility Sale via the Straddle/ Strangle: The Strangle Swap

A *strangle swap* is an advanced strategy that can provide some of the benefits of a short straddle/strangle sale but with less risk. With a strangle swap, you would typically buy a wide out-of-the-money strangle in a later month and sell a slightly narrower strangle in a nearby month. The risk/reward characteristics of the strangle swap largely depend on the strike prices you choose.

Your goal is to create a strategy that provides a positive theta, limited exposure to volatility, and a clearly defined risk profile.

Benefits and Disadvantages of the Strangle Swap

1. The strangle swap offers a limited risk/reward profile. You won't make a lot of money, but you won't lose much either.
2. If you add more legs to the trade, you increase the complexity of the trade and increase the risk. You will be less able to predict volatility for the strangle.
3. In general, a strangle swap leads to a position that is long volatility, long theta, and short gamma. However, the initial greek position depends on the strike prices you choose for the four options contracts included in the trade.
4. The strangle swap depends on both the volatility and the path. You can change the strangle swap's profit or loss potential by failing to correctly estimate the volatility or the change in price of the underlying asset.
5. Due to the complexities of the strangle swap, the greek values for resulting trades can change dramatically over time. Depending on the strike prices you choose, the strangle swap could shift from flat gamma to short gamma, long vega to flat vega, and so on.

Example of a Typical Strangle Swap

Strategy: Strangle swap based on stock in XYZ trading at $100 a share
Leg one: Sell thirty-day $104 calls and $96 puts (17 percent volatility, 2 percent interest rate; see table below)
Leg two: Buy fifty-day $108 calls and $92 puts (21 percent volatility, 2 percent interest rate; see table below)

Sell		
Thirty Day	$104 Call	$96 Put
Value	0.63	0.51
Delta	0.22	0.18
Gamma	0.06	0.055
Theta	0.025	0.021
Vega	0.079	0.07

Buy		
Fifty-Day	$108 Call	$92 Put
Value	0.73	0.49
Delta	0.17	0.12
Gamma	0.03	0.026
Theta	0.02	0.015
Vega	0.104	0.09

Net Strangle/Swap	
Value	0.08
Delta	0.01
Gamma	−0.059
Theta	0.011
Vega	0.045

Path-dependent outcome. The table below shows the theoretical net return on a strangle swap showing various share prices for the underlying stock. The net values for the strangle swap result only from changes in the stock price. The table below keeps volatility at 17 percent for the short position and 21 percent for the long position. The example also holds constant the number of days until the contracts expire— thirty days and fifty days, respectively.

Underlying Price	$90.00	$95.00	$100.00	$105.00	$110.00
Net Value	−2.28	−0.67	0.08	−0.52	−1.84
Net Delta	0.34	0.26	0.01	−0.23	−0.26
Net Gamma	0.01	−0.039	−0.059	−0.03	0
Net Theta	−0.016	0	0.011	0	−0.0145
Net Vega	0.096	0.024	0.045	0.049	0.107
Theoretical P/L	−2.36	−0.75	0	0.61	1.92

Comments Regarding Path-Dependent Outcome

1. The resulting profit/loss assumes that the volatility remains static over time, and that's pretty heroic. Don't rely on that assumption when you build your model.

2. The profit/loss also assumes that you won't hedge the deltas as share prices change—that is, you buy deltas as the share price of the underlying asset goes up or sell deltas as the price goes down. Hedging generally serves to limit your losses. On the other hand, hedging could *add* to your loss if the underlying share price is constantly moving up and down without any firm bias in direction.

3. The profit/loss assumes that the implied volatility skew remains fairly constant. This is also a large assumption. The volatility between the months could remain constant (4 percent), while the skew in the front month could climb to a level much higher than in the deferred month.

4. Although complex, the strangle swap, unlike the naked strangle or straddle sale, can limit the unlimited loss profile associated with any naked sale.

> *Rare event outcome.* Suppose a rare event causes the XYZ index to open down 30 percent. It may be impossible to predict how the volatilities will react. The scenario below illustrates what might happen to a strangle swap as a result of an extreme move in both volatility and the share price of the underlying stock.
>
> *Strategy:* Strangle swap based on stock in XYZ trading at $100 a share
> *Leg one:* Sell thirty-day $104 calls and $96 puts at $1.14 (17 percent volatility, 2 percent interest rate)
> *Leg two:* Buy fifty-day $108 calls and $92 puts at $1.22 (21 percent volatility, 2 percent interest rate; see the table that follows)
> *Scenario:* Due to a global rare event, XYZ index opens down 30 percent. The second table that follows shows a sampling of theoretical values for the thirty-day $104 call/$96 put versus the fifty-day $108 call/ $92 put strangle swap using various extreme volatilities and the new underlying price of $70 per share.

Value	0.08
Delta	0.01
Gamma	−0.059
Theta	0.011
Vega	0.045

Initial strangle swap values, XYZ = $100

	Thirty-Day $104 Call/ $96 Put Strangle	Fifty-Day $108 Call/ $92 Put Strangle	Thirty-Day Net	Naked Short $104 Call/ $96 Put Strangle
Volatility	0.99%	0.89%		99%
Strangle value	$28.29	$26.08	($2.21)	$28.29
Delta	73	−61	12	73
Gamma	−0.021	0.022	0.001	−0.021
Theta	0.13	−0.12	0.01	0.13
Vega	−0.084	0.133	0.049	−0.084
Profit/Loss			($2.29)*	($27.15)**

XYZ = $70 a share. P/L of strangle swap as compared with outright naked short straddle with XYZ down 30 percent along with a significant upward move in implied volatility.
P/L reflects thirty-day implied volatility rising from 17 percent to 99 percent.
P/L reflects fifty-day implied volatility rising from 17 percent to 89 percent.

	Thirty-Day $104 Call/ $96 Put Strangle	Fifty-Day $108 Call/ $92 Put Strangle	Net	Naked Short $104 Call/ $96 Put Strangle
Volatility	0.99%	0.99%		0.99%
Strangle Value	$28.29	$27.44	($0.85)	$28.29
Delta	73	−56	17	73
Gamma	−0.021	0.022	0.001	−0.021
Theta	0.13	−0.15	0.02	0.13
Vega	−0.084	0.133	0.049	−0.084
Profit/Loss			($0.93)*	($27.15)**

XYZ = $70 a share. P/L of strangle swap as compared with outright naked short strangle with XYZ down 30 percent along with a significant upward move in implied volatility.
P/L reflects thirty-day implied volatility rising from 17 percent to 99 percent.
P/L reflects fifty-day implied volatility rising from 21 percent to 99 percent.

Comments Regarding a Rare Event with Both Volatility and Movement in the Underlying Share Price

1. The resulting profit/loss assumes that the volatility remains static over time, and as stated previously, that's pretty heroic. Don't rely on that assumption when you build your model.
2. The profit/loss values also assume that you are not hedging deltas as share prices change. An attempt to sell is not considered in this example.

3. This example also does not consider the lack of liquidity that might prevail in a crisis. In this event, given the complexity of the strategy, selling out might provoke heavy losses.
4. Although the two trades shown previously are losing money, the results are by far not as destructive as the straight naked strangle or straddle sale.

CHAPTER 17

The Vertical Spread and Volatility

A vertical spread is a popular options investment strategy for the investor who wants to hedge his bets about how a given asset will perform over time. The vertical spread involves buying either a call or a put option contract and at the same time writing another call or put contract with the same expiration date but at a different strike price.

A vertical spread is dubbed a *bull spread* if the trader expects the price of the underlying asset to go up. In a bull spread with calls, the trader buys a call contract with one strike price and sells a call contract with the same expiration date but a higher strike price. In the case of puts, the trader sells a put contract with one strike price and buys another put contract with the same expiration date but a lower strike price.

A vertical spread is referred to as a *bear spread* if the trader expects the price of the underlying asset to drop. In a bear spread with calls, the trader sells a call contract with one strike price and buys a call contract with the same expiration date but a higher strike price. A bear spread with puts involves buying a put contract with one strike price and selling another put contract with the same expiration date but a lower strike price.

To confuse matters more, a vertical spread (aka bull or bear spread) is also referred to as a *debit* or *credit* spread and is named according to whether the spread involves an initial inflow (credit) or outflow (debit) of cash. If you purchase a bull or bear spread, you are buying a (debit) vertical spread. If you sell a bull or bear spread, you are selling a (credit) vertical spread.

All this bull, bear, debit, credit vernacular tends to confuse some investors into thinking of vertical spreads as pure directional strategies.

Vertical spread strategies are more complex than that. Furthermore, some popular literature inaccurately suggests that an investor can easily take advantage of high implied volatility by selling credit spreads and harness low volatility by buying debit spreads. Having an opinion on volatility and being willing to exploit that conviction through vertical spreads takes a lot more than what is usually disseminated to the masses.

The goal of this chapter is to clarify some of the nuances associated with vertical spread strategies. The investor will learn that buying a vertical spread does not necessarily mean buying volatility. In the same way, selling a vertical spread doesn't always equal selling volatility. This chapter addresses how to create a theoretical model for vertical spreads and how to design them to apply in real-world situations. In particular, it talks about how to build vertical spreads that account for the mystery of implied volatility.

Introduction to the Vertical Spread

With a bull spread strategy, an investor buys a call contract at one strike price and sells a call contract at a higher price, both with the same expiration date. The bull spread using calls is a debit spread for the investor, and requires an initial outflow of cash. The basic profit or loss for this strategy, assuming the spread is held to expiration, depends on the share price of the underlying stock, as shown in **Table 17.1**. As compared with the outright purchase of a call, the bull spread buyer gives up additional profits if the underlying asset price rises above the strike price on the call contract sold. However, the spread lowers, or subsidizes, the cost when compared with buying a call contract alone, without making it a part of a vertical spread. This therefore reduces the losses if the underlying asset price does not rise as expected.

TABLE 17.1   Vertical Spread—Sampling of Various Vertical Spreads with Calls

Call Strike Price	Call Price
$22.00	$1.92
$23.00	$1.20
$24.00	$0.67
$25.00	$0.33

Bull Call Vertical	Price	Maximum Risk	Maximum Reward
$22/$23	$0.72	$0.72	$0.28
$23/$24	$0.53	$0.53	$0.47
$24/$25	$0.34	$0.34	$0.66
$22/$24	$1.25	$1.25	$0.75
$23/$25	$0.87	$0.87	$1.13
$22/$25	$1.59	$1.59	$1.41

XYZ = $23.70.

TABLE 17.2 Vertical Spread—Sampling of Various Bull Put Spread Combinations

Strike Price		Call Price	Put Price
$22.00		$1.92	$0.22
$23.00		$1.20	$0.50
$24.00		$0.67	$0.97
$25.00		$0.33	$1.63

Bull Put Vertical	Price	Maximum Risk	Maximum Reward
$22/$23	$0.28	$0.72	$0.28
$23/$24	$0.47	$0.53	$0.47
$24/$25	$0.66	$0.34	$0.66
$22/$24	$0.75	$1.25	$0.75
$23/$25	$1.13	$0.87	$1.13
$22/$25	$1.41	$1.59	$1.41

XYZ = $23.70.

You can create an equivalent bull spread by buying a put contract with one strike price and selling a put with a higher strike (see **Table 17.2**). A bull spread using puts is a credit spread since the investor is selling the spread and thus receiving an initial inflow of cash. As compared with simply selling the put at the higher strike, the put spread lowers the net income but limits the losses if the underlying asset price declines.

A Trader's Reasoning for Trading a Vertical Spread

There appears to be large quantities of good option-trading literature available, yet too much of it is bogged down in theoretical clutter, causing the investor to miss the entire point of the practical application of a strategy in the first place. When straying from theoreticals, there are clear-cut reasons for applying a vertical spread.

Reason #1: Lowering Your Net Cost, Qualifying Your Risk

You are bullish regarding the share price for XYZ, so you decide to convert your opinion from buying a call contract to creating a bull spread, where you would buy a set of call contracts at one strike price and sell an equal number of call contracts with a higher strike price but with the same expiration date.

This call spread will lower your net cost and therefore your maximum possible loss. It will also decrease your break-even point, making profit more likely. The only problem in this strategy is that you have severely limited your profit if the underlying share price rises sharply. You should always think carefully when capping your potential profitability. To be profitable over the long haul, you must limit your losers while riding your winners.

Reason #2: Flexibility

You can implement a bullish strategy with puts or a bearish strategy with calls. You can go long on the market by selling options and short the market by buying.

Suppose you begin with a short put and convert it into a put bull spread by buying a second put at a lower strike price. In this case, you have reduced your risk exposure since possible losses (at expiration) are now limited to the difference in the two strike prices less the net price. Since possible losses are now defined, you also lower your margin requirement. The disadvantage of converting the sale of the put contracts to a bull spread is that you lower your maximum gain and raise the break-even point, and therefore the likelihood of a loss.

For the same strikes, both call and put bull spreads have identical deltas, vegas, gammas, and payoff patterns. But the net cash flow differs. For the put contracts, the resulting vertical spread is a credit spread. You receive cash when setting up the spread, because the price you paid for the contracts you bought is less than what you received from the contracts you sold. The call bull spread, however, is a debit spread. Setting up the spread has a net cost, because the price of the options you bought exceeds the price of the options you sold. This is also true of bear spreads. A put bear spread is a debit spread (you receive net cash), whereas a call bear spread is a credit spread (you have a net loss of cash).

Table 17.3 demonstrates the parity between a bull spread with calls as opposed to a bull spread with puts with the same strike price.

Reason #3: Taking Advantage of Direction and Greeks are Contained by a Predefined Risk Profile

A vertical spread can be implemented with the profile of being long the market while long theta, or long the market and short theta. A vertical spread

TABLE 17.3 Demonstrating Parity between a Bull Spread Implementing Both Ball Spreads and Put Spreads

Strike	Call	Delta	Gamma	Theta	Vega	Implied Volatility
$24.00	$0.77	50	0.21	−0.014	0.028	26.75%
$25.00	$0.42	33	0.17	−0.011	0.026	25.96%

Strike	Put	Delta	Gamma	Theta	Vega	Implied Volatility
$24.00	$0.77	−50	0.21	−0.014	0.028	26.75%
$25.00	$1.42	−33	0.17	−0.011	0.026	25.96%

Long 24/25 Bull Call Spread

	Price	Delta	Gamma	Theta	Vega	Risk	Reward
	$0.35	17	0.04	−0.003	0.002	$0.35	$0.65

Short 24/25 Bull Put Spread

	Price	Delta	Gamma	Theta	Vega	Risk	Reward
	($0.65)	17	0.04	−0.003	0.002	$0.35	$0.65

XYZ = $24, contracts expire in thirty-three days. Volatility = 26.75%, interest rate =.25%.

can be short the market while being either long or short gamma. Furthermore, you can devise a vertical spread that captures both your directional conviction and volatility conviction—simultaneously!

Vertical spreads are great tools, especially when you understand that greeks can help supplement a bad directional decision or increase a good one. Unfortunately, there are two sides to that coin—a vertical spreader can win on his directional call yet lose horribly due to the spread's delinquent greek position. That said, a vertical spread can potentially afford the trader many distinct advantages in terms of contained greek exposure. It's of key importance that the investor both understands and appreciates the possible implications of the greek exposure of any vertical spread.

Designing Your Vertical Spread

When you set up a vertical spread you have three design choices:

1. Selecting call or put contracts, for a debit or credit spread
2. The strike prices to use in relation to the underlying asset price
3. The difference in strike prices between the options contracts you buy and the contracts you sell

Choosing a Debit Spread or Credit Spread

It has already been noted that it doesn't matter much whether you use call or put contracts when building a vertical spread using the same set of strike prices. But cash flow patterns differ for calls and puts. Call bull spreads and put bear spreads are debit spreads. That means that you have to pay more to buy the calls or puts to set up the spread than you earn from selling the corresponding calls or puts. Put bull spreads or call bear spreads are credit spreads. You have net cash as a result of the trade, because you can earn more selling the call or put contracts in the spread than you have to pay to buy the matching call or put contracts.

The avoidance of early exercise may be of consequence, especially with dividend-paying equities. That difference would mean a slight preference for debit spreads—particularly for put spreads. With that, you would do better to create debit spreads, especially put debit spreads, to give yourself an advantage over the counter party in the trade. With a put bear spread (a put debit spread), you are buying put contracts at one strike price and selling put contracts at a lower strike price. This allows you to control the position; based on how you view the market, changes to the underlying share price are more likely to move your contracts to in the money than the contracts you sold. In this case, the contracts you hold would be the best ones to exercise, not the contracts you sold to another party. If put contracts are exercised against you, however, then your position becomes a bear position.

Choosing the Right Strike Prices on the Contracts in Relation to the Underlying Asset Price

One of the most cited advantages of creating a vertical spread rather than buying a put or call contract outright is that the vertical spread costs less. But this ignores two features of the strategy. A combined long/short position reduces your costs, but it also reduces your risk/reward ratio. Also, if you are trying to limit the amount of cash you invest initially, you can do that by creating a credit spread rather than a debit spread.

The net price of a debit spread corresponds to the maximum possible loss on the trade. The net price of a credit spread represents the maximum possible profit. Therefore, with a bull spread, using either call or put contracts, if you choose a higher strike price pair with the same gap, it reduces the maximum loss while increasing the maximum profit potential. However, higher strike prices also raise the break-even point, and this lowers the likelihood that you will realize a profit, as shown in **Table 17.4**.

TABLE 17.4 Vertical Spread—Risk/Reward and Break-Even Point Profile of Various Call and Put Vertical Spreads

Call Spread	Cost	Risk	Reward	Break-Even Point
$24/$25	$0.35	$0.35	$0.65	$24.35
$25/$26	$0.27	$0.27	$0.73	$25.27
$26/$27	$0.10	$0.10	$0.90	$26.10
Put Spread	Cost	Risk	Reward	Break-Even Point
$24/$25	($0.65)	$0.35	$0.65	$24.35
$25/$26	($0.73)	$0.27	$0.73	$25.27
$26/$27	($0.90)	$0.10	$0.90	$26.10

XYZ = $24, contracts expire in thirty-three days. Volatility = 26.75%, interest rate =.25%, no dividend.

Many traders tend to prefer positively skewed returns when choosing a pair of strike prices for contracts to buy and sell. A trader who prefers a positive skew looks for a small loss with high probability united with the potential for a large profit that is low probability. A positive skew vertical spread would have out-of-the money strike prices for debit spreads and in-the-money strike prices for credit spreads. For a negative skew, you are content with a large potential loss that is unlikely to happen and a much more likely potential for a small profit. In this case, the debit spreads have in-the-money strike prices and the credit spreads feature out-of-the money strikes. Make sure you recognize the consequences of the strike prices you select relative to the share price of the underlying asset. Any vertical spread you design will feature its own characteristics in terms of its net price, price skew, greek exposure risk, and risk/reward profile.

Selecting the Strike Price Gap between the Contracts You Buy and the Contracts You Sell

Carefully consider the difference between the strike prices in the contracts you buy and the contracts you sell when creating the vertical spread. If you increase the gap in strike prices for a vertical spread while holding the median strike constant, both the net price of the options contract and the absolute delta also increase. So if you want to set up a vertical spread to maximize the absolute delta, the spread should feature large differences between the two strike prices. If you want to limit the net price and/or maximize delta per

TABLE 17.5 Vertical Spread—Cost Basis, Net Delta, and Break-Even Point(s) of Various Call Vertical Spreads

Call Spread	Cost	Net Delta	Break-Even Point
$1,000/$1,050	$20.72	0.33	$1,020.72
$1,000/$1,100	$25.93	0.48	$1,025.93
$1,000/$1,150	$26.89	0.52	$1,026.89
$1,000/$1,200	$26.95	0.53	$1,026.95

XYZ Index = $1,004, contracts expire in thirty-three days. Volatility = 38.7%, interest rate =.25%, no dividend.

dollar, choose a small differential in the strike prices. **Table 17.5** demonstrates the spread differential as the spread is widened.

The gap, or differential, in the strike prices between the call or put contracts you buy and those you sell affects how the greek values will perform after you complete the trades to set up the vertical spread. Since gamma, vega, and theta are bell-shaped functions of the strike price with peaks close to the underlying asset price, whether they are increased, decreased, or unchanged as the gap in strike prices widens depends solely on whether the strike prices are at the money, in the money, or out of the money. If the geometric mean strike price is unchanged, if you increase the gap between the strike prices for the contracts bought and the contracts sold, vega and gamma remain unchanged at zero and theta is little changed. If both strikes remain out of the money or in the money, increasing this strike price differential increases vega, gamma, and theta in absolute terms. But if you increase the gap in strike prices between contracts bought and sold so that one of the contracts moves from out of the money to in the money or vice versa, projecting the future impact on the vega, gamma, and theta becomes unclear.

Vertical Spreads and Greek Exposure

Delta

Your goal in creating a vertical spread is to speculate on how the share price of a stock is going to change in the future. So it's logical to seek the maximum spread in the absolute delta. To this end, choose strike prices that are at the money. But if your goal is to seek the maximum delta per dollars invested, choose strikes that are out of the money.

Call SpreadStrikes	NetDelta
$95/$100	17
$100/$105	20
$105/$110	18
$110/$115	11
$115/$120	2

XYZ = $100.79, contracts expire in sixty-one days. Volatility = 23.37%, interest rate =.32%, no dividend.

Gamma

All other things equal, traders who set up long vertical spreads should prefer positions with positive gamma. That way, if the share price moves in the direction they were expecting, they profit more than they would lose if the share price changes by the same amount in the other direction. Like vega, an option's gamma is proportional. A vertical spread has a gamma of zero when the strike price is at the geometric mean. Vertical spread traders who want positive gamma should choose out-of-the-money strike prices for debit spreads and in-the-money strikes for credit spreads. Also, if your goal is to maximize gamma per dollar invested, you should have an even stronger bias for the out-the-money strikes on debit spreads.

Call Spread Strikes	Net Gamma
$95/$100	−0.02
$100/$105	0.02
$105/$110	0.02
$110/$115	0.01
$115/$120	0.005

XYZ = $100.79, contracts expire in thirty-three days. Volatility = 22.85%, interest rate =.32%, no dividend.

Theta

One advantage of creating a vertical spread over a standard call or put position is that you can build the spread so that theta is small, or even with a sign opposite of that of a standard option position with the same delta. If you buy a call contract because you believe that the share price of the underlying stock will increase, and instead the price of the underlying asset remains unchanged, over time the options contract loses value and the position loses money. Suppose instead that you create a bull call spread where both strikes are in the money. Initially the price of the spread is less than the strike price gap. But as expiration approaches, if the underlying asset value remains unchanged, the value of the in-the-money spread approaches the value of the strike differential, and you benefit as the bull trader.

- Debit spreads with in-the-money strikes generally have positive thetas. The value of the spread increases as expiration approaches.
- Debit spreads with out-of-the-money strikes have negative thetas.
- Debit spreads with at-the-money strikes have small absolute thetas.

For credit spreads, the relation is reversed. If you want positive theta, choose in-the-money options for debit spreads and out-the-money options for credit spreads.

Long Bull	Net	Theta
Call Spread Strikes	Positive	Negative
$23/$25	0.0291	
$24/$25	0.0173	
$24/$26	0	0
$25/$26		−0.0173
$26/$27		−0.0118

XYZ = $25, contracts expire in five days. Volatility = 29.67%, no dividend.

Vega

One of the benefits for vertical spreads is that they allow traders to build positions that are sensitive to some risk factors and not sensitive to others. Chapter 14 describes straddles and strangles, which are designed so that their deltas are near zero yet vega and gamma are high. In contrast, traders of vertical spreads prefer spreads with higher deltas while lowering exposure to vega risk. Vertical spread traders who seek to limit their exposure to vega risk should choose at-the-money strikes, or strike prices that straddle the underlying asset price. That is, for the contracts bought and sold, the higher strike price is greater than the share price, and the lower strike price is less than the share price.

Call Strikes	Vega	Long Bull Call Spread Strikes	Net Positive	Vega Negative
$800	$0.16	$800/$850		($0.25)
$850	$0.41	$850/$900		($0.24)
$900	$0.65	$900/$950		($0.32)
$950	$0.97	$950/$1,000		($0.22)
$1,000	$1.19	$1,000/$1,050	$0.33	
$1,050	$0.86	$1,050/$1,100	$0.56	
$1,100	$0.30	$1,100/$1,150	$0.24	
$1,150	$0.06	$1,150/$1,200	$0.04	
$1,200	$0.02			

XYZ Index = $1,004, contracts expire in thirty-three days. Volatility = 38.7%, no dividend.

Vertical Spreads as a Pure Volatility Play

Apart from directional risk and time decay risk, volatility risk is another crucial factor in deciding how to set up a vertical trade and the strike prices to select for contracts. You can set up a vertical spread to either moderate volatility risk or to have a very large exposure to it.

As volatility increases, an at-the-money option will increase more in price than an in-the-money or out-of-the-money option. At the same time, the at-the-money option will increase in price more than an in-the-money or out-of-the-money option with a lower vega. Conversely, the at-the-money option will lose value at a greater rate than an in-the-money or out-of-the-money option if implied volatility decreases. The question is how to use the vertical spread to take advantage of anticipated movements in implied volatility.

If you think that implied volatility is likely to increase, you can set up a vertical spread by buying an at-the-money option and selling either the in-the-money or out-of-the-money option against it. If you feel that implied volatility is artificially too high, you can set up a vertical spread by selling an at-the-money option and buying either an out-of-the-money or an in-the-money option against it.

Set up the vertical spread to take advantage of time decay (theta). If you think the share price of the underlying asset is likely to rise, decide between buying a vertical call spread and selling a vertical put spread. Either way, buy the at-the-money option if you sense volatility will increase and sell the at-the-money option if you believe volatility will decrease. The beauty (and danger) in all of this is that you can be correct in your assumption about

TABLE 17.6 Vertical Spread—Comparing Vertical Spreads with Varied Implied Volatilities

Call Strike	Implied Volatility	Theoretical Value	Implied Volatility Up.05%	Implied Volatility Up.10%
$17	36.20%	$6.26	$6.28	$6.29
$19	34.06%	$4.35	$4.37	$4.39
$21	33.31%	$2.64	$2.69	$2.74
$23	31.43%	$1.31	$1.37	$1.43
$25	30.20%	$0.51	$0.56	$0.61
$27	31.58%	$0.19	$0.23	$0.26
$29	31.58%	$0.06	$0.07	$0.09

Call Spread	Spread Value	Value Up 5% Volatility	Value Up 10% Volatility
$17/$19	$1.91	$1.91	$1.90
$19/$21	$1.71	$1.68	$1.65
$21/$23	$1.33	$1.32	$1.31
$23/$25	$0.80	$0.81	$0.82
$25/$27	$0.32	$0.33	$0.35
$27/$29	$0.13	$0.16	$0.17
$17/$21	$3.62	$3.56	$3.55
$19/$23	$3.04	$3.00	$2.96
$21/$25	$2.13	$2.13	$2.13
$23/$27	$1.12	$1.14	$1.17
$25/$29	$0.45	$0.49	$0.52

XYZ Index = $23.25, contracts expire in sixty days. Volatility = 31.4%, no dividend.

direction and wrong in your assumption about volatility, and still win. **Table 17.6** compares vertical spreads with varied implied volatilities.

Comparing Volatility's Effect on Vertical Spreads

To better understand how volatilities affect vertical spreads, consider these three examples. The examples use three different implied volatilities while keeping the share price of the underlying stock constant at $27.50.

1. *Spread #1: XYZ thirty-day $20/$25 call.* For this in-the-money call spread, as volatility increases, the value of the spread decreases. This is because with the increased volatility, the underlying share price will tend to change, and that leads to a higher likelihood of the share price reaching a level where the $20/$25 call spread will no longer finish in the money.

The rule of thumb is that as volatility increases, the value of in-the-money vertical spreads decrease. As volatility decreases, an in-the-money vertical spread's value increases.

2. *Spread #2: XYZ thirty-day $25/$30 call.* For this at-the-money call spread, we see little if any effect with changes in volatility. With the underlying asset price located equally distant from the strike prices of the two options contracts, the volatility component for each strike price will be very similar. Thus, when volatility increases, both options will increase equally. With the spread set up so that the trader owns one contract and sells the other, the increase in values will offset each other so the value of the spreads will remain constant.

   The rule of thumb with at-the-money spreads is that when volatility increases or decreases, the value of an at-the-money vertical spread will remain constant.

3. *Spread #3: XYZ thirty-day $30/$35 call.* For this out-of-the money spread, as volatility increases, the value of the out-of-the money call spread increases. This is simply because the increase in volatility assumes that the share price of the underlying stock will be more likely to move, and thus the out-of-the-money vertical spread will have a greater chance of becoming in the money.

   The general rule is that when volatility increases, the value of an out-of-the-money vertical spread also increases. When volatility decreases, the spread's value decreases.

Summary: Comparing Vertical Spreads and Implied Volatility

An in-the-money call spread has the same net implied volatility exposure as its corresponding out-of-the money put spread. With XYZ at $40, selling the thirty-day $25/$30 put spread will have the exact same implied volatility exposure as purchasing the thirty-day $25/$30 call spread.

An easy way to remember volatility's effect on a spread is to think in terms of the spread's median value. For example, the median value of a $5 vertical spread will be $2.50, whereas a $10 spread will have a median value of $5. *An increase in volatility will cause vertical spreads to move toward their median value.* The higher the volatility, the closer the spread will move toward its median.

In other words, if a $5 vertical spread has a value over $2.50, it will lose value and move toward its median price *when volatility increases.* Meanwhile, the increased implied volatility will cause a spread with a value less than its

TABLE 17.7 Convergence and Divergence of Bull Spreads to Median with Increase in Implied Volatility

Bull Call Spread		Spread Values	
Strikes	Volatility 26.05%	Volatility 28.65%	Volatility 31.26%
$98/$103	$2.34	$2.41	$2.47

Bull Put Spread		Spread Values	
Strikes	Volatility 23.73%	Volatility 26.1%	Volatility 28.47%
$98/$103	$2.62	$2.57	$2.52

XYZ Index = $98.31, contracts expire in sixty days. Volatility = 26.05%, no dividend.

median value to increase, moving up toward the median price. If implied volatility goes down, you can expect the opposite to occur. That is, the value of a $5 spread will move away from the median price of $2.50. With that, when implied volatility decreases, all the spreads valued above $2.50 will increase in value (toward maximum value), while spreads valued below $2.50 will lose value (see **Table 17.7**).

Changes in Implied Volatility during the Trade

After you buy or sell the contracts you need to set up any kind of vertical spread, you can't change the maximum amount of potential profit or the amount of risk. Changes in the implied volatility won't affect the profit potential.

The time decay (theta) curves of the spreads, however, are affected by changes in implied volatility.

If the implied volatility increases after the vertical trade, the theta or time decay curve is flattened. The value of the spread approaches the ultimate value at expiration more slowly. Therefore, the probability of closing the trade early to take the maximum profit is reduced significantly.

If implied volatility decreases after the vertical spread trade, the theta curve spreads out so that the value of the spread approaches the ultimate value at expiration more quickly, which should be intuitive. If the implied volatility goes down, it suggests that the price range will be tighter in the future for the underlying stock. This means an in-the-money option contract will be more likely to remain in the money, and an out-of-the money contract will probably stay out of the money and thus expire as worthless.

Generally, sound trading practice involves buying low-volatility options and selling high-volatility options. But that doesn't necessarily mean that you should set up credit spreads when implied volatility is high and debit spreads when implied volatility is low.

When thinking of capturing the directional move with a vertical spread strategy, the choice of using a debit or credit spread should be nothing but personal preference.

The risk or return for credit and debit spreads is always the same. The implied volatility levels will have no effect on their returns. So implementing a vertical spread could be an excellent way to trade high-volatility options contracts, as compared with simply trading in high-volatility options contracts without using them to set up a vertical spread. Trading options contracts in this way can be both expensive and risky.

CHAPTER 18

Calendar Spreads: Trading Theta and Vega

Market-neutral strategies and their close relatives—long-short, relative-value, and option-spread strategies—have long held out the promise of high returns, low drawdowns, and low volatility. These strategies tend to grow in popularity when a financial calamity results in both volatility and wider market spreads. Normally, a period of comparative market calm and stable correlations between markets follows, and at that point spread strategies appear almost too good to be true. Traders and investors alike envision hedged portfolios with fat spreads and a high likelihood of those spreads conveniently and profitably converging at expiration.

In the mid- to late 1990s there seemed to be a wide variety of funds that went down in flames while promoting such market-neutral strategies. These funds were based on studies of previous market-neutral programs and were backed by Nobel Prize–winning theorists using high-speed computers who scanned the globe for opportunities in market-neutral trading opportunities. In the end, each fund failed for one or more of the following reasons:

- A liquidity squeeze
- Too much leverage
- A fund manager's inability to meet margin calls
- A fund being short put contracts during a market correction

And yet, a new hedge fund would appear, fresh with someone else's cash, ready to pick up the baton and run with the same investment strategy.

Fortunately, there are options strategies that really are market-neutral. The *calendar spread* can be used as an approach to use both theta and vega to your advantage. If implemented wisely, the calendar spread can provide you with a market-neutral strategy without the entanglements that often turn up with other types of investment schemes.

Calendar Spreading—Trading Time

To set up a calendar spread, also called a "time spread," the trader buys either a call or a put contract and then writes (sells) another call or put contract with the same strike price but a different expiration date. Note that with a calendar spread position, both contracts will be either puts or calls.

With a *long calendar spread*, the trader sells a call or put contract in a front month and buys a call or put contract for a back month with the same strike price. You might use a long call calendar spread when you believe that the share price for a stock is likely to remain stable in the near term but is likely to moderately increase later. You would sell a call contract due to expire in thirty days and buy a call contract due to expire in sixty days. Setting up a long calendar spread is also called *buying* a calendar spread.

For a *short calendar spread*, the opposite applies, in that the trader buys a call or put contract in the front month and sells a call or put contract for the deferred month. You would use a short call calendar spread if you believe that the underlying stock is likely to increase in value in the short term but then level out—in other words, you believe that the share price will be stable closer to the time that the contracts you sell are due to expire. Setting up a short calendar spread is also called *selling* a calendar spread.

Calendar spreads include a unique risk profile that other option strategies do not, because one contract in the spread expires before the other. For example, with XYZ trading at $28 a share, you could set up a calendar spread by buying the XYZ fifty-day $28 calls at $1.50, and selling (writing) the XYZ thirty-day $28 calls for $1 (see **Exhibit 18.1**). In terms of risk, the most you can lose with a calendar spread is the difference between how much you spend to buy the call contracts and the amount you earn to sell the matching call contracts. In this case, the net debit is 50 cents per contract ($1.50 less $1).

With the first leg of this spread, the contracts you sold that expire in thirty days, you seek to benefit from time decay. As time passes, the value of the option slowly declines as the contract nears expiration, allowing you to pocket the premium you received from the sale. With the second leg, the contracts you bought, you benefit if your hunch is right and the price of the underlying shares changes in the twenty days after the contracts you sold expire. In essence, this spread not only helps you play the time value in your favor, but could help you subsidize the cost of buying the second option.

EXHIBIT 18.1 Long Call Calendar before Expiration

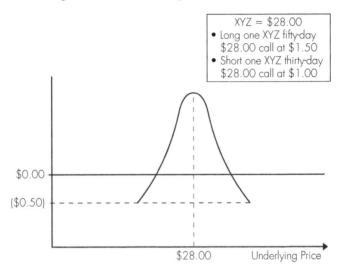

XYZ = $28.00
• Long one XYZ fifty-day
$28.00 call at $1.50
• Short one XYZ thirty-day
$28.00 call at $1.00

$0.00

($0.50)

$28.00   Underlying Price

Note: Prior to expiry, the maximum loss of the long calendar spread is the loss of the original debit paid.

Risks and Rewards of the Calendar Spread

Calendar spreads, whether they are call calendars or put calendars, work for the party holding the spread when the share price of the underlying stock matches the strike price of the options contracts at the time that the front-month options are expiring. If you *buy* a calendar spread, you want the stock price to be at the strike price at expiration. If you *sell* a calendar spread, you want the stock price to be as far away as from the strike price as possible at expiration. The following table shows various calendar spreads with the underlying at $24.56.

Strike	Short XYZ 26-Day Call	Long XYZ 54-Day Call	Calendar Spread Value
$19.00	$5.65	$5.70	$0.05
$20.00	$4.65	$4.75	$0.10
$21.00	$3.70	$3.85	$0.15
$22.00	$2.64	$2.86	$0.22
$23.00	$1.75	$2.05	$0.30
$24.00	$1.00	$1.36	$0.36

(Continued)

Strike	Short XYZ 26-Day Call	Long XYZ 54-Day Call	Calendar Spread Value
$25.00	$0.47	$0.83	$0.36
$26.00	$0.17	$0.44	$0.27
$27.00	$0.05	$0.19	$0.14
$28.00	$0.03	$0.10	$0.07
$29.00	$0.02	$0.06	$0.04

XYZ = $24.56

A long calendar works if you are right in assuming that underlying price of a stock is going to move to and then stay at a specific price until the front-month option expires. The greatest risk of a long calendar spread is the price you pay for it. The maximum value depends on the value of the deferred-month option contract when the front-month option contract expires. And that value depends largely on the implied volatility of the deferred-month options.

Another risk, albeit remote, is that you are assigned on your short option. For example, with a long put calendar spread, you would sell a put contract that expires in, say, thirty days, and buy a put contract that expires in fifty days. If the short put is assigned, you will need to buy the shares of stock at the strike price stated in the contract. With this long position in the shares of stock, plus the put contract that you bought but that has yet to expire, your strategy changes from a calendar spread to a synthetic long call. This position features limited risk, but you might need a great deal of cash or margin in your account to be able to hold the long stock position.

Options contracts with less time remaining until they expire have more time decay (theta) than contracts that expire in later months. That is, the front month will have a higher theta value. The calendar spread profits from this sharp difference in decay rates between the front month (short option) and back month (long option). This trade seems to work best when implied volatility is low and when an implied volatility skew appears between the two expiration months—specifically, when the contract you sold with the near-month expiration date has a relatively higher implied volatility than the contract you bought with the later-month expiration. Also, keep in mind that a call calendar spread is virtually identical to a put calendar when using the same strike price.

A Calendar Spread with a Bullish Expectation

Suppose you believe that XYZ, currently trading at $100, is going to rise gradually over the next thirty days. With that confidence, you review data such as that in the table below, which gives you the various (call) fair values of the XYZ index.

Call Strike	Three Days till Expiry Value	Thirty-One Days till Expiry Value	Fifty-Nine Days till Expiry Value
$95.00	$5.05	$5.88	$6.78
$100.00	$1.30	$3.17	$4.34
$105.00	$0.01	$1.00	$1.95

XYZ = $100

You review data such as that in the table below and decide to buy the $105 call calendar spread for a net price of $.95. In this case you would buy the fifty-nine-day call for $1.95 and write a call contract for thirty-one days for $1.

Strike	Calendar	Index	Spread Value	Spread Delta
$95.00	Call	XYZ	$0.90	−0.05
$100.00	Call	XYZ	$1.17	0.01
$105.00	Call	XYZ	$0.95	0.07

XYZ = $100. Long option, fifty-nine days until expiration, at-the-money volatility = 24.5%. Short option, thirty-one days until expiration, at-the-money volatility = 24.1%.

Twenty-eight days go by. Your $105 long calendar spread now has thirty-one days for the long contract and three days remaining for the short. But you were incorrect on your outlook of XYZ. The share price has remained largely unchanged (at $100) over the course of the past twenty-eight days. The table below demonstrates what happens to the price of the calendar spread with time decay but no movement in the underlying share price.

Strike	Calendar	Index	Spread Value	Spread Delta	Spread P/L
$95.00	Call	XYZ	$0.83	−0.24	−$0.07
$100.00	Call	XYZ	$1.87	0.01	$0.70
$105.00	Call	XYZ	$0.95	0.25	$0.00

XYZ = $100. Long option, thirty-one days until expiration, at-the-money volatility = 24.21%. Short option, three days until expiration, at-the-money volatility = 27.59%.

Now consider the table below, which shows a typical outcome of the effect on the price of various calendar spreads with time decay and with the stock price climbing from $100 to $105 a share.

Strike	Calendar	Index	Spread Value	Spread Delta	Spread P/L
$95.00	Call	XYZ	$0.45	−0.07	($0.45)
$100.00	Call	XYZ	$1.10	−0.25	($0.07)
$105.00	Call	XYZ	$1.91	0.01	$0.96

XYZ=$105. Long option, thirty-one days until expiration, at-the-money volatility = 22.25%. Short option, three days until expiration, at-the-money volatility = 27.03%.

Considerations and Observations for Calendar Spreads and Volatility

Like any other options strategy, the calendar spread has its limitations.

1. Time Value and Volatility in Calendar Spreads Are not Necessarily Connected

The link between time value and volatility in a calendar spread is not as clear as it seems. Buying a calendar spread is not the same as buying volatility. Volatility refers to the likelihood of the price of an underlying asset to change significantly. When you're trading options, the vega determines whether you are buying or selling volatility.

The point is that with a *long calendar position*, you can theoretically be long volatility with long vega, but you absolutely do not want the underlying asset to move very much. A long calendar spread—in this case, an at-the-money calendar spread—makes the most money if the underlying share price remains within a narrow range or matches the strike price of the contracts you sold close to the date those contracts expire. But the calendar spread can lose money if the implied volatility changes, or with relative changes in volatility between the front- and back-month expiration dates.

Exactly how much net vega you get between the contracts you buy and sell in a calendar trade depends on the time until those contracts expire. The implied volatility for the contracts expiring in the back month (later) will not drop as much as the implied volatility for the contracts expiring in the front month, but the back-month contracts can have much larger vegas. So if you sold one contract with fifty days to expiration and bought another that expires in thirty days, a small move in implied volatility can impact the option with fifty days until expiration as much, or more, as a larger change in implied volatility on the contracts that expire in thirty days.

2. Implied Volatility Affects Calendar Spreads Mostly with At-the-Money Options

Vega estimates how much the value of an option will change when implied volatility moves up or down by 1 percent. Vega is higher, with all other things being equal, when there is more time to expiration. Vega in a calendar spread is highest for at-the-money options and drops as a contract moves out of the money. A change in volatility has little impact on the value of a contract that is out of the money because the contract is less likely to be exercised or to be in the money prior to expiry. So the impact of a change in volatility largely depends on how close the underlying share price stands relative to the strike price of the calendar spread.

For example, XYZ trades at $50. Assume you bought the XYZ sixty-day $50 call and sold the XYZ thirty-day $50 call. As both the thirty-day and sixty-day options move away from being at the money, the vega values drop for both, and the values of the options contracts tend to converge. With the vega values approaching roughly the same value, an increase or decrease in the implied volatilities for the contracts included in the spread will not have much of an impact on the value of the calendar spread itself.

In a long at-the-money calendar spread, the value of the spread will increase more quickly if the implied volatility for the back-month contract goes up than if the implied volatility of the front-month contract goes down. That's because the back-month option contracts (sixty days to expiration, in the example above) will have a higher vega than the front-month contracts (thirty days to expiration). The longer the amount of time until the front-month contract expires, the more the implied volatility decreases for that same front-month contract. As the front-month contract approaches the expiration date, the vega of the contract becomes significantly smaller.

3. Avoid Assuming Too Much about Front-Month versus Back-Month Vega

For most calendar spreads, it may not be wise to assume that the front-month implied volatility will increase or decrease by the same amount as the back-month volatility. A calendar spread that appears to have positive vega in fact may not have a positive vega at all if you take into account the different sensitivities of the implied volatilities of the front-month contracts versus back-month contracts. Simply put, even though back-month vega is larger than front-month vega, back-month implied volatility may increase less than front-month implied volatility.

On the other hand, this could all be an illusion. The vega of an options contract decreases steadily the closer you get to the expiration date for that contract, especially if the contract is out of the money. With that, it appears logical that it takes large changes in implied volatility to translate into any real change in the market value of a short-dated option. So for a front-month options contract to change in value by 10 cents requires a greater change in implied volatility than would be needed for a similar change in value for a back-month option.

A calendar spread is typically long vega. Normally, an overall increase in implied volatility will help the position, and an overall decrease in implied volatility will hurt the position.

4. At Extreme Prices for an Underlying Stock, Differences in Parity Appear

Suppose you bought a calendar spread in XYZ stock which is currently trading at $60 per share. You bought the XYZ fifty-nine-day $60 call and sold the XYZ thirty-day $60 call. If you run a risk/reward profile for this calendar spread, you should notice that the value of the calendar spread drops to zero if the stock price falls low enough, but it seems to retain some residual value no matter how high the stock price moves up. For a call calendar, as the stock price rises above the calendar spread's mean strike price, both options approach parity. Yet the back-month option retains a small portion of early exercise value.

If a stock price falls to $0, all of the put contracts will be at parity. But no matter how high the stock goes, it can theoretically go higher still. So call contracts can still carry a value.

5. Pay Attention to Long-Term Trends in Volatility

When volatility goes up, it may theoretically help your position, but it also increases the possibility that the underlying share price will move away from the strike price. In short, it may be better to choose the correct strike price when trading a calendar spread than correctly estimating implied volatility.

Stating that a calendar spread has positive vega is futile without accounting for how the implied volatility might change for the options contracts included in the calendar spread. The implied volatility for an options contract may not change with general market volatility. There is no rule regarding how implied volatility may differ between the options contracts in a calendar spread.

Some traders believe that the implied volatility for each contract appears to have some sort of mean reversion, and that can provide insight when creating a strategy for a calendar spread. Mean reversion refers to the tendency for a traded security to return to its average price over time. For example, a stock may suddenly soar in value, but a wise investor should keep in mind that stock might return to the five-year average share price. But with a mean reversion, you must be able to define the mean value and the appropriate time period to consider. It is probably true that implied volatility can exhibit more mean reversion in shorter time periods—say, thirty days or so.

You should consider investing in a calendar spread as long as the volatility difference between the back-month and front-month options contracts isn't far from where it has been in the past. If the two sets of implied volatilities are too different, whether too close or too far apart, you should assume that you are probably missing something that everyone else understands, and so avoid the spread.

6. Don't Put Too Much Emphasis on Greek Values

When it comes to calendar spreads, you should generally stay away from the terms "overpriced" and "underpriced" because they imply that the markets are not rational. In general, it's good to believe that options are fairly priced, assuming the market's volatility assumptions are correct. Keep in mind that greek values are imperfect when attempting to model prices for real options contracts. You should never consider buying or selling a calendar spread solely because of the net greek values. There are no parameters that say volatility is too high or too low, or that your net vega is too flat or too wide. Rather, the information simply makes the calendar spread cheap or expensive relative to the values you think you might reach before the contracts in the calendar spread expire.

The greeks and implied volatilities are both fascinating and useful calculations. But in the end, they are simply theoretical risk-measurement tools. Over the long haul, they won't necessarily help you find good calendar spreads.

CHAPTER 19

Ratio Spreading: Trading Objectives Tailor Made

When working with options contract spreads, think of the spread as an asset. Treat the spread, however you build it, however many options contracts you buy or sell, and however you design the strategy, as a position in itself, as if it were two thousand shares of stock or twenty call contracts. Your spread will be more than the net income or cost to set up the position, more than the average strike price between the contracts you buy and the contracts you sell, and more than the likely volatility. This is especially true with a back spread or a ratio spread, as this investment strategy tends to be a lot more complex than a vertical spread or a calendar spread. For a back spread or ratio spread you might be tempted to add layers of complexity, mull over your opportunities, and tinker with expiration dates, strike prices, and quantities in order to control for greek values and implied volatilities. The problem with this approach is that no matter how sophisticated your strategy, your spread will tend to take on a life of its own. The spread will behave as unpredictably as any other investment in a complicated marketplace, and the more complex you make a spread, the more this unpredictability applies.

How Back Spreads and Ratio Spreads Work

With a back spread or ratio spread, you are buying and selling complementary options contracts, as with a vertical spread, where the expiration date is the same but the strike prices differ, or with a calendar spread, where the strike prices are the same but the expiration dates differ. But with a *back spread*, you are buying more options contracts than you are selling by a fixed ratio. Commonly, you will be long two contracts for every contract you are short, for a ratio of 2:1. A *ratio spread* is just the opposite—you write more contracts than you buy. Both back spreads and ratio spreads are made up of either both calls or both puts at two different strike prices in the same expiration month.

For example, with a ratio spread you might buy one call contract with a strike price of $45 and sell two call contracts with a strike price of $50. With a back spread, you might buy two $45 call contracts and sell one $40 call contract. By selling contracts, you finance part or all of the cost to create the spread, and this can serve to limit risk. But with either type of spread, you can also enjoy a better (if riskier) potential for profit if the underlying share price moves in the direction you expect it to move than you can expect with a simpler vertical spread.

A few more examples are provided below. All the examples use the strike prices and call and put values shown in the table below.

Strike Price	Call Value	Put Value
$22	$2.70	$0.10
$23	$1.80	$0.20
$24	$0.96	$0.36
$25	$0.40	$0.80
$26	$0.10	$1.50
$27	$0.05	$2.45

XYZ = $24.60, eighteen days to expiration.

Call Back Spread

- Sell one $24 call, buy two $25 calls. You gain a 16-cent credit by selling the call contract for 96 cents and buying two calls at 40 cents each ($.96 − $.80).
- Sell one $25 call, buy two $27 calls. You gain a 30-cent credit by selling the call for 40 cents and buying two calls at five cents each ($.40 − $.10).

Put Back Spread

- Sell one $25 put, buy two $24 puts. You gain an 8-cent credit by selling the put contract for 80 cents and buying two puts for 36 cents each ($.80 − $.72).
- Sell one $24 put, buy two $22 puts. You gain a 16-cent credit by selling one put contract for 36 cents and buying two put contracts for 10 cents each ($.36 − $.20).

Call Ratio Spread

- Buy one $24 call and sell two $26 calls. The position costs you 76 cents (76-cent debit) because the call contract you buy costs 96 cents and the two contracts you sell net you 10 cents each ($.20 − $.96).
- Buy one $26 call and sell two $27 calls. The transaction nets to zero. The $26 call contract costs 10 cents, and the $27 calls sell for 5 cents each.

Put Ratio Spread

- Buy one $25 put and sell two $24 puts. The position leads to an 8-cent debit. The put you buy costs 80 cents, and you sell two for 36 cents each ($.72 − $.80).
- Buy one $25 put and sell two $23 puts. This leads to a 40-cent debit, as the put contract you buy costs 80 cents, and you sell two puts for 20 cents each ($.40 − $.80).

Any percentage of long to short options is theoretically possible. You can buy twenty-two call contracts and sell seven if you like. But for the most part, 1:2 ratios will be used as examples in this chapter. When referring to the back spread or ratio spread, the lower strike is generally stated first, no matter whether it is long or short—for example, the XYZ $40/$50 call back spread (or ratio spread), and the XYZ $30/$40 put back spread (or ratio spread). Note that a back spread or ratio spread can result in a credit, in which you earn more income from the sale of contracts than you spend to buy contracts, or in a debit.

Back Spreads

You would set up a call back spread if you believe that the share price of the underlying stock will change rapidly. A call back spread profits if the price rises above the strike price in the contracts you are holding, and the higher the better. A put back spread is most profitable if the underlying share price falls sharply, and the further below the strike price of the contracts you bought, the better.

Back spreads result in selling one options contract and buying two or more options contracts with a strike price that is further out of the money. The contracts are either both calls or both puts. Similar to the ratio spread, the ratio of the back spread is the number of long options contracts divided by the number of short options. If you buy two contracts for every one you sell, the ratio is 2:1. You can use the money you gain by selling contracts to cover or at least help offset the cost of buying the matching contracts in the spread.

The risk with a back spread is that if the contracts you sell move closer to being in the money, they might increase in value faster than the out-of-the-money options contracts you buy if the underlying share price moves more slowly than you expect. This happens even more rapidly as expiration draws near. The out-of-the-money options contracts you bought might lose value even if the share price of the underlying asset moves in the way you expected. That same move in the underlying price may boost the value of the options contracts you sold and make it more likely that those contracts will be exercised against you. This is when the back spread position loses value most rapidly.

This consequence is portrayed in the valley of the break-even graph shown in **Exhibit 19.1**.

In Exhibit 19.1, the current day shows no valley, but one appears over time, and it grows deeper and deeper, symptomatic of larger and larger losses. The cost of the underlying at the base of the valley, by the way, is the strike price of the long option.

However, if you can set up a back spread for a credit, the position can nonetheless be profitable if the underlying price falls (for a call back spread) or climbs (for a put back spread) enough to escape the "valley" of losses.

EXHIBIT 19.1   Call Back Spread Break-Even Graph

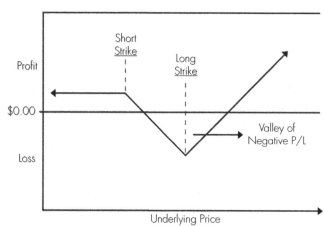

Ratio Spreads

Ratio spreads involve buying one options contract and selling two or more options contracts with a strike price that is further out of the money than the contracts you buy. The options are either both calls or both puts. The ratio of the spread is the quantity of short options divided by the quantity of long options. If you sell two XYZ January $50 calls and buy a single XYZ January $35 call, it is a 1:2 ratio spread. Some traders prefer to convert the ratio so that the first number always equals 1, and so express a 2 to 5 ratio as 1 to 2.5, to make it easier to compare one ratio spread to another. Generally, you will set up a ratio spread if you buy an options contract because you believe that the market is going to move up or down for a given stock, and then you sell additional contracts for the same stock in order to cover the cost to buy the options contracts, or at least limit the net expense. The contracts you sell will be further out of the money than the contracts you buy.

A call ratio spread works best when the share price of the underlying stock moves close to the strike price of the contracts you sold just before the contracts expire, and the same is true of a put ratio spread. You may want to set up a credit ratio spread, where the income you receive in premium from the contracts you sell is greater than the cash you have to spend to buy contracts. But the options you sell are probably going to be considerably cheaper than the options you need to buy, so to create a credit spread you will likely need to sell additional contracts. This generally is not a good idea. The larger the ratio of short options to long options in a ratio spread, the greater the risk involved. As a result, most traders generally set up a spread with the ratio of short options to long options no more than 1:2, even if the ratio spread results in a net debit.

More important, with the ratio at 1:2, you can more easily convert the ratio spread position into another strategy that limits your risk if the underlying share price starts to move against you. For example, with a 1:2 ratio spread you can buy one call or put contract and convert the ratio spread into a butterfly trade. Also, if you buy back one of the contracts you sold to build a 1:2 ratio spread, it becomes a vertical spread. In a crisis you might find it easier to buy a call contract with a higher strike price (for a call ratio spread) or a put with a lower strike price (for a put ratio spread) to form a butterfly trade than to try to get out of the position altogether. Or it may be cheaper to reduce a ratio spread from 1:2 to 1:1 to create a vertical spread. This will be addressed in more detail later in this chapter.

Call ratio spreads lose money when the underlying share price rises sharply (see **Exhibit 19.2**). Put ratio spreads lose money when the underlying

EXHIBIT 19.2   Call Ratio Spread Break-Even Graph

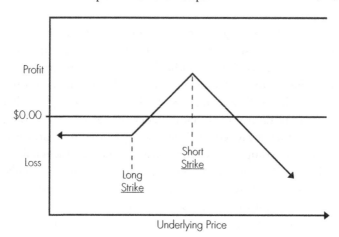

price drops sharply. Either can lose money when volatility rises. And in fact, both call and put ratio spreads can lose a lot of money if you aren't careful. If you are going to invest in call ratios, you need to monitor your positions closely and decide before you start on a fast strategy to limit risk that you can implement in an emergency. Be prepared for the worst. The ratio spread is the options strategy that could quickly finish your career!

Greek Values and the Back Spread or Ratio Spread

The greek values related to the back spread and ratio spread are influenced by these factors:

- The underlying share price relative to the strike prices of the long and short options contracts
- The distance between the strike prices in the options contracts
- Time remaining until the contracts expire
- Changes in implied volatility
- The ratio of long options to short options

Back and ratio spreads are precarious investments, and so the greek values for the spread can vary dramatically, as these kinds of spreads are more vulnerable when the underlying share price or implied volatility changes abruptly. Make sure you understand the risks inherent with these types of spreads, and make sure that you are prepared with an exit strategy before you start buying and selling contracts in case things go wrong.

Delta

The delta of a back spread or ratio spread is by and large dominated by the option further from expiration. This is simply because as the expiration date approaches, the delta tends to move up toward 1.0 if the contract approaches being in the money, or down toward 0 if it is moving out of the money.

Suppose the share price for XYZ is at $50 with seventy days remaining till expiration. The XYZ seventy-day $50 calls have a delta of .54, and the XYZ seventy-day $55 calls have a delta of .43. The net delta of the XYZ seventy-day $50/$55 call 1:2 back spread would be .32, or two times the delta of .43 (.86) minus the delta of .54. The delta is clearly focused on the long options. Yet with three days remaining to expiration, the XYZ three-day $50 call (with XYZ trading at $50) has a delta of .51, whereas the XYZ three-day $55 calls have a delta of .12. This means the net delta of the XYZ three-day $50/$55 call back spread would be −.27, or two times the delta of .12 minus the delta of .51. With fewer days remaining, the delta of the back spread shifts toward the short option contracts.

This is the reason that call back spreads, for example, are typically always net long delta as long as there are an adequate number of days to expiration. But with fewer days to expiration, the delta of the call back spread is further responsive to where the underlying price is relative to the strike prices. Recall that a back spread loses the most value when the underlying is at or near the long strike price at expiration. As expiration draws near, if the underlying is close to the short lower strike, the call back spread will flip from a net positive delta position to one with a negative delta.

If the share price of the underlying stock rises, the share price will approach the value of the contracts you bought that have the higher strike price. As a result, the spread itself will lose value. After the share price reaches the higher strike price, the delta of the back spread will tip from negative to positive. In other words, the delta of the contracts you sold with the lower strike price will approach −1, and the delta of the contracts you bought, with the higher strike price, approach +.50. Given this is a 1:2 back spread—you sold one contract with a lower strike price and bought two contracts with higher strike prices—the spread will commonly yield a positive delta. If the share price increases beyond the strike price of the contracts you hold, the delta of the spread will increase and approach a delta of +1. This will counteract a negative delta for the contracts you sold. Put back spreads and call and put ratio spreads work the same way, but in reverse.

Gamma

The gamma of back spreads and ratio spreads respond very much like delta with regard to the amount of time to expiration. Back spreads normally have positive gamma if the expiration date is far away, so when the underlying share price moves it will result in favorable deltas for the spread.

As expiration draws near, however, if the underlying share price approaches the strike price of the contracts you sold, the gamma turns negative. If the underlying price moves, unfavorable deltas result. Remember that a back spread is at its lowest value when the stock price matches the strike price of the long contracts at the expiration date. The short gamma indicates that deltas will turn negative if the underlying stock price rises and positive if the underlying price falls.

If the share price for XYZ is at $25 with fifty days to expiration, the XYZ fifty-day $25 calls have a gamma of .16, and the XYZ fifty-day $27 calls have a gamma of .12. The net gamma of the XYZ fifty-day $25/$27 call back spread would be .08, or two times the gamma of .12 (.24) minus the gamma of .16. With fifty days remaining, the gamma of this back spread is clearly dominated by the long $27 strike. But with five days remaining to expiration, with the underlying unchanged at $25, the XYZ five-day $25 call now has a gamma of .59, and the XYZ five-day $27 strike has a gamma of .10. The net gamma of the XYZ five-day $25/$27 call back spread changes to −.39, or two times the gamma of .10 minus the gamma of .59. With five days remaining, the gamma of the back spread is heavily concentrated on the short $25 strike.

Theta

The theta of back and ratio spreads is the opposite of gamma. As a rule, if gamma is positive, theta will be negative. When a call back spread is further from expiration, the theta is negative; as time passes, the back spread loses value. The purpose of the call back spread is to take advantage of a large increase in the underlying share price. As the expiration date draws closer, the probability of a major change in the share price decreases, and thus the back spread position itself steadily declines in value.

Near the expiration date, if the share price of the underlying stock is close to the strike price of the contracts you bought, the theta for the back spread becomes increasingly negative. As a result, the net value of the spread drops as well. A back spread makes money at expiration when the underlying share price either matches the strike price of the contracts you sold or is far enough above the strike price of the contracts you bought to cover the initial trading cost to create the spread. But if the share price is close to the strike price of the contracts you sold, the theta increases, and the value of the spread improves too. Finally, if the underlying price falls to the point at which it is well below the strike price for the contracts you sold to form the back spread, theta becomes increasingly positive, and the price of the back spread falls to zero.

If XYZ has a share price of $25, the XYZ fifty-day $25 calls have a theta of.009, and the XYZ fifty-day $27 calls have a theta of.006, the net theta of the XYZ fifty-day $25/$27 call back spread would be −.003, or.009 minus two times.006, or.009 −.012. With fifty days remaining, the theta of this back spread is clearly dominated by the long $27 strike. But with five days remaining to expiration with the underlying unchanged at $25, the XYZ five-day $25 call now has a theta of.028 and the XYZ five-day $27 strike has a theta of.007. So the net theta of the XYZ five-day $25/$27 call back spread would be positive at.014, or.028 minus two times.007, or.028 −.014. With five days remaining until the contracts expire, the theta of the back spread is heavily concentrated on the short $25 strike.

Vega

Generally speaking, the more time until expiration, the greater the vega will be for a back spread. If the expiration date is further in the future, the vega values for the long and short contracts in the spread will be close to matching. But as time passes and the expiration date draws closer, several things typically take place. First, the vega loses value and can turn negative, depending on whether the share price of the underlying stock approaches the strike price of the contracts you sold or the strike price of the contracts you bought. Second, the vega values for the strike prices for the two sets of options contracts move farther and farther apart. When these two vega values are averaged, you might expect a back spread to have a flat vega. The vega depends on how closely the underlying share price approaches the strike prices in the position itself.

If the share price of XYZ is $40, the XYZ 140-day $40 calls have a vega of.0981, and the XYZ 140-day $45 calls have a vega of.0826, the net (average) vega of the back spread for the XYZ 140-day $40/$45 call would be.0671. This is two times the vega of.0826 minus the vega (.0981). With 140 days remaining, the net vega of this back spread is closer to the $45 strike price—the strike price of the contracts you bought. But with forty days remaining to expiration and the share price of the underlying unchanged at $40, the XYZ forty-day $40 call now has a vega of .0528, and the XYZ forty-day $45 strike has a vega of .0192. So the net vega of the XYZ forty-day $40/$45 call back spread would be −.014, or two times the vega of .0192 minus the vega of .0528. With forty days remaining, the vega of the back spread approaches the vega of the short $40 strike price.

Configuring and Pricing a Back Spread or Ratio Spread

There is a simple way to think about a back spread—it is really a vertical spread in which you buy an extra options contract. Likewise, a ratio spread is a vertical spread in which you write an extra options contract. To provide a more specific example, a call back spread is really a short call vertical spread (also known as a call bear spread) with an additional options contract purchased, though the extra contract will have a higher strike price than the other long contract in the position.

A 1:2 back spread or ratio spread is one option contract away from being a butterfly. Consider the XYZ thirty-day $25/$30 call ratio spread. To form it, you buy one XYZ thirty-day $25 call contract and sell two XYZ thirty-day $30 call contracts. If you then buy one XYZ thirty-day $35 call contract, the call ratio spread changes into a long XYZ thirty-day $25/$30/$35 call butterfly. This is important, for the butterfly (as explained in Chapter 20) has a limited amount of risk, whereas the ratio spread has unlimited risk.

Second, consider an XYZ forty-day $55/$60 put back spread. In this case you sold one XYZ forty-day $60 put contract and bought two XYZ forty-day $55 put contracts to create the spread. If you were to sell one more XYZ forty-day $50 put, you would alter the XYZ forty-day $55/$60 put back spread into a short XYZ forty-day $50/$55/$60 put butterfly. Even if you are comfortable with your back spread position, if you are concerned that the share price of the underlying stock is not moving, you can transform your position without completely giving up on your objective. Keep in mind, however, that even if you turn a losing back spread into a short butterfly, you may only postpone what turns out to be a trade that loses money in the end.

A 1:2 back spread or ratio spread is one option contract away from being a bull or bear vertical spread. You can convert a 1:2 call back spread into a call bear spread by selling one of the call contracts you originally bought to form the position. Likewise, if you decide to sell one of the put contracts you bought to form a put back spread (1:2), you can turn the position into a put bull spread. In either case, you have a short 1:1 vertical spread.

For ratio spreads, the opposite rule applies. Buy an additional call contract to turn a call ratio spread (1:2) into a call bull spread. A put ratio spread (1:2) turns into a put bear spread after you buy another put contract. For both calls and puts, buying the additional short strike contract turns your ratio spread into a long (bull or bear) 1:1 vertical spread.

This can serve to get you out of trouble in a hurry, either to reduce risk or reduce loss. But you must weigh transforming a position against getting out entirely. Any trader struggles to accept loss, but when working with options contracts, knowing how to lose well is one of the keys to success.

Pricing a Back Spread or Ratio Spread

One of the more confusing things about back spreads and ratio spreads is how you can set them up as either credit or debit spreads. As a debit spread, you spend more to buy the options contracts than you earn in premiums from the contracts you sell. With a credit spread, you earn a net income from the contracts you sell because the premium more than offsets the money you spend to buy contracts. If all of the contracts expire as worthless, the credit will represent your total profit for the trade.

There are three factors that determine the relative cost of a back spread or ratio spread:

1. The distance between the long strike and short strike of the spread. Assume XYZ is trading at $58 a share:
   - The XYZ twenty-day $58 call contracts are selling for $1.40 each.
   - The XYZ twenty-day $59 calls are selling for 95 cents each.
   - The XYZ twenty-day $60 calls are selling for 55 cents each.

   The XYZ twenty-day $58/$59 back spread would cost you 50 cents per contract to set up—that is, two $58 call contracts ($1.80 total) minus $1.40 for the $59 contract. So this would be a debit spread.

   With an XYZ twenty-day $58/$60 back spread, however, you would earn a net return of 30 cents (a credit spread), as you would spend $1.10 to buy two $60 call contracts and earn $1.40 for the $58 calls.

   If you set up a credit back spread, the position will make money if the underlying price moves far enough beyond the strike price of the contracts you bought. It will also make a profit if the options contracts all expire as worthless. If a back spread is established for an initial debit, the position will make money only if the underlying price moves far enough past the strike price of the contracts you bought.

2. *Time to expiration.* If the expiration date for the options contracts included in a back spread or a ratio spread is several months into the future, the contracts will trade at close to the same price. As the expiration date approaches, the prices for the contracts will tend to diverge. Consider XYZ, currently trading at $58 a share. At twenty days to expiration, a $59 call contract might sell for 95 cents, whereas a $60 call contract would draw 55 cents. This close to expiration, the likelihood that the share price will change enough to make either contract in the money is starting to grow more remote. Because the $59 contract is closer to the $58 share price, it has a better chance, so the contract is worth more. With the same strike price and share price but at ninety days until expiration, the $59 contract might trade at 45 cents and the $60 contract at 40 cents.

3. *Increase in volatility.* An increase in implied volatility will have the same effect on back spreads and ratio spreads as an increase in time. The higher the implied volatility, the wider the perceived future price range will be for the shares of underlying stock. If the implied volatility is high, the contracts bought and sold to set up a back spread or ratio spread will tend to have sale prices that are closer together. For example, consider again XYZ trading at $58 a share. With volatility at 24.5 percent, a $59 call contract could sell for $1.40 and a $60 call contract for $1.38. But if volatility drops to 9.2 percent, the $59 call might sell for 80 cents and the $60 call for 44 cents.

Reconciling Volatility and the Back Spread or Ratio Spread

A lot of investment material talks about how a back spread or ratio spread can be designed to profit from anticipated changes in implied volatility. But from the point of view of a trader who has actually traded hundreds of these spreads, no one should be encouraged to use this strategy as a means to enhance or reduce volatility. The usefulness of a back spread or a ratio spread for managing volatility is unclear.

First, most traders set up back and ratio spreads so that the net price of the spread is small, the position tends to be delta neutral, and the combined vega is fairly trivial. The only way to alter that would be to choose contracts to buy and sell with strike prices that are far apart, making one in the money and the other out of the money. You would get a better vega value, but you would also dramatically increase your risk. Professional traders typically set up back spreads and ratio spreads using either one at-the-money strike against an out-of-the-money strike or two out-of-the-money strikes.

Second, think of these strategies as mostly dependent on the actual performance of the underlying asset, with some effect from implied volatility. This means that the vega for the back spread or ratio spread is a secondary value. In a typical 1:2 trade, you can be correct in predicting the implied volatility but still lose money on the trade if you fail to accurately forecast what happens to the stock price itself. You aren't going to successfully trade in back and ratio spreads if you don't focus first on what is likely to happen with the underlying asset.

CHAPTER 20

The Butterfly Spread

So far you have learned about options spreads that involve buying and selling contracts with just two different strike prices. The butterfly spread is a strategy that involves four contracts with three strike prices. These are somewhat complicated trades, but they can be quite useful in either taking advantage of implied volatility or reducing your exposure to volatility. The butterfly spread offers low risk but also low reward. More important, the butterfly strategy can be a good investment in a time of high volatility because as implied volatility increases, the butterfly spread becomes less expensive to create. Hence you don't have to fear the butterfly spread because of its complexity. You aren't likely to lose much if the market goes south in any case, and in an unpredictable marketplace the butterfly can offer a measure of security. The butterfly spread makes a profit if the share price for the underlying stock remains mostly unchanged when the contracts in the spread expire.

Setting up a Butterfly

When you make a risk chart of a butterfly spread, you see an investment strategy that looks like a butterfly, with a body and a pair of wings. In a long butterfly contract, the strike prices for the contracts you buy form the wings, and the lower price for the contracts you sell make up the body. For a short butterfly, the short contracts make up the wings. Setting up the butterfly involves four different options contracts with three strike prices, and all of the contracts expire at the same time. The contracts can be either calls or puts, but the three strike prices must be equally spaced. The ratio of the number of contracts in the butterfly is always 1:2:1. For example, you could set up a butterfly buying a $50 call contract, selling two $55 call contracts, and buying a $60 call contract.

EXHIBIT 20.1   Long Butterfly—Expiry Break-Even

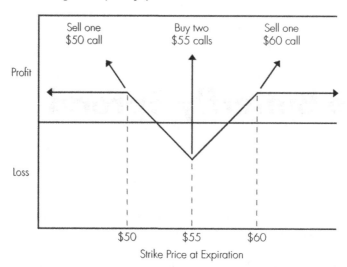

Strike Price at Expiration

   If you set up a butterfly spread in which you spend more to buy contracts than you gain in premium from the contracts you sell, you are said to be *buying* the butterfly, also called a *long* butterfly (see **Exhibit 20.1**). In this case, you are buying the outside strike prices ($60 and $50) and selling the inside strike prices (two for $55). When the contracts expire for a long butterfly, your loss will never be more than the net price you paid to set up the butterfly. If you sell the contracts with the outside strike prices and buy the contracts with the inside strike prices, you have *sold* the butterfly, also called a *short* butterfly (see **Exhibit 20.2**). Thus, with a short butterfly you will receive net income when you place the trades to set up the strategy.
   A long butterfly tends to behave like a ratio spread, and a short butterfly tends to behave like a back spread (see Chapter 19).

The Long Butterfly and the Ratio Spread

Consider a trader who buys a $50/$55/$60 call butterfly (buys a $50 call, sells two $55 calls, and buys a $60 call). If the share price of the underlying asset falls below $50 when the contracts expire, none of the contracts will be exercised; all of them will expire as worthless. The value of the butterfly position will be zero. If the share price rises above $60 at expiration, the value of the $50 and $60 call contracts together will match the value of the two $55 calls. Again, the value of the butterfly will be zero. This is because all of the

EXHIBIT 20.2 Short Butterfly—Expiry Break-Even

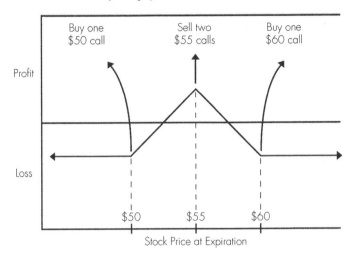

contracts could reasonably be exercised, so the profit the trader gains from exercising the $50 and $60 call contracts, which will offset the expense of having the two $55 contracts exercised against him. Suppose the stock price reaches $62 a share. The trader would exercise the two long contracts and earn $14 per share ($12 for the $50 contract and $2 for the $60 contract). But the two $55 contracts would also be exercised, forcing the trader to sell shares at $55 each to the other trader at a $7 loss in value per share. Because he sold two contracts, his loss equals $14. The butterfly is worthless.

Now suppose the share price of the underlying asset is $55 at expiration, between the strike prices of the two outside contracts—$50 and $60—and matching the strike price of the inside contracts. The $50 call contract will be worth $5 a share, whereas the $55 and $60 calls will expire as worthless. If the share price equals the strike price on the short contracts ($55), no one will bother to exercise them against the trader who wrote the contracts. So the butterfly spread is worth $5 a share. If the underlying moves away from $55, the value of the butterfly will decline, but its value can never fall below zero.

When the contracts expire, the butterfly spread will always have a value somewhere between zero and the range of strike prices between the two outside contracts ($50 and $60 in the table below). As you can see **Table 20.1**, the butterfly will have a value between $0 and $5. It will be worth $0 if the share price for the underlying asset is below the lowest strike price ($50) or above the highest strike price ($60). The butterfly can earn the most when the share price equals the inside strike price ($55) when the contracts expire.

TABLE 20.1   Butterfly—Profit and Loss Table at Expiration (Long One $50 Call; Short Two $55 Call; Long One $60 Call)

XYZ Closing Price	Butterfly Value
$30.00	$0.00
$40.00	$0.00
$50.00	$0.00
$51.00	$1.00
$52.00	$2.00
$53.00	$3.00
$54.00	$4.00
$55.00	$5.00
$56.00	$4.00
$57.00	$3.00
$58.00	$2.00
$59.00	$1.00
$60.00	$0.00
$70.00	$0.00
$80.00	$0.00

A long butterfly spread compares well to a ratio spread.

1. You should set up a long butterfly spread if you believe that the share price for the underlying asset is likely to remain within a narrow range until the contracts expire.
2. The long butterfly position reaches its highest possible value if the market is quiet and the share price remains stable.

The Short Butterfly and the Back Spread

Now consider the opposite strategy. If you sell a butterfly spread, you have a lot in common with a trader setting up a back spread because you want the underlying share price to move as far from the inside exercise price as possible. When the contracts expire, you want the share price to be either below the lowest strike price (less than $50) or above the highest strike price (above $60). A short butterfly acts like a back spread in that it tends to increase in value if the market is moving.

To return to the original example, assume a trader sells a $50/$55/$60 call butterfly (sells a $50 call, buys two $55 calls, and sells a $60 call). If the share price of the underlying asset falls below $50 when the contracts expire, none of the contracts will be exercised but will expire as worthless (see Table 20.1). The butterfly will be worth $0, but the trader will profit in that he gets to keep the net premium from selling the contracts. If the share price rises above $60, all of the contracts will be exercised, but the amount earned from the $50 and $60 contracts together will offset the cost to satisfy the $55 contracts when they are assigned. So the short butterfly works the same way as the long butterfly if the share price climbs—the net value of the butterfly is $0, but the trader keeps the net premium earned.

Now suppose the share price of the underlying asset is $55 at expiration, between the strike prices of the two outside contracts—$50 and $60—and matching the strike price of the inside contracts. The $50 call contract will be worth $5 a share, whereas the $55 and $60 calls will expire as worthless. The $50 call contract would be exercised against you, so you would lose $5 a share, minus the amount of premium earned when completing the trades to set up the spread. If the underlying moves away from $55, the value of the butterfly will decline, but its value can never fall below zero.

As with a back spread, you would set up a short butterfly if you feel that the share price of the underlying stock will change significantly before the contracts expire so you can record the net premium earned in the trade as a profit.

The Butterfly Spread as a Volatility Investment

The risks and rewards of butterflies are limited. If you buy a butterfly, the most you can lose is the amount you paid for it. If you sell a butterfly, the most you can earn is the net amount of premium you received from placing the trades to create the spread. For either type, the most you can make is the difference between the inside strike price and outside strike price minus the amount you paid to buy the contracts.

Butterfly Spreads and the Expiration Date

The closer a butterfly is to expiration, the more sensitive its price will be to a change in the price of the underlying asset (see **Table 20.2**). Far from the expiration date, if the underlying share price changes, it doesn't necessarily affect the value of the butterfly spread. This means that trading in butterfly spreads is not a sound strategy if you want to exploit long-term changes in an underlying asset value. A butterfly spread can be long volatility or short volatility, and either a bull or bear strategy. But these descriptions don't mean much unless you are fairly close to the expiration date.

TABLE 20.2 Butterfly—Theoretical Value of XYZ Butterfly with Regard to Time Structure

Butterfly	Expiry 6 Days	Expiry 57 Days	Expiry 113 Days
$61/$62/$63	$0.25	$0.15	$0.10
$57/$62/$67	$3.20	$1.40	$1.06

Theoretical value of XYZ butterfly with term structure; XYZ = $61.77.

TABLE 20.3 Butterfly—Intrinsic Value of Various Strike Prices at Expiration

XYZ = $30			XYZ = $35			XYZ = $40		
Expiry Values			Expiry Values			Expiry Values		
Call	Strike	Put	Call	Strike	Put	Call	Strike	Put
$0.00	$30	$0.00	$5.00	$30	$0.00	$10.00	$30	$0.00
$0.00	$35	$5.00	$0.00	$35	$0.00	$5.00	$35	$0.00
$0.00	$40	$10.00	$0.00	$40	$5.00	$0.00	$40	$0.00

TABLE 20.4 Butterfly—Demonstration of Parity between Call and Put Butterfly with the Same Strikes

$30/$35/$40 Call Butterfly Value	$30/$35/$40 Call Butterfly Value	$30/$35/$40 Call Butterfly Value
$0.00	$5.00	$0.00

$30/$35/$40 Put Butterfly Value	$30/$35/$40 Put Butterfly Value	$30/$35/$40 Put Butterfly Value
$0.00	$5.00	$0.00

Call and Put Butterfly Spreads Work the Same Way

All butterflies are worth their maximum amount when the underlying share price matches the strike price of the inside contracts. Therefore, you could achieve the same result using either a call or a put butterfly as long as the expiration date and strike prices are the same.

Both the thirty-day $30/$35/$40 call butterfly and the thirty-day $30/$35/$40 put butterfly will be worth no more than $5 if the share price of the underlying asset reaches $35 at expiration. The butterfly has a minimum value of $0 if the share price falls below $30 or climbs above $40. The table that follows demonstrates the likeness—or parity—of a call or put butterfly given three different price scenarios at expiration (see **Table 20.3** and **Table 20.4**).

Greek Values and the Butterfly

The price of the butterfly spread becomes more sensitive to changes in the share price of the underlying stock with thirty days or less to go until expiration. The greeks of the butterfly respond the same way, in that they can also change dramatically with less time to expiration. Therefore, closer to expiration you can calculate the greek values for a butterfly and use these values to help estimate the price and performance of the butterfly itself.

But for all of the greek values, keep in mind that the delta, gamma, theta, or vega is not of much interest if the contracts in the spread are ninety days or more away from expiration. Far away from expiration, the greek values are negligible; they become significant only when the contracts are within thirty days of expiring.

Delta

For a long butterfly, such as the $50/$55/$60 spread in the example, the delta will be as follows:

- Positive when the underlying share price falls below the inside strike price ($55)
- Neutral when it matches the inside strike price
- Negative when it climbs above the inside strike price

The butterfly reaches its maximum value when the price of the underlying share equals the inside strike price. Therefore, if the share price falls below the middle strike, that share price must rise for the butterfly to make money—hence the positive deltas. If the price of the underlying asset is above the middle strike price, it must fall for the butterfly to make money. That leads to a negative delta value (see **Table 20.5**).

TABLE 20.5 Butterfly—Net Delta of $50/$55/$60 Call Butterfly with Varied Days till Expiration and Varied Underlying Prices

XYZ Price	$50.00	$55.00	$60.00
50 Days	0.19	0	−0.19
20 Days	0.38	0	−0.38
10 Days	0.51	0	−0.51

TABLE 20.6 Butterfly—Net Gamma of XYZ $50/$55/$60 Call Butterfly with Various Closing Prices and Days till Expiration

XYZ Price	$50.00	$55.00	$60.00
50 Days	0	−0.07	0
20 Days	0.06	−0.2	0.06
10 Days	0.17	−0.36	0.17

XYZ long $50/$55/$60 call butterfly, gamma with various closing prices and days till expiration.

Gamma

The gamma value of a long butterfly flows from positive to negative, or vice versa. When the stock price reaches the outer strike prices of the butterfly, the gamma is positive. This shows that the butterfly would produce positive deltas if the underlying share price rises, and negative deltas if that share price falls, albeit to the extent that the underlying is close to a long strike. This matches the behavior of the delta of the long butterfly as shown in **Table 20.6**.

Meanwhile, the gamma of the long butterfly is negative when the underlying share price matches the inside strike price (see **Table 20.6**). This shows that the butterfly will create negative deltas if the underlying share price rises and positive deltas if the share price falls. But you want your delta to be neutral; you want the share price to match the inside strike price and stay there.

Theta

Theta is the opposite of gamma. If a long butterfly is negative gamma, the theta will be positive; if a short butterfly is positive gamma, it will have a negative theta. For any butterfly, the theta will be positive if the stock price approaches the inside strike price. As the expiration date approaches, a positive theta is good for a long butterfly and bad for a short butterfly. If, however, the stock price trades either high or low, and thus near one of the outer strike prices, the theta is positive for a short butterfly and negative for a long butterfly (see **Table 20.7**).

That is, if the share price is close to one of the outer strike prices, it benefits the holder of the short butterfly, because the theta will be positive, but the theta will be negative for the long butterfly. With the short butterfly, remember, you sold the contracts with the outside strike prices (say, $60 and $50), bought two contracts with inside strike prices ($55 each), and earned a net premium in the transaction. With a short butterfly, you make a profit if

TABLE 20.7 Butterfly—Net Theta of XYZ Long $50/$55/$60 Call Butterfly with Various Closing Prices and Days till Expiration

XYZ Price	$50.00	$55.00	$60.00
50 Days	0	0.013	0
20 Days	−0.014	0.047	−0.014
10 Days	−0.036	0.086	−0.036

XYZ long $50/$55/$60 call butterfly, theta with various closing prices and days till expiration

TABLE 20.8 Butterfly—Net Vega of Long XYZ $50/$55/$60 Call Butterfly with Various Closing Prices and Days till Expiration

XYZ Price	$50.00	$55.00	$60.00
50 Days	−0.02	−0.054	−0.02
20 Days	0.022	−0.069	0.022
10 Days	0.028	−0.061	0.028

XYZ long $50/$55/$60 call butterfly, vega with various closing prices and days till expiration.

the share prices climb toward the highest strike price ($60) or fall toward the lowest strike price ($50). The short butterfly profits if the market is active, and the theta tends to reflect that.

Vega

When the underlying share price matches the inside strike price, the vega of a long butterfly is negative (see **Table 20.8**), and it is positive for a short butterfly. That means that any increase in the implied volatility of the underlying share price decreases the value of the long butterfly. This should make sense. The long butterfly's value depends on the likelihood that the share price will approach the inside strike price when the contracts expire.

The lower the implied volatility, the more likely it is that the share price will stay close to the inside strike price. Therefore, in this situation, the price of the butterfly falls if the implied volatility increases. On the other hand, if the share price is high or low and closer to one of the outside strike prices, an increase in the implied volatility increases the value of the butterfly. If the implied volatility is high, it suggests that the share price is going to move somewhere, either up or down. So if the share price is likely to move at all, it is more likely that the share price will move back toward the middle—closer to matching the inside strike price—before the expiration date. In this event, vega will be positive for a long butterfly.

Structuring and Pricing a Butterfly

You can think of a butterfly spread as two combined vertical spreads—that is, a bull spread at one strike price and a bear spread at a higher strike. You can also change a strategy from a back spread, ratio spread, or vertical spread into a butterfly spread and thus reduce your risk and likely loss. For example, suppose you have a thirty-day $25/$30 call ratio spread for XYZ. You bought one XYZ thirty-day $25 call contract and sold two XYZ thirty-day $30 call contracts. If you then buy one XYZ thirty-day $35 call contract, the call ratio spread would be converted into a long XYZ thirty-day $25/$30/$35 call butterfly.

Recall that with vertical spreads, you can set up a bull spread by buying a call contract or selling a put contract, whereas with a bear spread you can either sell a call contract or buy a put. So, any way in which you combine a bull spread at the lower strike and bear spread at the higher strike results in a long butterfly. A bear spread at the lower strike and a bull spread at the higher strike results in a short butterfly. Consider the example above again, a long thirty-day $25/$30/$35 call butterfly. You bought the $25 and $35 call contracts and sold two $30 call contracts. To form a call bear spread, you would buy a $35 call and sell a $30 call; to form the bull spread, you would buy a $25 call and sell the $30 call. Combine the two vertical spreads to form a single butterfly spread.

The value of the butterfly spread depends on the relationship of the share price to the strike prices in the spread before the contracts expire. The more time you need to wait until the contracts expire, the less confident you can be in predicting where the underlying share price will land when the expiration date arrives. But as you get close to expiration, you can estimate the share price with some certainty. This means that you can't accurately estimate the final value of a butterfly spread either until the expiration draws near.

Trading Butterflies in a Volatile Market

Butterflies are a fine investment strategy when volatilities are high. When volatilities climb, it costs much less to set up a butterfly, especially one at the money. A butterfly spread is one of the few types of investments that, in a turbulent market, is both cheap and offers limited risk. Also, you can use the butterfly to capture short-term volatility without having to be completely accurate in predicting the direction of the share price of the underlying stock. This is partly because you can only effectively project prices or values for a butterfly spread within about thirty days of when the contracts included in the spread expire. Also, you can design a butterfly to work even in a time of volatility; even if share prices spike or fall, you don't risk losing much money, and if prices become stable close to expiration, you make a modest profit.

This is not to suggest that a (long) butterfly trade is a surefire winner in a high-volatility environment. There is no such thing as a surefire investment. Usually, if volatility is high, it is high for a reason. Implied volatility numbers generally predict more movement in a share price in the mid-term than actually tends to happen. More important, no matter how carefully you calculate the implied volatility for a stock, no matter how good you are at considering historic trends and the current marketplace, you are unlikely to predict the possibility of an enormous, hundred-year swing in a market. And these days, hundred-year events seems to happen every five years or so. When you face a market earthquake, as in October and November 2008, there's not much you can do but turn off your laptop and stare at it in wonder.

In short, butterflies are usually valued accurately whether implied volatilities tend to be low or high. When markets are volatile, butterfly values tend to get pushed lower. That's because a higher implied volatility suggests a wider range of movement in the underlying share price, leading to ever more uncertainty as the volatility itself climbs. Higher volatility tends to lead to ever higher volatility; in particular, the more violently the market responds to current events or a bursting bubble, the more likely traders and investors are to panic and start dumping assets on the market to cash out as best they can, driving prices still lower. The same can happen in reverse—a frenzy of buying driving prices up rapidly—but this tends to take longer. And in either case psychology trumps both technology and people with PhDs in mathematics when the market becomes volatile. Anyone with experience in a trading room or on the floor knows how hard it is to let experience, judgment, and a predefined strategy remain in control during a crisis.

Hence the value of the butterfly strategy; you don't have to panic when the market is in turmoil. In fact, if volatility climbs high enough, the values of all of the different butterfly spreads you are holding will tend to converge. If you are convinced that the implied volatility for a stock is likely to climb in the mid-term, you can set up a butterfly for the spread at a bargain price, break-even, or possibly suffer a small loss if the volatility remains high, and profit if the share price ends up approaching the inside strike price shortly before the contracts expire. The butterfly depends far less on the performance of the underlying stock than do most other kinds of investment strategies. It's not a flawless approach to investing, but a butterfly spread is about as good an approach as you are going to find in a marketplace where you need to step carefully.

CHAPTER 21

Wingspreads

Capturing Convergence and Divergence

In options parlance, an albatross, condor, and pterodactyl are otherwise known as "wingspreads" as their expiration date risk/reward profiles resemble that of either a giant seabird, a new world vulture, or even an extinct flying reptile. This likeness may require substantial imagination to picture, but it does add a bit of welcome atmosphere to the otherwise lifeless world of options strategy. However, to be clear, this expiry date risk/reward resemblance to something that flies does serve to offer specific clues on both how and when they should be traded. And, by the end of this chapter, this seemingly complex subject will—with any luck—become somewhat intuitive to you.

When talking about wingspreads you'll hear the option contracts involved described as "body" and/or "wings." The body refers to options with strikes in between the two outermost strikes (exoskeleton). The wings refer to options at the outermost strikes (farthest tip of the wing). Basically, I use the term wingspreads to identify old-school option positions such as albatrosses, condors, and pterodactyls, which resemble butterflies (Chapter 20) that have been stretched out either a little (condor) or quite a lot (pterodactyl). They can also be viewed as being made up of a row of butterflies! The more butterflies that one has in a row, the wider the wingspread is and the more the risk/reward zone is being stretched out. Before describing the individual characteristics of each winged-creature spread, I thought it would be beneficial to provide an overview—sewing the common thread that all of these strategies are simply an extrapolation of the butterfly!

Wingspreads: Risk/Reward

It's essential to recognize that both the potential risks and rewards of wingspreads are limited. If you purchase a wingspread, the most you can lose is the premium you paid for it. The most you can make is the difference between the body strike and a wing strike, subtracting the amount you originally paid for it. If you sell a wingspread, the profit and loss potential is the exact opposite. If short a wingspread, the most you can lose is the difference between the body strike and a wing strike, potentially adding back some or the entire premium you originally received.

Wingspreads: Sensitivities

Wingspreads' reaction to change in the underlying price is related directly to the time left to expiration. For example, the nearer a wingspread is to expiry, the more sensitive its price is to an alteration in the price of the underlying price. What this implies is that wingspreads that are far off from expiration don't always change in value very much when the underlying price moves. This could suggest that far-term wingspreads aren't necessarily the best tool for profiting from changes in the underlying price. Wingspreads may be bullish or bearish, long or short volatility, or positive or negative one of the Greeks. The point is the nearer a wingspread is to expiration, the more pronounced that effect can/will be.

Wingspreads achieve their greatest value when the underlying price is between the middle or body strike(s) at expiration. Wingspreads are at their lowest value when the underlying price is either at or above the higher wing strike or at or below the lower wing strike at expiry. Consequently, wingspreads can be efficient tools when you believe that the underlying price will settle inside a particular range and within a precise time frame.

Let's assume you are convinced that the underlying price will hang somewhere between two defined prices, long wingspreads with middle body strikes at the low and high prices of the underlying price range might work best. Let me challenge you to consider it this way: Long wingspreads are likened to short straddles and strangles—without the unlimited risk. Glance at **Exhibit 21.1** showing the value of a long wingspread at expiration. You should notice that the middle of the spread resembles that of a short straddle. Alternatively, if you should sense the underlying price is ready to move away from a particular point or beyond a specific range of prices, short wingspreads may well be a respectable option. They perform in the vein of long straddles and strangles, but without the unlimited profit/loss potential. They are also normally much less expensive. Look

EXHIBIT 21.1   Long Condor Spread

EXHIBIT 21.2   Short Condor Spread

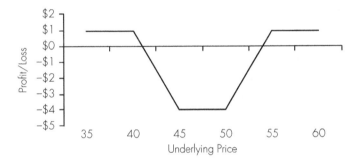

at **Exhibit 21.2**, which show the value of a short wingspread at expiration, and you'll notice the middle of the butterfly looks a lot like a long straddle.

Wingspreads and the Greeks

Traders beware! The value of a wingspread can grow to be quite sensitive to changes in the underlying price with fewer than two weeks to go. The Greeks of the wingspread also can vary considerably as the underlying price moves up and down. This sensitivity can be applied to all wingspreads.

Delta

The delta associated with a wingspread is not necessarily intuitive and is somewhat of an interesting concept once grasped. A long wingspreads delta is positive when the underlying price is below the middle strike of the butterfly, neutral when the underlying price is at the middle strike, and negative when it's above the middle strike. In addition, the delta will go away once the underlying price has gone beyond the upper and lower limits of the spread. The insight behind this is that the long wingspread gets the most out of its value when the underlying price is at the middle strike. Therefore, if the underlying price is below the middle strike, it has to rise for the long wingspread to make money, thus the positive deltas. If the underlying price is above the middle strike, it has to fall for the wingspread to make money—therefore the negative deltas. The reverse would be true for a short wingspread.

Gamma

On a theoretical level, gamma is what's causing the long wingspreads delta to potentially change direction from positive to neutral to negative as the gamma of a long wingspread flows from positive to negative. At the external strikes of the long wingspread, gamma is positive, indicating that the long wingspread would produce positive deltas if the underlying price rises, and negative deltas if the underlying price falls. This consistently matches with the manner in which the delta of the long wingspread operates as depicted above. The gamma of the long wingspread is negative when the underlying price is at the middle strike. This points to the reality that the long wingspread will, in fact, create negative deltas if the underlying price rises and positive deltas if the underlying price falls. This is precisely what you don't want to happen!

Theta

The theta of the long wingspread is the mirror reflection of the gamma. Alongside negative gamma comes positive theta and vice versa. Theta is positive when the underlying price is at the middle strike, indicative of the passage of time helping the long wingspread reach its highest value. At the outer strikes theta is negative, demonstrating that the wingspread is losing value as time presses on.

Vega

Wingspreads can be a decent choice to take advantage of changes in implied volatility when one wishes to do so in a limited risk manner. Like the other

Greeks, the vega of a wingspread varies depending on where the price of the underlying is compared to the strike price of the wingspread. When the underlying price is at the middle strike, the vega of the long wingspread is negative. That suggests that any increased implied volatility in the underlying price will decrease the value of the wingspread. This should make particular sense, since a wingspread's value depends on the probability that the underlying price will be at its middle strike at expiry. Higher implied volatility diminishes the possibility and perception that the underlying price will remain at the middle strike price; consequently the value of the wingspread would decrease with an increase in implied volatility. Vega is positive for the long wingspread at the outer strikes. Hence, an increase in the implied volatility of the underlying increases the value of the wingspread because of the greater likelihood that the wingspread will move toward the middle strike by expiry.

Wingspreads: Various and Sundry Details

The price of a wingspread depends by and large on the likelihood of the underlying being at or between two prices at expiration. The more time there is to expiration, the less confident you can or should be of where the underlying price will land at expiry. The less time there is to expiration, the more certain you can and should be of where the underlying price will remain at expiration.

This concept suggests that if you were to list the prices of various strike wingspreads in each expiration month, the graph would look rather flat in the months far from expiration due to the increased vagueness about which wingspread will have the maximum value at expiration. (Remember: a wingspread reaches maximum value when the underlying price is at the middle or body strike of the butterfly at expiration.) Consequently, wingspreads far from expiration all share very similar values, because only one or two of them can be of any value at expiration, and which one or two will have value is at best vague and uncertain.

When there is a reduced amount of time to expiration, there is a bit more certainty where the underlying price is going to land at expiration. As a wingspread comes closer to expiration, the graph would begin to develop a bulge at or near the current underlying price. The bulge on the graph is the price of the most expensive butterfly. It's the most costly because it's at the money, which has a middle strike that is the most likely price of the underlying at expiration.

Generally speaking, wingspreads will be more costly than butterflies because they have a much bigger profit range. That is, a butterfly maximizes its value if the underlying price is exactly at the middle strike price of the butterfly. But a wingspread maximizes its value over a range of underlying prices. Since a wingspread has a greater perceived likelihood of maximizing its value, it has a larger price than a butterfly.

The Condor Spread

Think of the condor spread as an ever so slightly stretched out butterfly. The condor is similar to a butterfly, except that the contracts in the middle (whether long or short) do not have matching strike prices as they would in a butterfly. With a long call condor, the trader might buy a $40 call, sell a $45 call, sell a $50 call, and purchase a $55 call—implementing equally spaced strikes with the same expiration date (see Exhibit 21.1). This would be a debit transaction. A short condor would be the reverse where you would sell a $40 call, buy a $45 call, buy a $50 call, and sell a $55 call (see Exhibit 21.2).

It is often helpful to think of a condor in terms of two consecutive vertical spreads: one bullish, the other bearish. This may help you to calculate both your risk and price faster. When long a call condor, think of yourself buying a bull vertical spread and subsidizing its cost by selling a bull vertical spread directly on top of it. On the other hand, when selling a condor, think of it in terms of selling a bear vertical spread and buying a bull vertical spread on top of it. Bear in mind that a true condor always uses equally spaced strike prices sharing the same expiration date.

Limited Risk/Reward Profile

Maximum profit for the long condor options strategy is achieved when the underlying price falls between the two middle strikes (your short strikes) at expiration. In other words, the most you can make on a long condor is the difference between the strikes in the spread minus the debit paid. If you paid $1.00 for the $40/$45/$50/$55 call condor, the most you can make is $4.00 ($5.00 − $1.00 = $4.00). Maximum loss for the long condor is the original premium paid. That would occur if, at expiration, the underlying price settled at or below $40.00 or at or above $55.00.

The short condor would be the exact opposite. Refer to **Table 21.1** to see an exact expiration profit/loss break-down of the long condor spread.

TABLE 21.1 Expiration Profit/Loss Detail

$40/$45/$50/$55 Call and Put Condor Expiration Profit/Loss Detail		
Underlying Expiration Price	$40/$45/$50/$55 Call Condor Expiration Value	$40/$45/$50/$55 Put Condor Expiration Value
$100.00	$0.00	$0.00
$60.00	$0.00	$0.00
$55.00	$0.00	$0.00
$54.00	$1.00	$1.00
$53.00	$2.00	$2.00
$52.00	$3.00	$3.00
$51.00	$4.00	$4.00
$50.00	**$5.00**	**$5.00**
$49.00	**$5.00**	**$5.00**
$48.00	**$5.00**	**$5.00**
$47.00	**$5.00**	**$5.00**
$46.00	**$5.00**	**$5.00**
$45.00	**$5.00**	**$5.00**
$44.00	$4.00	$4.00
$43.00	$3.00	$3.00
$42.00	$2.00	$2.00
$41.00	$1.00	$1.00
$40.00	$0.00	$0.00
$35.00	$0.00	$0.00
$0.00	$0.00	$0.00

At expiration, if the underlying price should settle below $40.00, all of your options will expire as worthless—the original premium paid will be lost. Similarly—but not exactly—if at expiration, the underlying price should settle above $55, all your options will be in-the-money; your long strikes ($40 and $55) would be exercised while your short strikes ($45 and $50) would be assigned. However, the net result would be the same—your long condor would expire as worthless as your two long calls would match in value with your short calls. Recall, you in effect purchased the $40/$45 call bull spread and subsidized it by selling the $50/$55 call bull spread—both your long and short spread settled at parity: $5.00.

The Condor Strategy

Presented here is the Condor Strategy with regards to time to expiration, underlying path, and volatility.

The condor is a multidimensional trade—one that requires the trader to think both critically and perceive details in a three-dimensional manner. In an effort to help you cut through the clutter, I would encourage you to think of the condor in light of three principal factors: the condor's time to expiry (term structure), where the condor is placed relative to the underlying price, and the prevailing implied volatility of the options position. Getting to that point—where your mind and risk management skills can manage multidimensionality is no easy feat. The straightforward explanations that follow should help you begin that process of orchestrating the risk of time-to-expiration, underlying price, and volatility.

In the subsequent examples, the book will describe being long the XYZ $40/$45/$50/$55 call condor.

The Condor and Time Structure

In **Exhibit 21.3** notice the convergence—the similarity—of prices the further you go out along the time horizon. In contrast, observe how quickly the

EXHIBIT 21.3   Condor Pricing with Regard to Time till Expiration—Underlying $134.50

Underlying : $134.50					
Condor	1 day till Expiry	8 days till Expiry	15 days till expiry	57 days till expiry	134 days till expiry
130/131/132/133	0.02	0.11	0.14	0.08	0.05
131/132/133/134	0.05	0.28	0.17	0.09	0.05
132/133/134/135	0.52	0.32	0.19	0.11	0.06
133/134/135/136	0.95	0.38	0.26	0.11	0.08
134/135/136/137	0.44	0.26	0.21	0.11	0.07
135/136/137/138	0.02	0.11	0.16	0.12	0.06

prices diverge—especially within the last month of the contract's life. Do understand that the speed of the condor's price convergence is also influenced by the implied volatility of the options.

The Condor and Various Points in the Underlying Environment

Condors tend to be more sensitive to changes in the underlying when:

- Volatility is low or trending lower.
- Time to expiration lessens.

In that regard, these points apply to one degree or another depending on a mix of:

- How low implied volatility actually is.
- How close the contract is to expiration.
- Which condor you have relative to the underlying.

This myriad of factors—things that need to go right—is implied in the pricing of the condor. In other words, condors can, at first glance, appear extremely cheap or incredibly expensive—almost too good to be true. However, it goes back to the adage that you do get what you pay for. **Table 21.2** demonstrates the price change of the $40/$45/$50/$55 call condor with different points in the underlying price.

The Condor within Various Volatility Environments

Generally speaking, condors will be priced relatively cheaper in a higher volatility environment than in a lower one. Again, this phenomenon—when you stop and think of it—should hopefully be somewhat logical as higher volatility implies larger path uncertainty, whereas low volatility—by extension—suggests a small, more predictable range of the underlying price. Using the $40/$45/$50/$55 call condor, take note of **Table 21.3**, which shows the price differentials inputting a variety of implied volatilities.

The Albatross Spread

Don't let the name alarm you. The albatross is really an extension of the condor. In fact, the albatross spread is simply a condor spread with longer wings created by placing the legs of the strategy with a wider strike

TABLE 21.2 The Condor and Various Points in the Underlying Price

XYZ = $44.00 XYZ $40.00/$42.50/$45.00/$47.50 Condor		
Underlying Price	Condor Price 14 days till expiration	Condor Price 42 days till expiration
$37.00	0.21	0.09
$38.00	0.35	0.11
$39.00	0.81	0.31
$40.00	1.11	0.43
$41.00	1.21	0.51
$42.00	1.24	0.71
$43.00	1.31	0.76
$44.00	1.42	0.81
$45.00	1.22	0.81
$46.00	1.22	0.74
$47.00	1.21	0.73
$48.00	1.14	0.42
$49.00	0.76	0.22
$50.00	0.44	0.14
$51.00	0.12	0.11

TABLE 21.3 The Condor within Various Volatility Environments

XYX = $596.00 Days till expiration: 20	Condor value @ 18% implied volatility	Condor value @ 24% implied volatility	Condor value @ 30% implied volatility
Condor Strike Prices			
580/585/590/595	0.81	0.62	0.41
585/590/595/600	0.95	0.65	0.44
590/595/600/605	1.05	0.72	0.44
595/600/605/610	1.05	0.71	0.44
600/605/610/615	0.91	0.64	0.41

differential. Recall, that with a condor the body and wings are consecutively placed. With the albatross they are not. Allow me to take it one step further in making the albatross strategy even easier to understand. With the long call albatross, as shown in **Exhibit 21.4**, imagine purchasing one bull vertical call spread and subsidizing its cost by selling another bull vertical spread closely (but not directly) above it. For instance, XYZ is trading at $50.00 per share. The long albatross would involve purchasing something such as the $40.00/ $45.00 call spread against selling the $55.00/$60.00 call spread. What should be apparent is there is the arithmetic gap at the $50.00 strike. The short call albatross is the exact opposite as displayed in **Exhibit 21.5**.

In general and in theory (both distasteful words in options trading) the albatross will be priced at a higher premium relative to its condor cousin. In return for that higher premium, the albatross does not require you to be as perfect in your conviction compared to the condor as there is just a

EXHIBIT 21.4   Long Albatross Spread

EXHIBIT 21.5   Short Albatross Spread

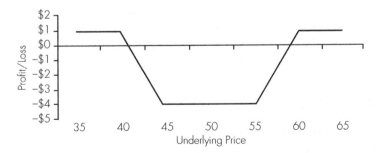

bit more wiggle room between the "body" strikes and the "wing" strikes of the strategy.

Limited Risk/Reward Profile

Maximum profit for the long albatross is realized when the underlying price falls anywhere between your two body (short) strikes at expiration. Assume you paid $2.00 to be long the $40/$45/$55/$60 call albatross. The most you can make is $3.00 ($5.00 − $2.00 = $3.00). The most you can lose is the premium paid. However, keep in mind, your potential range for profit is wider—you'll collect the full profit/loss potential if the underlying price expires anywhere between $45.00 and $55.00. If the underlying price should rise above $55.00 or fall below $45.00 your loss will be 1:1 up through and including the premium paid.

Maximum loss for the long albatross takes place if, at expiry, the underlying price lands at or below the $40.00 strike or at or above the $55.00 strike. The albatross will start to lose value once the underlying price settles anywhere away from your short body strikes. The short albatross is the exact opposite. Refer to **Table 21.4** for an exact expiration profit/loss detail.

Purchased (Long) $40/$45/$55/$60 Call Albatross

At expiration, if the underlying price should settle at or below $40.00, all of your options will expire as worthless—the original premium will be gone. Similarly—but not exactly—if, at expiration, the underlying price should settle at or above $60.00, all your options will be in-the-money; your long strikes ($40.00 and $60.00) would be exercised while your short strikes ($45.00 and $55.00) would be assigned. However, the net result would be the same: your long albatross would expire as worthless as your two long calls would match in value with your short calls. Recall, you in effect bought the $40.00/$45.00 bull call vertical spread and subsidized the purchase price by selling the $55.00/$60.00 bull call vertical spread against it. In short, both your vertical spreads settled at parity.

The Albatross Strategy

This section describes the Albatross Strategy with regards to time to expiration, underlying path, and volatility.

TABLE 21.4 Expiration Profit/Loss Detail

40/45/55/60 call and put albatross expiration profit and loss detail		
Underlying Expiration Price	40/45/55/60 Call Albatross Expiration Value	40/45/55/60 Put Albatross Expiration Value
$100	$0	$0
$70	$0	$0
$60	$0	$0
$59	$1.00	$1.00
$58	$2.00	$2.00
$57	$3.00	$3.00
$56	$4.00	$4.00
$55	$5.00	$5.00
$54	$5.00	$5.00
$53	$5.00	$5.00
$52	$5.00	$5.00
$51	$5.00	$5.00
$50	$5.00	$5.00
$49	$5.00	$5.00
$48	$5.00	$5.00
$47	$5.00	$5.00
$46	$5.00	$5.00
$45	$5.00	$5.00
$44	$4.00	$4.00
$43	$3.00	$3.00
$42	$2.00	$2.00
$41	$1.00	$1.00
$40	$0	$0
$30	$0	$0
$0	$0	$0

The comprehension of any options spread with multiple break-even points (e.g., albatross) requires discipline, patience, and a thorough understanding of multiposition management. And, it is true that the albatross is a simple extension of the condor and a distant relative of the butterfly. However, as risk/reward goes, the further the wingspread is removed from the butterfly, the hazier position awareness becomes. Let the next few tables (**Tables 21.5** to **21.7**) assist you in understanding both the similarities and

TABLE 21.5 Condor Pricing with Regard to Time till Expiration

Underlying: $45.00			
Albatross	14 days till expiry value	42 days till expiry value	168 days till expiry value
30/35/45/50	3.70	3.10	1.80
35/40/50/55	4.65	3.75	2.20
40/45/55/60	3.85	3.35	2.35
45/50/60/65	1.30	1.75	2.05
50/55/65/70	0.05	0.45	1.45

TABLE 21.6 The Albatross and Various Points in the Underlying

	XYZ = $134.50	XYZ 125/130/140/145 call albatross	
Underlying Price	Albatross Price 10 days till expiration	Albatross Price 55 days till expiration	Albatross Price 130 days till expiration
115.00	0.10	0.25	0.80
120.00	0.70	1.56	0.95
125.00	1.43	1.41	1.25
130.00	2.92	2.68	1.80
135.00	3.87	3.47	2.15
140.00	3.28	3.22	2.43
145.00	1.75	1.95	2.14
150.00	0.42	0.62	1.43
155.00	0.10	0.12	0.70

TABLE 21.7 The Albatross within Various Volatility Environments

XYZ = $595.00 Days till expiration: 35	Ablatross value @ 15% implied volatility	Albatross value @ 25% implied volatility	Albatross value @ 35% implied volatility
Abatross Strike Prices			
570/575/585/590	1.00	0.60	0.20
575/580/590/595	1.20	0.65	0.20
580/585/595/600	1.45	0.70	0.25
585/590/600/605	1.50	0.80	0.30
590/595/605/610	1.50	0.75	0.25
595/600/610/615	1.45	0.70	0.25
600/605/615/620	1.20	0.65	0.20

differences of the albatross and how they can react to changes in time, path, and volatility.

Conclusion

This chapter could go on endlessly addressing pterodactyls along with various and sundry broken wingspreads, to name a few. However, it seems the point has been made—the trends have been set—and I trust this chapter has lent a hand in laying the foundations of better understanding how and why a wingspread may or may not work. There is no such thing as an all-weather options strategy. What might work this month could be next month's disaster. Understanding the inner workings of any spread will provide you with some confidence—a good head start indeed.

About the Author

Larry Shover has been a firm and proprietary options trader for more than 25 years and can be seen three times per week on networks such as: Bloomberg, BNN, CNBC, CNN, FOX Business, Phoenix Television, and SKY. He is currently chief investment officer and portfolio manager of Solutions Funds Group Inc., a managed futures mutual fund. A large portion of his career has been dedicated to developing his own proprietary trading firm, and he has also served as director of education, senior vice-president of trading at several commodities and options firms. Shover was a member of the CME and the Chicago Board Options Exchange and holds several Financial Industry Regulatory Authority licenses.

Index

Printed and bound by CPI Group (UK) Ltd, Croydon, CR0 4YY

16/04/2025